Why We Gesture

Gestures are fundamental to the way we communicate, yet our understanding of this communicative impulse is clouded by a number of ingrained assumptions. Are gestures merely ornamentation to speech? Are they simply an "add-on" to spoken language? Why *do* we gesture? These and other questions are addressed in this fascinating book. McNeill explains that the common view of language and gesture as separate entities is misinformed: language is inseparable from gesture. There is gesture–speech unity.

Containing more than 100 illustrations, *Why We Gesture* provides visual evidence to support the book's central argument that gestures orchestrate speech. This compelling book will be welcomed by students and researchers working in linguistics, psychology and communication.

DAVID MCNEILL has taught at the University of Michigan, Harvard University, Duke University and the University of Chicago, where he is now an Emeritus Professor.

Why We Gesture

The surprising role of hand movements in communication

David McNeill

University of Chicago

CAMBRIDGE
UNIVERSITY PRESS

University Printing House, Cambridge CB2 8BS, United Kingdom

Cambridge University Press is part of the University of Cambridge.

It furthers the University's mission by disseminating knowledge in the pursuit
of education, learning and research at the highest international levels of excellence.

www.cambridge.org
Information on this title: www.cambridge.org/9781316502365

First published 2016

Printed in the United Kingdom by Clays, St Ives plc

A catalogue record for this publication is available from the British Library

Library of Congress Cataloguing in Publication data
Names: McNeill, David, 1933–
Title: Why we gesture : the surprising role of hand movements in communication /
David McNeill.
Description: New York : Cambridge University Press, 2015. | Includes
bibliographical references and index.
Identifiers: LCCN 2015028157| ISBN 9781107137189 (hardback) |
ISBN 9781316502365 (paperback)
Subjects: LCSH: Gesture. | Speech and gesture. | Psycholinguistics.
Classification: LCC P117 .M36 2015 | DDC 153.6/9–dc23
LC record available at http://lccn.loc.gov/2015028157

ISBN 978-1-107-13718-9 Hardback
ISBN 978-1-316-50236-5 Paperback

To my dear family, Nobuko, Cheryl and Randall

Contents

Figures

Tables

Preface

Why We Gesture capstones three previous books—an inadvertent trilogy spanning 20 years—*How Language Began* (Cambridge University Press, 2012), *Gesture and Thought* (Chicago University Press, 2005) and *Hand and Mind* (Chicago University Press, 1992). In *Why We Gesture* the three merge into a single multifaceted hypothesis.[1] It has many facets but is one hypothesis. To present it in its fullness is the purpose of the book. The integration itself—that it is possible—is part of the hypothesis. Integration occurs because of a central idea—implicit in the trilogy, explicit here—that gestures orchestrate speech. In simplest terms, this answers the implicit question of our title: *to orchestrate speech is why we gesture.* We gesture because we speak—not that speech triggers gesture but that gesture orchestrates speech; we can speak because we gesture, rather than we gesture because we speak. To present such a package takes time and an ordering of parts but the whole is the important thing, to be grasped as such, considered all at once and all together. To this end, brevity is a virtue, and I have held the book to the main points. My impression is that many readers know one book of the trilogy or the other, but few have read them all, let alone have worked out the conceptual framework they collectively create. This is hardly surprising: it has nowhere been spelled out as such. *Why We Gesture* does it for the reader. The hypothesis in all its facets is here in one place, rendered as briefly as I can manage without losing intelligibility and completeness. Moreover, *Why We Gesture* has uncovered connections that had earlier escaped notice —the integrative role of gesture-orchestrated speech is one (mentioned in passing in *Gesture and Thought* but now on center stage). Equal

---

[1] With additions from a blog (Linguist List, Cambridge extras, Gesture–Speech Unity at the Origin, in 6 parts, Fall 2012), McNeill (2014b) and Levy and McNeill (2015). When I speak of "hypothesis." I use the word in a broader and more traditional sense than its statistical understanding by many psychologists and social scientists. The *Oxford English Dictionary* captures this sense—a supposition made as a starting point for further investigation from known facts.

in importance and pervasiveness is the idea of "new" gesture-actions and how they differ from "old" action-actions, these last assumed widely as the core of gesture but that, if admitted, would decisively roadblock gesture-orchestrated speech. The principal new finding of the book is that much material coalesces naturally around these concepts.

Acknowledgments

I thank Elena Levy for her insights and gratefully followed advice on presentation as I strove to unpack the first forms of this book and equally for our collaboration on children's gesture and narrative coherence (Levy and McNeill 2015), which plays such an important part at several points in this book. Her understanding of the arguments of the book reassures me that the ideas are in what Merleau-Ponty called the world of shared meanings. Renia Lopez-Ozieblo, in a nearly year-long email exchange, raised questions and counterarguments that have done much to shape and clarify the chapter on phylogenesis. Susan Duncan has been a participant in all the "trilogy." Her insights and methods have been so thoroughly absorbed it is impossible to sort them all out. I have acknowledged her contributions wherever I can.

Maya Hickmann and Marianne Gullberg have played more of a role in the origin of this book than they perhaps realize. They kindly invited me to write a paper for their journal, *Language, Interaction, and Acquisition*, which I did (McNeill 2014b). I thank them for offering this excellent venue. In writing the paper, I saw suddenly how this book could be mutated into the form now before you. From *LIA* to the book was one step.

Without artwork, a book with gesture in a center place would hardly be possible. I thank three artists, first in time Laura Pedelty who made all the illustrations in *Hand and Mind* and is now a professor of neurology at the University of Illinois Medical School; Fey Parrill whose computer art filled *Gesture and Thought* (and much of the current book), now a professor of cognitive science at Case Western Reserve University; and for this book, Dusty Hope, a professional designer who rendered ancient videos into elegant line drawings.

The National Science Foundation, the Spencer Foundation, and the University of Chicago Beck Fund at different times supported the research from which the observations reported herein derive.

Finally, above all I thank my precious family. This book is dedicated to them. They have always been at my side. It is impossible to overstate how important their support, intellectual as well as lovingly personal, has been. Without them this book and the three earlier books it capstones would never have begun, let alone finished. I thank them for everything they bring—joy, humor, wisdom, history, stability, motivation, beauty, music, inspiration and a wonderful shining intelligence that brightens everything.

Part I

Gesture-orchestrated speech

1   Why we gesture

Why do we gesture? Many would say it brings emphasis, energy and ornamentation to speech (which is assumed to be the core of what is taking place); in short, gesture is an "add-on."[1] However, the evidence is against this. The lay view of gesture is that one "talks with one's hands." You can't find a word, so you resort to gesture. Marianne Gullberg (2013) debunks this ancient idea. As she succinctly puts it, rather than gesture starting when words stop, gesture stops as well. So if, contrary to lay belief, we don't "talk with our hands," why do we gesture? This book offers an answer.

The reasons we gesture are more profound. Language itself is inseparable from gesture. While gestures enhance the material carriers of meaning, *the core is gesture and speech together*. They are bound more tightly than saying the gesture is an "add-on" or "ornament" implies. They are united as a matter of thought itself. Even if, for some reason, the hands are restrained and a gesture is not externalized, the imagery it embodies can still be present, hidden but integrated with speech (and may surface in some other part of the body, the feet for example).

As stated in the Preface, the purpose of the current book is to present the multifaceted hypothesis that *to orchestrate speech is why we gesture*. Gestures of course do not always occur. This is itself an aspect of gesture; there is a natural variation of gesture occurrence. Apart from forced suppressions (as in formal contexts), gestures fall on an elaboration continuum, their position an aspect of the gesture itself.[2] The degree of elaboration is the extent to which the gesture adds communicative "push" to the utterance, what Firbas (1971) called

---

[1] Kendon (2008), who also argues against the view.
[2] Forced suppressions only shift the gesture to some other part of the body – the feet or an overactive torso. We once taped an individual who had been highly recommended to us as an elaborate and vigorous gesturer. Somewhat maliciously, when asked to recount our cartoon stimulus, he sat on his hands yet unwittingly began to perform the gestures typical of the experiment with his feet insofar as anatomically possible—foot up for Sylvester's ascent, other foot next to it for his ascent inside a pipe, etc. James Goss (personal communication) undertook a systematic study of foot gestures (never published).

"communicative dynamism." At one end, very elaborate gestures participate at the highest levels of communicative dynamism; at the other end, where communicative dynamism or "push" is minimal, elaboration reaches zero, ending with no motion at all; yet this is not a disappearance of the gesture and its imagery; it is the minimum of its concrete enactment. The reality is imagery with speech ranging over the entire continuum. It is visuoactional imagery, not a photo. Gesture imagery linked to speech is what natural selection chose, acting on gesture–speech units free to vary in elaboration. As communicative dynamism varies, the gesture–speech unit moves from elaborate movement to no movement at all. To speak of gesture–speech unity we include gestures at all levels of elaboration.

1.1   What is a "gesture"?

The term "gesture" covers a range of phenomena. We focus on one in particular: gesture in our sense is *the intrinsic imagery of language*. Language is inseparable from it. Inseparable, because gesture orchestrates speech; it and speech (and all the language forms speech includes) cannot be sundered. Such gestures are not exotic or rare. They are the ordinary gestures of daily speech and by far the most abundant of any kind of gesture.

A journalist's cliché portrays gesture as pretense, fake action for show and not for substance—for example, "[t]here is also the suggestion of a [story] plot, or rather a gesture in the direction of a weave of narratives" or "a small gesture stirs giving on a big scale" (both *New York Times*). The cliché is worse than irrelevant. I do not say that it is meaningless, but if adopted it misleads or worse, positively interferes with understanding. In our discussion a gesture is the very fuel of language and thought. Moreover, language could not have evolved without it. Gesture and speech were "equiprimordial" (a term from Liesbet Quaeghebeur, pers. comm.). Gesture and language are inseparable, and the journalist's cliché hides this deep relationship.

I occasionally say "gesticulation" to designate the gestures that orchestrate speech, but the word is far from satisfactory. It conveys a picture of windmilling arms (the *Oxford English Dictionary* confirms), but the gestures we observe are nearly all small, confined to a space in front of the torso. When the ambiguity is harmless, I will say simply "gesture." Speech-synchronized gestures (and not windmilling arms) are by far the most common form of gesture in narratives and conversations.

Adam Kendon (2004) placed gestures in the category of "actions that have the features of manifest deliberate expressiveness." I adopt this definition with the qualification that speech-orchestrating gestures cannot be deliberate. Kendon may have meant by "deliberate" non-accidental, and with this I agree; but the word also conveys, "done for a purpose," and with this I do not

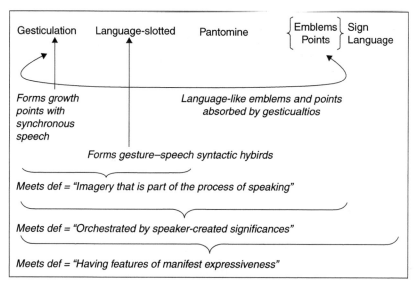

Figure 1.1 Gesture continuum. Cambridge University Press, reprinted with permission.

agree—orchestration of speech via a gesture is not the goal of any speaker in making a gesture. If the speaker intends anything it is to "communicate," not to perform a speech-orchestrating gesture. Pantomime, which can be deliberate, is not able to orchestrate speech, as will become clear later.

1.2   A gesture continuum

Figure 1.1 shows a gesture continuum and how places along it relate to Kendon's definition and to the others indicated in the figure.

1.3   Notation

In addition to semiotic properties, a gesture can be described in terms of movement. This mode is incorporated into our notation. One complete "manifestly expressive action" is what Kendon (1980) called a gesture phrase, a "gesture" in normal parlance. For the gesture illustrated in Figure 1.2,

(1.1)   he goe[ss **/ up / through** the pipe] this time #

the *gesture phrase* as a whole is marked by "[" and "]" (the "/" marks a silent hesitation of speech, the "#" an audible breath intake, and large font prosodic stress). A gesture phrase has up to five *phases*. Not all phases need be present,

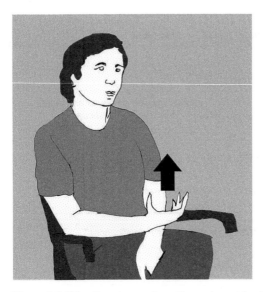

Figure 1.2 "New" gesture-action. Computer art by Fey Parrill, now on the faculty of Case Western University. Used with permission of University of Chicago Press.

but one or more *strokes*—the image-bearing phase—is obligatory; without a stroke a gesture is not said to have occurred. This is marked in boldface ("up through"). The *preparation* is the hand getting into position to make the stroke and is indicated by the span from the left bracket to the start of boldface (during "goes"). Preparation shows that the gesture, with all its significance, is coming into being—there is no reason the hands move into position and take on form than to perform a stroke yet to come. *Holds* are cessations of movement, either *prestroke* (the "*I*"), the hand frozen awaiting the stroke, or *poststroke* (the "the"), the hand frozen in the stroke's ending position and hand shape after movement has ceased. Holds of either kind are indicated with underlining. They show the precise synchrony of stroke and orchestrated speech. *Retraction* is also an active phase, the gesture not simply abandoned but closing down (in this case, during "pipe"). Not atypically, the gesture phase in Figure 1.2 did not align with a syntactic constituent of the sentence, preparation beginning in the middle of "goes." We will see later salient examples of disconnection and explain why an imperfect alignment of gesture and linguistic form will happen, but the Figure 1.2 example suggests even now the reason is that the gesture has orchestrated the speech—the gesture does not spring from the sentence constituent structure but instead this structure fits or tries to fit the gesture.

1.3.1 Storytelling

The gesture examples described in this book are spontaneous, unsolicited and unrehearsed, recorded during storytelling. A participant watches an approximately eight-minute-long animated Tweety and Sylvester cartoon or a full-length Hitchcock film, *Blackmail* (1929), then retells the story, without notes, to a listener who has not seen it. For readers unfamiliar with the genre, Tweety is a feisty, large-headed canary belonging to a feisty elderly grandmother. Sylvester, an enterprising cat with culinary goals, endlessly pursues Tweety; his unchanging lot is frustration and disaster. The genre was familiar to our narrators but not the specific cartoon ("Canary Row," Warner Brothers, 1950). The cartoon consists of eight episodes, all with the same pursuit-catastrophe theme in amusing variations. McNeill and Levy (1982) chose it originally to show to children, but adults, university-educated and professional, also find it engaging.

One participant (the "speaker"), chosen at random at the start of the session, is shown the cartoon/film in its entirety. The speaker is told in advance that immediately after viewing the cartoon/film he or she will tell the story to the second participant "as accurately and completely as possible, as your listener will have to retell the story based on your narration," or words to this effect. The second participant was a genuine listener, not one of the experimenters (usually a friend or spouse, never a stranger). The performance was recorded on video with the seated speaker in full camera view and at least the front half of the listener as well. The instructions emphasized that the experiment was about storytelling. Gesture was not mentioned.

1.3.2 Coding validity

Gesture coding requires close attention to kinesic details and an accurate and detailed transcription of speech. Unlike some researchers who, fearing "contamination," code gesture and speech separately, our method requires them to be coded jointly. Ultimately we are coding *gesture–speech units*, not "gestures" alone (see also Chapter 2). Separating the streams removes the very phenomenon we want to code. Each narration is coded by at least two coders working independently, who then agree on the final coding (a finished transcript includes notes of any disagreements). The development of this method and notation is the achievement of two researchers, Susan Duncan and Karl-Erik McCullough.

How are gestures interpreted? The answer is not obvious. I am of the view that "true" interpretation of a gesture is a hypothesis to be judged for its correspondence to observable facts. These facts include the form and timing of the gesture, and (equally important) how it fits into the immediate context of speaking. The exact timing of the gesture with speech is important. An example is in the "it down" gesture in the following graphic (the two hands, facing down and curved as if around an object—the bowling ball, and thrusting down), timed as shown:

(1.2) "and Tweety Bird runs and gets a bowling ba[ll and Ø$_{tw}$ drop<u>s</u> **it do<u>wn</u>** the drainpipe]"

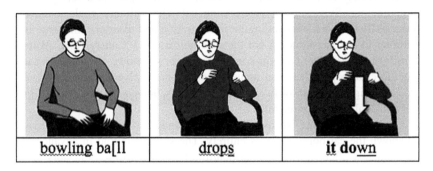

| bowling ba[ll | drops | it do<u>wn</u> |

The square brackets mark the beginning and end of motion; the boldface the image-bearing stroke, when the arched hands moved down; the underlining two holds, a prestroke on the final sibilant of "drops" and a poststroke at the end of "down." This example illustrates a number of points and will be analyzed in full in Chapter 4. However, we can make the point now that the syntax of co-occurring speech—"it" and "down" in different constituents—is dominated by the gesture, as gesture-orchestrated speech implies, and is not a guide for rendering it.

1.4   The beat

One type of gesture, the "**beat**," may seem an exception. A beat appears to be a gesture without an image-bearing stroke. Rather than embodying meaning, beats appear to synchronize with speech rhythm. Bressem (2010) has tracked different hand shapes and orientations of beats with shadings of this function. If anything, beats appear to show the reverse of gesture-orchestrated speech—speech-orchestrated gesture. Indeed, Kevin Tuite (1993) argued that iconic gestures contain rhythmic pulses, in effect inner beats, deriving from speech rhythmicity.

Rhythmicity is unquestionably a factor in all forms of gesture but it does not operate autonomously. Both beat and rhythm arise from meanings on the discourse level. They share a source in contextual highlighting. For example, the beats and rhythmic emphasis in the following shift successively to follow what is new in each speech unit: "his gírlfriend– Álice—Alice Whíte"—first her role in the story, then her first name, then her last (beats in boldface and rhythmic pulses in enlarged font with accents).

The principle seems to be that highlighting draws effort in both speech and gesture. We can go further and say that an observed beat is a reduced version of a full gesture. It contains its meaning on this level. Some beats stand alone, but many ride on an imagery-bearing gesture stroke—the hands depicting something and, while depicting it, moving up and down or in and out, in beats. The added effort takes this form. We will see an example of such beats later in Figure 1.5. These beats seem to be replications of the gesture on which they ride. They are the gesture made twice or thrice, all at the same time, and have the function of emphasizing the gesture for the significance it has in the discourse beyond its speech unit (as with "Alice White").

1.5   Emblems and pointing

Two other slots on the gesture continuum, the **emblem** and the **point**, have yet other features. Although usually thought of as different gestures, they are surprisingly similar on these features and can be described together.

First, standardization of form. The upward movement of Figure 1.2 indicates the location of the pipe, its position relative to the character and the location inside. This deixis was accomplished not with a dedicated point but was built into the gesticulation itself. A dedicated, stand-alone point, however, has properties that make it more like an emblem than a gesticulation, and the gesture continuum combines it with the emblems. Like an emblem, a point meets form standards—while all kinds of gestures can be used to indicate a locus, the extended index finger is standard in North American and Northern Europe; a flat hand is standard in some British Isle uses (Kendon 2004); and lip points are standard in Laos (Enfield 2001). All have in common depicting an iconic vector from a zero point or "origo" (Bühler 1982) to some target. The vector is the image, and cultures standardize different forms of it. This is one similarly of points to emblems.

The other similarity, less obvious but more profound, is how points and emblems relate to speech. While points and demonstrative pronouns ("this," "that," etc.) can synchronize (Levelt et al. 1985) and thus appear to be like gesticulations, in fact the timing is different and more like that of an emblem. The similarity appears when gesture and speech are asynchronous. For both points and emblems, the asynchronies are meaningful, and are so in both directions. Say "that" and then point; point and then say "that"; or say and point simultaneously—each combination is meaningful and different (the meanings seem metapragmatic, indicating how speech and gesture are being used pragmatically). The same asynchronies and differences appear with emblems, for example, do the same experiment, with "OK" and the OK sign. Asynchronous gesticulations, on the other hand, are merely slovenly and not meaningful. Duplicate the experiment with the "rising hollowness" gesture of Figure 1.2, either synchronized with speech ("up through") or not, and the meaning is the same until the asynchrony grows so great that the gesture and speech lose unity and seem to be repetitions. So pointing joins the emblem slot far from gesticulation as one of the most language-like of the non-sign language gestures. This has implications for gesture-orchestrated speech. Points and emblems play a metapragmatic part. They can act on their own or can join speech being organized by something else. The arrow in Figure 1.1, from the "Emblem/Point" slot to the "Gesticulation" slot, shows the possibility that the latter can absorb the former, and in this way endow the emblem or a point with the power of orchestration. At the same time, points bring a metapragmatic indication to "Gesticulation"; the arrow accordingly is two-headed. As a quick example, imagine a gesture with "he barrels up it," in two versions that we compare; first, the fingers resting together in a relaxed pose as the hand rotates left and right and rises up: the meaning is co-expressive with "barrels up," its deixis inherent to the gesticulation; next, the forefinger extended, the others folded into the palm (the classic point) while the hand rotates right and left and rises up, like the first: again co-expressive with "barrels up" with inherent deixis but with the addition of a specific point, the utterance not just about the cat's motion in a certain direction but also calling attention to ascent itself as a discourse relevant dimension.

1.6   The conception of language and gesture in this book

The motto is, "abandon all presuppositions, ye who enter here." Language and gesture as described here need to be grasped as a totality. The conception is non-reductive. It is important to think of words, grammar, sentences, etc. not separately, and gesture–speech unity not as something built out of "parts," but to see gesture as the orchestrating force of the whole. If you set aside reductive expectations, you can easily follow the logic. You see language in a new (or perhaps an old but forgotten) way. Wilhelm von Humboldt, two centuries ago, saw language in the right way to follow the arguments here and avoid a hell of concepts that slide past each other without fixing into a form. I can do no better than start with Humboldt's distinction between *Ergon* and *Energeia*:

"An important distinction ... kept reemerging"; this was Humboldt's distinction between language as *Ergon*—language viewed as structure—and as *Energeia*—language as an "embodied moment of meaning located both in the organism and in the medium that the organism uses for expression." The latter is language at the moment of its use, "alive, in an actor." (Elena Levy, pers. comm., quoting Glick 1983)

The sense of such a seemingly innocent remark as, "when people talk, they often gesture," illustrates what you must avoid if you are to follow the arguments herein. From the vantage point of this book, such a way of speaking is like saying, "when people talk they often add speech." The absurdity equally applies to "gesture"— the remark presupposes that what actually is a gesture–speech unit is divided into an essential and an accidental part, with gesture the accident. In the conception of this book, however, gesture-orchestrated speech is *essential* to speech.

Ergon and *Energeia* are conceptualized as **dimensions of language** that cross in the **growth point**, henceforth "GP" (described in full in Chapter 2). The two dimensions have classically been called "linguistic" (*Ergon*) and "psychological" (*Energeia*) but better if less colorful (and less proprietary) terms are "**static**" and "**dynamic**." Some phenomena are more accessible or prominent on one dimension, others on the other, but the dynamic and static cannot be isolated. They intersect and interact. This is the starting point of our investigation. The dimensions are organized on different principles and require different methods of description and analysis (the field of linguistics specializing on the static) but both are part of "language."

Saussure (1959, in lectures around 1910), crystalized the static dimension into *langue*, or the "system of language," which must be observed **synchronically**, in a kind of panorama at one theoretical instant. In *langue*, Saussure said, there are only differences, and to see them a panoramic view is required. The synchronic approach is fundamental to much of the work of linguists, and a century of insights attests to its vigor. In a trenchant remark concerning the "poetic function," Roman Jakobson concisely explained the two principal axes of the *langue* static dimension. He wrote: "The poetic function projects the principle of equivalence from the **axis of selection** into the **axis of combination**" (Jakobson 1960, p. 358, boldface added). By poetic function, he means a process whereby sequences come to have contrastive values. His "axis of selection" is the **paradigmatic** axis—the contrasts established when a linguistic form is selected from a set of equivalents ("sheep" and "mutton" are equivalents that contrast on an axis of selection in English). The "axis of combination" is the **syntagmatic** axis—by combining words, higher linguistic units and new syntagmatic values emerge (combining "hit" and "ball" into "hit the ball" generates a verb phrase, a higher level unit, and a direct object, a syntagmatic value that "ball" does not have on its own).

Saussure's formula for *parole* is: *langage* (the semiotic totality of language) minus *langue* equals *parole*. The dynamic dimension, however, is not *parole* or its modern counterpart, performance. The concept of *parole* relies on a separation of speaking and language, the first an individual fact (*parole*) and the

second a social fact (*langue*).The definition of "performance" is inappropri-
ate for a different reason. It uses a metaphor of manipulation: the "use" of
language that does not fit our model where the static and dynamic *jointly* fuel
an imagery–language dialectic. The dynamic and static are dimensions of one
"thing," *Energeia*. When we consider the growth point in Chapter 2 we will see
how the two dimensions form dynamic units of speaking.

The question of why we gesture is answered on the dynamic dimension. The dynamic dimension, cross-cutting the static, could be termed the
"activity" of language, but I am calling it "inhabiting" language. Inhabiting
is a broader concept, done with one's thought and action in an immediate
context, and becomes part of the speaker's cognitive Being at the moment
of speaking (Merleau-Ponty 1962). It is more than making language your
own. Inhabitance is all-encompassing: organizing thought and action,
effecting goals, creating and fulfilling presuppositions. The "inhabiting"
terminology has the advantage of alluding to both *langue*—Saussure's
static system synchronically revealed—and whatever animates it, the
dynamic dimension. Besides Merleau-Ponty, a historical figure associated
with language regarded dynamically is Vygotsky (1987). On the dynamic
dimension, units come and go, emerge and disperse in real time. It crosses
the abstractions from time in the unmoving totality of synchronic *langue*
at 90 degrees.

1.6.1   Inhabitance

We inhabit gesture-orchestrated speech dynamically. The concept of "inhabitance" will arise often in our discussion. It is an idea from Merleau-Ponty
(1962) and phenomenology in general. A further concept of the **material carrier** goes with it (Vygotsky 1987)—a phrase referring to the embodiment of
meaning in enactments or material experiences.[3] Inhabitance and the material
carrier add greatly to our understanding of gesture and gesture-orchestrated
speech.

Inhabitance of a motor execution, a gesture or writing something down, for
example, the *very act of it*, enhances a symbol's experiential power. Inhabitance
brings these material carriers to life, ushering them into the dynamic realm.
Gesture materialization implies that the gesture, this natural material carrier,
the actual motion of the gesture itself, is a dimension of meaning. Such follows
from the role of gestures in orchestrating speech. Experiential enhancement
of language is possible since the gesture *is* the image in an imagery–language
dialectic, not an "expression" or "representation" of it, but *is* it. From this

---

[3] Pointed out to me originally by Elena Levy. The quote itself, recovered by Tae Kunisawa, is in
Rieber and Carton (1987, p. 46).

Communicative Dynamism (CD)

Most Continuous/Predictable				Least Continuous/Predictable
Less Materialization	⟶			More Materialization
Linguistic Form Continuum				
∅	Unstressed Pronoun	Noun Phrase	Modified Noun Phrase	Clause or Verb Phrase
Gesture Form Continuum				
Referring term included in ongoing iconic	Referring term excluded from adjacent iconics	Iconics that cover clause or Verb Phrase	O-VPT iconic with Noun Phrase	Deictics with Clause or VP O-VPT iconics (one hand) O-VPT iconics (two different hands) C-VPT iconics

Figure 1.3 Communicative dynamism. From McNeill (2005, p. 55). Linguistic continuum based on Givón (1985). "O-VPT" = observer viewpoint, the hands are the character or event; "C-VPT" = character viewpoint, the hands the hands of a character. Used with permission of University of Chicago Press.

viewpoint, a gesture, the global-synthetic whole, is an image in its most developed—that is, in its most naturally embodied—form. The material carrier concept explains how an imagery–language dialectic is still possible in the absence of a visible gesture. The "absence" is the gesture in its least materialized form. If there is no visible gesture there is still global-synthetic imagery and a dialectic with linguistic categorization, the simultaneous rendering of a meaning in opposite semiotic modes—the dialectic in its essentials—but it is bleached, experienced at the lowest level of materialization. This leads us to expect that gestures are more elaborate, more materialized and more frequent—in a word, more *inhabited*—when the gesture has greater newsworthiness. In Figure 1.3 we see a range of materializations, from zero to full, on two continua—speech and gesture. The continua correlate positively with communicative dynamism in terms of the elaboration of the quantity of "substance" involved (Firbas 1971; see also Chapter 4). The most elaborate noun phrases are accompanied by the most developed gestures, the least with the least. So the more discontinuous an utterance is with the previous context, the greater the communicative dynamism, the more probable a gesture, the more internally complex it will be, and the more complex the synchronous speech as well.

Inhabitance itself

The concept of a material carrier is raised to a whole new level when we turn to Merleau-Ponty (1962) for insight into the unity of gesture and language and what we can expect of gesture in a dual semiotic process. It is here that inhabitance is made clear. The material carrier is inhabited and takes a position in the speaker's "world of meaning." The degree of materialization is the extent of this inhabitance or, better, the energy with which the speaker takes up the position. Merleau-Ponty introduces several important ideas:

> The link between the word and its living meaning is not an external accompaniment to intellectual processes, the meaning inhabits the word, and language "is not an external accompaniment to intellectual processes."[4] We are therefore led to recognize a gestural or existential significance to speech ... Language certainly has inner content, but this is not self-subsistent and self-conscious thought. What then does language express, if it does not express thoughts? It presents or rather it *is* the subject's taking up of a position in the world of his meanings. (Merleau-Ponty 1962, p. 193, emphasis in the original)[5]

A deeper answer to the query of why we gesture, therefore, is that we are updating our current cognitive Being, our very mental existence, while it is occurring. By performing the gesture, a core idea is brought into concrete existence and becomes part of the speaker's existence at that moment. The Heideggerian echo in this statement is not accidental. Following Heidegger's emphasis on Being, a gesture is not a representation, or is not only such: It is a form of Being. From a first-person perspective, the gesture is part of the immediate existence of the speaker. Gestures (and words, etc. as well) are thinking in one of its many forms—not only expressions of thought, *but thought, that is, cognitive Being, itself* (see Dreyfus 1994). To the speaker, gesture and speech are not only "messages" or communications, but are a way of cognitively existing, of cognitively Being, at the moment of speaking. This "H-model" avoids the homunculus problem encountered by the third-person perspective inherent to the concept of a "representation" and with it the "theater of the mind" problem highlighted by Dennett (1991). The theater of the mind is the presumed central thinking area in which representations are "presented" to a receiving intelligence. The possibilities for homunculi—each with its own theater and receiving intelligence—spiraling down inside other homunculi are obvious. In the H-model, there is no theater and no extra being; the gesture is, rather, part of the speaker's momentary mode of Being itself, and is not "watched."

The speaker who creates a gesture of Sylvester rising up fused with the pipe's hollowness (Figure 1.2) is, according to this interpretation, embodying thought in gesture, and this action—thought in gesture-action over the thought–language–hand link—was part of the person's Being cognitively at

---

[4] Merleau-Ponty's quote is from Gelb and Goldstein (1925, p. 158).
[5] I am indebted to Jan Arnold for this quotation.

that moment. To make a gesture, from this perspective, is to bring thought into existence on a concrete plane, just as writing out a word can have a similar effect. There is not a causal sequence of thought → speech/gesture; speech and gesture *are* the thought coming into being at that instant. The greater the felt departure of the thought from the immediate context, the more likely its materialization in a gesture. Thus, gestures are more or less elaborated depending on the importance of material realization to the existence of the thought (Figure 1.3).

Elena Cuffari (pers. comm. 2014) writes: "Heidegger could easily dismiss units, and psychological and linguistic analysis as such, as elements of the 'ontic' rather than ontological realms of Being." I replied (I confess impetuously): "The irony is that Being can be examined empirically if you don't insist on the 'ontic'/'ontological' distinction. Being then takes on depth and unit properties. I always say the 'moment' of Being, and I have in mind this thickness." Cuffari also warns that neither Heidegger nor Merleau-Ponty favors dichotomies—"both were trying to avoid dichotomies as much as possible." While a field of equivalents is not a set of dichotomies, it does inherently have the ideas of alternatives and opposition. In this I follow Saussure and Jakobson, extending their concept of opposition to the very workings of thought with language. The most pernicious aspect of any squeamishness over empirical grounding, however, is that it hides the dynamic dimension. Contrast, not "dichotomy," is the core—an essential part of dual semiosis, the dialectic of gesture imagery and linguistic form, the minimal unit and the psychological predicate, and nothing can be understood of the arguments of this book without the concept.

1.6.2   *"New" versus "old" actions*

Further clarification comes from distinguishing two kinds of action—"new" *gesture-actions* and practical *action-actions*, the "old" kind (adjectives referring to phylogenesis, "new" in human evolution versus primate "old"). The inhabitance of language on the dynamic dimension enters "new" gesture-actions. "Old" action-actions have a different relationship to the individual, who "performs" them, carrying them out to achieve goals. Chapter 3 focuses on the "new" and "old" difference and the opposed worldviews they occupy regarding language.

1.7   Self-demonstrations

To experience gesture–speech unity oneself is the best means to bring these abstract arguments down to ground. If you ask of what context this or that gesture–speech unit could have been the differentiation, you can see how

Figure 1.4 Gesture to be mimicked A: speaker saying "he's like," conveying alarm. Hands start palm down and then rock up once in a quick motion. Cambridge University Press, reprinted with permission.

Figure 1.5 Gesture to be mimicked B: speaker saying "the grandmother // instead of Tweety," highlighting the plot twist. Hands move upward in unison, then downward in small beats. Cambridge University Press, reprinted with permission.

Figure 1.6 Gesture to be mimicked C: speaker was saying "pulls off // the cover of the cage," presenting the denouement. Two hands, palms facing up in lower right space, shove forward. Cambridge University Press, reprinted with permission.

gesture infuses language with life. You directly experience the GP and the context it is differentiating. This is a method gesture coders also adopt, mimicking the gesture and speech they code to clarify its meaning. The effect can be dramatic: a GP and its context arising before you as if by magic but it is not magic—it is because the original gesture had absorbed this context and mimicry recreates it wholly or in part. The exercises that follow demonstrate that contexts and GPs can be brought into your own experience this way.

In Figures 1.4–1.6, cartoon narrators are describing an episode where Sylvester, disguised as a bellhop, has run off with what he believes is Tweety in his covered birdcage. However, Sylvester is the victim of a ruse. He removes the cover to discover, too late, that it is his umbrella-wielding nemesis, Granny, instead. The narrators were recounting this moment of revelation, and you are invited to recreate the gesture and speech combination, and to introspect whether this clarifies the significance of the gesture–speech unit. I have selected gestures where the significance seems at first obscure, before mimicry brings it into focus. The context of each gesture is the entire episode. It is important to bear it in mind with each example, since you are mimicking a full gesture–speech unit, not a gesture by itself.

1 The gesture (Figure 1.4) occurred with "he's like" and is plausibly a metaphor of alarm—both hands rise upward, palms forward (more broadly,

a metaphor of blocking incoming energy; compare with the "emblem" in Chapter 5). The speech is a metapragmatic reference to Sylvester's alarm, and the gesture a metaphor of it. However, at first glance, the gesture is ambiguous (it could be the shape of the cage, Granny's location or other interpretations), but with mimicry of the gesture and accompanying speech, the "alarm" conception dominates. The hands should start palm down and then rock up once in a quick motion.

2 Beats highlighting the plot twist of "the grandmother // instead of Tweety" (Figure 1.5). The hands are held motionless in the position and location shown except for small up–down beats as the speaker says "instead of," separated from the preceding speech by a pause (slashes). The GP concerns Granny's unexpected appearance. Beats, especially superimposed beats, in general indicate the relevance of the gesture on which they ride and the speech with which they synchronize to a larger discourse theme, and such appears to be the case here. Raising and extending the two parallel hands "placed" the grandmother in the gesture space. The beats (a kind of miniature reactivation of the gesture) highlight the grandmother's popping up, contrary to expectation.

3 A denouement metaphor, deictically placed, with "pulls off // the cover of the cage" (Figure 1.6). This gesture is also set off by a hesitation (slashes). The two-handed gesture with "the cover," I find, makes little sense without mimicry, but with it the significance of a denouement emerges (the metaphor is a classic conduit gesture "presenting" the denouement). The position of the gesture in the lower space (reinforced by the speaker's lowered head-tilt) links it to several previous gestures (not shown) for the birdcage in this gesture space.

1.8   The synchrony test

How various gesture–speech theories handle **synchrony** exposes in the clearest way the differences among them.

In a **GP**, synchrony is a matter of thinking itself, of inhabiting language. Gesture and speech synchronize where they co-express the same idea. Synchrony establishes the dual semiosis of this imagery–language dialectic, which is why it is intrinsic to thought. The speech side may or may not be a syntactic unit ("it down" broke syntax apart—"it" going with "drops" and "down" with "drainpipe"), but this synchrony is an essential aspect of the GP. Contrasting the GP's synchrony to other hypotheses elucidates the hypothesis. In none of the alternatives is gesture–speech synchrony intrinsic. It is introduced arbitrarily or simply ignored as a phenomenon.

1.8.1   Lexical affiliates

The lexical affiliate is the word to which the gesture corresponds most closely in meaning. Schegloff introduced the concept in his 1984 paper, "On some gestures' relation to talk," to identify, via a gesture, upcoming topics in conversations. Like the growth point, the lexical affiliate posits a tight speech–gesture linkage. However, unlike the GP, the lexical affiliate ignores context, a difference that produces an incorrect expectation of what synchronizes with what in gesture-orchestrated speech. A lexical affiliate is discovered from the semantic content of the word the gesture is identified with alone, in contrast to the GP, where the linguistic side can be identified by reference only to the field of meaningful equivalents that it along with the co-expressive gesture differentiates. In *Gesture and Thought* (2005), to demonstrate this distinction, I analyzed in GP terms one of Randi Engle's (2000) examples, whose data has been cited as "proof" that gesture and speech are not synchronous; however, she had used the lexical affiliate concept:

A clear illustration of the lexical affiliate/co-expressive speech distinction appears in Engle (2000). A gesture anticipated a lexical affiliate, consistent with Schegloff's original observation, but the immediate context of speaking suggests that the gesture and the co-expressive speech were actually synchronous. This is the example: Attempting to explain how a lock-and-key mechanism works, the subject said, "lift them [tumblers] to a // height, to the perfect height, where it [enables] the key to move," and appeared to turn a key as he said, "enables." The lexical affiliate is "key" or "key to move" and the key-turning gesture clearly occurred in advance of it. But from the vantage point of what would be newsworthy content in context, the synchrony of "enables" with the key-turning gesture embodies an idea this speaker might be expected to highlight—that by lifting the tumblers up, you are able to turn the key; and this thought is what the combination of a turning gesture plus "enables" captured. (McNeill 2005, pp. 37–38)

1.8.2   Conversational agent

In the design of conversational agents, synchrony is not ignored but it is artificial. "Max," a conversational agent perfected at the University of Bielefeld by Ipke Wachsmuth and colleagues (Wachsmuth and Sowa 2002), can engage in social interactions with humans about selected topics (such as how to put together a model airplane) and display convincing social, verbal and visual abilities. The way "he" produces speech-synchronized gestures, however, is in sharp contrast to the GP. My colleague, Susan Duncan, succinctly describes how Max synchronizes gesture with speech:

Max works as follows—looks ahead, sees what the linguistic resource will be, calculates how far back the preparation will have to be in order for the stroke to coincide with this. Then speech and gesture and generated on their own tracks, and the two assembled into a multimodal utterance. (Susan Duncan, pers. comm.)

In contrast, in the GP, gesture image and linguistic categorization comprise one idea unit, and synchrony is inherently part of how this unit is created in an imagery–language dialectic. The start of preparation is the dawn of the idea unit, which is kept intact and is unpacked, as a unit, synchronously into the full utterance.

1.8.3   Various psycholinguistic models

With models derived from Levelt's (1989) *Speaking*, synchrony is again artificial and contrived. Modular theories (Kita and Özyürek 2003; de Ruiter 2000) are non-dialectic and assign no special meaning to gesture–speech synchrony. For them it is a fact to be modeled but devoid of function, one that is present and to be engineered, usually by sending signals between a "gesture generator" and "message generator," two separately functioning "modules" (which do not exist in the GP theory). In these modular models, unlike the GP, synchrony has no meaning and is a problem to be solved than a source of insight.

1.8.4   The growth point

This synchrony is internal: the embodiment of meaning in merging global-synthetic (gesture) and analytic-combinatoric (linguistic form) semiotic modes simultaneously. The term "synchrony" also refers to external (observable) synchrony—speech and gesture occurring at the same time. External synchrony must be true in general to observe GPs but we also allow for variation of alignment. Our rule of thumb: within a third of a syllable, or about 80ms. If a gesture and its co-expressive speech are this close or closer they are deemed "synchronous." More precise alignments with instrumental methods are conceivable but more precise may not equal more accurate. As resolution increases, non-GP factors such as different conduction times from the brain's motor areas to the vocal tract and limbs become important. Internal speech–gesture synchrony may then be concealed behind external asynchrony at this level of precision. The 1/3 syllable rule thus may yield more accurate (if not more precise) data. fMRI may seem to be a way to get at internal synchrony, but gestures introduce motion artifacts that disrupt the method.

2 The growth point

The **growth point** or GP is the minimal gesture–speech unit in Vygotsky's (1987) sense of a unit opposed to an element. It is the core of its individual utterance, a "new" gesture-action unified with some linguistic content (word or words), which the speaker inhabits. Table 2.1 shows how, in a GP, a meaning is simultaneously cast in **opposite semiotic modes**. This opposition, or **dual semiosis**, creates the conditions for a dialectic and is the engine driving language and thought forward in social and mental life. In a nutshell: when we see a gesture and the co-expressive speech with which it synchronizes, we see a dynamic unit of speech and thought. Combining the dynamic and static, the GP becomes the minimal unit of the dynamic dimension itself. This is the nexus at which the static and dynamic dimensions cross, and in forming a GP they have equal weight.

It is called a *growth* point because it is meant to be the initial pulse of thinking-for-speaking from which a dynamic process of organization emerges (see McNeill and Duncan 2000). Growth begins with a unification of a gesture with some linguistically encoded information. Neither speech nor gesture is the "source." The imagery in the gesture is visuospatial-actional. It is not photographic. As Table 2.1 shows, this imagery is global-synthetic and non-combinatoric. The linguistic component categorizes this imagery. Linguistic categorization is important since it brings the imagery into the system of language. Gesture is important since it grounds the linguistic categories in an imagery frame. The gesture image provides the GP with the property of "chunking," a hallmark of expert performance (see Chase and Ericsson 1981). A chunk of linguistic output (not necessarily a grammatical chunk) is organized around the presentation of the image. It is the source of gesture–speech orchestration. Synchronized speech and gesture is the key to this theoretical unit.

The GP is shaped, as Michael Silverstein (2003, p. 195) makes clear in another context, not by causes flowing through it but by a "complex and mediated absorption of indexically linked values and presuppositions." The GP is in a middle zone where its basic factors are not understood as causes and effects. A GP may "activate" a later GP, but the state is inhabitance rather than

Table 2.1 Semiotic contrasts within GPs. Cambridge University Press, reprinted with permission.

Imagery side	Language side
Global: Meanings of parts dependent on meaning of whole.	**Compositional:** Meaning of whole dependent on parts.
Synthetic: Distinguishable meanings in single image.	**Analytic:** Distinguishable meanings in separate linguistic forms.
Idiosyncratic: Forms created by individual on the fly.	**Conventional:** Forms regulated by sociocultural standards.
Additive: Images combine to add new details, but do not create new "higher" gestures or syntagmatic values.	**Combinatoric:** Linguistic elements combine into new higher units with syntagmatic values created in the process.

a cause–effect sequence. Later GPs arise as part of this ongoing, ever-changing inhabitance.

To sum up, a growth point is inhabited, belongs to a speaker's "world of meaning," is a "new" gesture-action and is a minimal unit of gesture–speech unity and gesture-orchestrated speech. It is the nexus at which the static and dynamic cross, the two dimensions of language receiving equal weight. Observing it we see a dynamic unit of speech and thought in its momentary existence. A GP exists for only this moment, yet during this time it cannot be broken apart or reduced to smaller elements, its separate words and gestures (see Chapter 4, Section 4.4 "The 'strong prediction' ").

The "rising hollowness" gesture in Figure 1.2 (repeated in Figure 2.1) illustrates a typical GP. In the stroke phase, the speaker raised her hand upward, palm facing up and fingers and thumb spread apart in a kind of upward moving open basket shape, as illustrated (the clip caught the moment she is saying the vowel of "through" with prosodic emphasis). Speech and gesture are co-expressive but semiotically non-redundant. Each has its own means of packaging the shared idea of Sylvester's upness and interiority. Co-expressively with "up" the speaker's hand rose upward; co-expressively with "through" her fingers spread outward to create an interior space. The upward movement and the opening of the hand took place concurrently, not sequentially, and these movements occurred synchronously with "up through," the linguistic package that carries the same meanings. The contrastive emphasis on "through," highlighting interiority, is matched by the added complexity of the gesture, the spreading of the upturned fingers. What makes speech and gesture co-expressive is this joint realization of the idea of upward motion by a figure (Sylvester) and interiority.

Figure 2.1 "Upward hollowness" showing gesture–speech unity (repeats Figure 1.2). Computer art by Fey Parrill. Used with permission of University of Chicago Press.

The idea unit can be called "rising hollowness." How do the semiotic frameworks of the idea unit differ? Speech divides the event into semantic units—a directed path ("up"), plus the idea of interiority ("through"). Analytic division further requires that direction and interiority be combined to obtain the composite meaning of the whole. In gesture, this composite meaning is fused into one symbol and the semantic units are simultaneous—there is no combination (meaning determination moves from the whole to the parts, not from the parts to the whole).

Finally, while speech is combinatoric, gestures are not. Linguistic units and gestures combine on different principles. Unlike gesture, two speech elements, when joined, form a new, higher level element with syntagmatic values from the "axis of combination"(Jakobson). The familiar tree diagram captures these

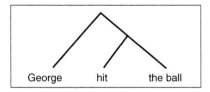

(a)

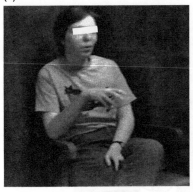

Figure 2.2 Gestures merging. "Down the pipe" at different levels of detail. The hallmark is that a gesture combination provides new detail but not new syntagmatic value, on both scores unlike a linguistic combination (in a transitive verb phrase, "hit the ball," there is no new detail—both the act and the object are what they are independently—but there is a new value, "ball" becomes a direct object.

Figure 2.2a, the speaker's initial description, one hand showing Tweety's 'hand' shaped over the bowling ball as it is thrust into a drainpipe; the downward thrust occurred three times (* = speech interruption):
SPEAKER: [and throws **a bow**<u>ling</u> ball] [down in **the***] [the **thing**]

relationships. "Hit" and "the ball" combine to form a new unit, a verb phrase, and "the ball" acquires the syntagmatic value of a direct object, a value it does not have outside the combination. Two gestures, however, merge and the result is an expansion of detail without a higher gesture unit or new syntagmatic value. Figure 2.2 illustrates two gestures merging without forming a higher gesture or acquiring syntagmatic values.

To be clear about certain concepts:

- By "image" I do not mean a photo or pictogram. I mean a mode of semiosis that is "global" and "synthetic." The "rising hollowness" gesture shows both properties.
- By "global" I mean that the gesture's parts (= the hands/fingers/trajectory/ space/orientation/movement details) have meanings dependent upon the meaning of the gesture as a whole. The parts do not have their own meanings, and the meaning of the whole is not composed out of the parts; rather, significance flows downward, whole to parts. We understand that the hand

(b)

Figure 2.2b, the second description after the listener requested clarification, an elaborated gesture together with an expanded verbal description (the downward thrust now occurring six times):
LISTENER: where does he throw the bowling ball?

SPEAKER: [it's one of those*] [the] [gu][tter pip<u>es</u>] [an' he t][hrows the ball into th<u>e top</u>]
In 2.2b, the left hand adds pictorial detail but the value is intrinsic to the imagery and does not arise from the left hand–right hand combination, unlike the way that a direct object arises when a noun is combined with a transitive verb in a verb phrase.
Cambridge University Press, reprinted with permission.

as a rising whole is Sylvester ascending; from this whole, the fingers are the pipe and the spreading of the fingers is hollowness.
- By "synthetic," I mean that meanings are synthesized into one symbolic form (the rising hollowness hand).
- The linguistic semiotic is the opposite in every respect. In the synchronous speech, the gesture's synthetic meaning is analytic separated into elements spread over the surface of the sentence ("goes" + "up"). The meaning of the linguistic whole (the sentence or other unit) is composed out of parts, and these have their own meanings—"goes," "up," "through"; and in addition "this time" for contrast to a preceding attempt in the cartoon story (where Sylvester climbed the pipe on the outside).
- Gesture–speech synchrony, co-expressive of the shared idea (and where not co-expressive, the gesture and speech will not be synchronous), is an essential part of thought. It brings together, at the same moment, these semiotic opposites, imagery and linguistic form, without which there is no dialectic.
- There is, moreover, an "all-at-onceness" in a GP's formation (a concept from Quaeghebeur 2012). All-at-onceness, as it says, means that the GP concept

must be taken literally all at once, not piecemeal and not sequentially. This has more than methodological significance. It explains the resistance to breakdown into elements of GPs.

To summarize, the speaker in Figure 2.1/1.2 illustrates global and synthetic gesture properties combined with analytic and combinatoric speech properties, and these were simultaneous. The gestures do not admit any decomposition. There are no sub-units with independent meanings, no repeatable significances for the outspread fingers and upward palm of Figure 2.1/1.2. Only upward motion has independent meaning. It means upward, but that is all, and it is not enough to generate the meaning of the gesture whole. And even this upward meaning acquires significance as a part of the whole (it means *rising hollowness*, which comes from the whole, not from upward simple). The gesture is not composed out of parts: the parts are (de)composed out of it. Also, the gesture is more a unified whole than just the combination of up and through. I have tried to convey this unity with the expression "rising hollowness," but whatever the phrase, the gesture has interiority, entity and upward motion in one undecomposable symbolic form. The gesture synthesized ideas that in speech required separation—the figure in motion, the direction and the idea of interiority were unified in the gesture, while the same ideas were distributed into "he," "goes up" and "thrOUgh" in speech.

2.1   Absorbing context

In addition to dual semiosis, dynamic dimension change arises from the constantly updated, itself dynamic, immediate context of speaking. Regarding the GP as a **psychological predicate** in a field of equivalents clarifies the sense we use for the term "context." The word has a host of meanings (see Duranti and Goodwin 1992) but for our purposes, "context" is the background from which a psychological predicate is differentiated. This absorption is also a vehicle of change. This section explains absorption, how it takes place and presents a natural experiment demonstrating its reality.

2.1.1   The psychological predicate

An implication of the GP is that *one meaning is two things*. It is (1) a point of differentiation and (2) the context, the field of meaningful equivalents, that it differentiates: "one meaning" is both. This makes the GP inherently dynamic. Merely intending, recalling or associating something is not enough. The field of meaningful equivalents must also be included. This conception differs from familiar "one-thing" conceptions such as "signified content," "association," etc. that regard meaning without absorbing context. Why meaning takes this form when "one thing" seems enough is explained by how language began, the very existence of language depended on it (how is explained in Chapter 6).

These conceptions of context and sense or meaning are subsumed under the Vygotskian concept of a **psychological predicate**. In a psychological (as opposed to a grammatical) predicate, newsworthy content is differentiated from a context. One of Vygotsky's examples is a crashing clock (1987, p. 250): there is a crash in the next room—someone asks: "What fell?" (the answer: "The clock"), or: "What happened to the clock?" ("It fell"). Depending on the context—here crystallized in the questions—the newsworthy reply (the psychological predicate) highlights different elements.[1]

This logic also applies to the GP. In forming a GP, the speaker shapes the background in a certain way, in order to highlight an intended differentiation within it while fulfilling "two things," much as the questioner about the falling clock shaped the context of the replies.

A psychological predicate:

- marks a significant departure in the immediate context; and
- implies this context as background.

Regarding the GP as a psychological predicate suggests that the mechanism of GP formation is differentiation of a newsworthy point of focus from a background. The GP is differentiation of a "figure" from a "ground." Such differentiation is validated by the very close temporal connection of gesture (strokes) with the peaks of acoustic output in speech, which also highlight newsworthiness (Nobe 1996).

Echoing the Jakobson (1960) paper already cited, I use the terms, "field of meaningful equivalents" and "significant (newsworthy) contrast" to refer respectively to the background and the differentiation of the "figure" within it. *The background is itself a part of thought and is adjustable by the speaker to make the differentiation meaningful.* All of this is meant to be a dynamic, continuously updated process in which new fields of equivalents are formed and new psychological predicates are differentiated in ongoing cycles of thinking for speaking.

2.1.2 A natural experiment

The bowling ball episode is the second of Sylvester's attempts to reach Tweety by climbing the drainpipe in our cartoon stimulus. In the first, which appeared immediately before, he climbs the pipe on the outside, using it as a kind of ladder. As usual, his effort fails. He immediately tries again, now a stealth

---

[1] Wallace Chafe suggested the term "newsworthy."

approach on the inside, leading to the bowling ball and its aftermath. This quirk in the cartoon lends itself to a natural experiment showing that GPs are psychological predicates that differentiate newsworthy information within immediate contexts.[2]

The experiment is the following: describing the first attempt, the field of meaningful equivalents would be something like *ways of using the drainpipe* (this is first mention of the pipe) and the psychological predicate something like *climb it*. With the second attempt, climbing itself is no longer newsworthy. It has become background and the field of meaningful equivalents would be updated to something like *ways of climbing the drainpipe*. In this field, interiority is newsworthy: *on the inside*.

If a speaker recalls both attempts in the correct outside–inside order, the psychological predicate relating to the second attempt should focus on interiority. This follows from the psychological predicate concept; in the updated field of meaningful equivalents, interiority becomes the newsworthy feature.

However, if a speaker recalls only the inside attempt and fails to recall the outside attempt, or recalls both attempts but reverses their order, interiority should not be newsworthy. This also follows from the psychological predicate concept. Interiority, lacking a field of meaningful equivalents, should not be a psychological predicate, even though the speaker has registered and recalls it as a fact. Speakers omit many details and interiority without exteriority, even when observed and remembered, is just one more. The field of meaningful equivalents would be about climbing, and interiority would not form a psychological predicate in this field.

Of the six original subjects in McNeill and Levy (1982), two recalled only the inside attempt. For them, interiority had no newsworthy significance and their gestures did not contain it, even though they went on to describe the bowling ball and its aftermath, demonstrating that they had in fact recognized interiority as an element of the story. Three speakers recalled both attempts in the correct order, and in each case their gestures highlighted interiority.

The sixth speaker also recalled both attempts but incorrectly remembered Sylvester's first ascent as by a non-existent ladder (no ladder appeared in the cartoon). For the second try the speaker did recall the pipe. So this speaker remembered not contrasting paths (inside versus outside), but contrasting *grounds* (using Talmy's 2000 terms), "ladder" versus pipe. Here is an exception that proves a rule. Interiority, a path property, would not be part of the psychological predicate for either ascent, and the speaker included interiority neither in speech ("he tries **cli**mbing up_ the <nn> dra**inspout**") nor gesture (it showed direction only). No GP differentiation of interiority took place.

---

[2] Susan Duncan discovered the logic of the natural experiment.

Nonetheless, she went on to describe the bowling ball event, and so showed that she had noticed and remembered it.

The natural experiment shows the psychological predicate, as the essential point of the GP, capturing exactly what is newsworthy in the immediate field of meaningful equivalents but ignoring the same information even if it was perceived and remembered when, through narrative mischance, it is not newsworthy. Again, this selectivity follows from the psychological predicate concept of "one meaning" being two things, one the context, the other the differentiation of it.

2.2   The dialectic

Static and dynamic intersect in GPs and create an opposition of global-synthetic, non-combinatoric versus analytic combinatoric semiotic modes and an imagery–language dialectic. This dialectic seems to go beyond Humboldt, who wrote, "In itself it [language] is no product—*Ergon*)—but an activity—*Energeia*. Its true definition can therefore only be a genetic one" (Humboldt 1999, p. 49). One agrees that the true definition of language must be "genetic," but Humboldt seems to dismiss *Ergon* as having no more than descriptive interest. We are considering it to be functional, with *Energeia* part of an imagery–language dialectic. It is functional also in that it supplies "stop-orders," intuitions of good form signaling that the dialectic has achieved stability. In these intuitions, the speaker directly experiences the static dimension. In the intended sense of the term, as fuel of speech in context, a dialectic arises from the following:

• A GP involves an opposition of the semiotic modes of imagery and linguistic categorization when they embody the same underlying idea, at the same time, as illustrated in the Figure 2.1/1.2 example.
• Having one idea in two semiotic modes at the same time is unstable. A GP seeks stability, which it achieves through unpacking itself into one or more syntactic constructions or approximations thereto, these providing a stopping point and completing the process of growth (a new cycle normally starting immediately, a preceding GP often reappearing as the new field of equivalents).
• The unpacking renders the GP as a socially validated entity in *langue*, gesture–imagery providing the framework within which the unpacking proceeds.
• The imagery–language dialectic is thus a model of the animation of language.

Why must the GP be unstable? I had supposed that instability was self-evident in a dual semiosis and have never spelled it out, but I will attempt it here.[3] One way to articulate it is in the classic dialectic triad of thesis (gesture)–antithesis (language form)–synthesis (a construction with the gesture in the right place). This captures the GP: there is a "contradiction" between gesture and form in terms of their semiotic modes; the unpacking with a construction is a resolution through the synthesis of form and gesture.

Another way to say it is that one idea wants one form, not two forms. The GP is compelled by its own logic to take two forms *and* is equally compelled to find a single form that will cradle it (a new object, stable as object, from the system of *langue*).

The instability is of a gesture–speech *unit*. The dialectic refers to this unit. The GP, the unit, is the whole, yet within it the meaning takes two modes, opposed yet tied together; this is the dialectic and the force for change and growth. The gesture itself is dynamic in that it is context-dependent and created on the spot, but this isn't the instability we have in mind. This instability comes from having one idea in two semiotic forms at the same time, when it "wants" one form. And the endpoint is found in a single form, a syntactic construction with the GP cradled in it and gesture attached. The construction itself is no longer just a static form in *langue* but a form with a gesture attached at the right place, and has joined the dynamic dimension.

Wundt's **simultaneous/successive awareness** distinction clarifies how the minimal gesture–speech GP unit spans both the whole utterance and is also located at a specific point within it:

From a psychological point of view, the sentence is both a simultaneous and a sequential structure. It is simultaneous because at each moment it is present in consciousness as a totality even though the individual subordinate elements may occasionally disappear from it. It is sequential because the configuration changes from moment to moment in its cognitive condition as individual constituents move into the focus of attention and out again one after another. (Blumenthal 1970, p. 21)[4]

The cognitive core, the GP, is the **simultaneous awareness** of the whole but it is also in **successive awareness** at a particular point in the sentence. If you visualize a suspension bridge with a tower in the middle and cables on either side supporting it, this tower is the GP in successive awareness, the supporting cables the GP in simultaneous awareness. "Gesture–speech unity" accordingly has a dual temporal reference, and does so for a reason. The GP is the simultaneous awareness of the sentence, an awareness often beginning even before the sentence begins and covering the whole. The sentence structure, however, also unpacks the GP. This unpacking is *of* the simultaneous GP and depends on it. Unpacking is in successive awareness and locates the GP

---

[3] I am indebted to Renia Lopez-Ozieblo for alerting me to this problem.
[4] I am grateful to Zenzi Griffin for calling my attention to this all-important passage.

within it. So the GP is also in successive awareness, *at* a particular place in its own unpacking.

A note on terms: the seeming contradiction when I say that imagery "opposes" language and also say that imagery is "part" of language is illusory. Different senses of "language" are involved, senses which Saussure's French clarifies, *langue* or the system of language for "opposes" and *langage* or the semiotic totality of language for "is part of." It would be tedious to always use the French terms, and I rely on context and say "language."

2.3   Minimal units

A gesture–speech unit is what Vygotsky (1987) termed a "minimal psychological unit"—the smallest package that retains the quality of a whole, in this case the whole of a GP and imagery–language dialectic. At the unit level, the properties of the whole include global-synthetic semiosis and the dual semiosis of this and linguistic form. Vygotsky contrasts units to "elements," the latter (in this case) the result of reducing the GP to sub-personal events (words, gestures, considered separately) that do not have the property of gesture–speech unity, the whole. And now we also see that units (but not elements) perfuse simultaneous and successive awareness. Awareness is awash with this semiotic package, as gesture-orchestrated speech is taking place. All these qualities reside irreducibly in the minimal gesture–speech unit.

By a unit we mean a product of analysis which, in distinction from elements, possesses all the basic properties of a whole. Further, these properties must be a living portion of the unified whole which cannot be broken down further. (Vygotsky, *Thinking and Speech*, 1934, quoted by Zinchenko 1985, p. 97)

Vygotsky thus contrasts units to "elements," the latter the result of reducing (in this case) the GP to sub-personal events that do not preserve an imagery–language unity (sub-personal events, as they are termed by Quaeghebeur and Reynaert (2010), are word retrievals, true/false judgments and many others, because they are relatively easy to measure and simulate that figure in experimental studies and in computer models; none are Vygotskian units). We adopt Vygotsky's anti-reduction position and stay on the unit level. For this reason, to access minimal units, methods in which gesture and speech are coded independently ("to avoid contamination") mislead. They conceal the very thing we want to see, a gesture–speech unit. The concept can be empirically studied only if we code gesture and speech together.[5]

So, why posit units at all? I am told that Heidegger and Merleau-Ponty managed without them. A unit pertains to phenomena in which apparently they

---

[5] The methods Susan Duncan and Karl-Erik McCullough pioneered have this goal.

had little interest.[6] But units are important for the psychology of language. Units speak to beginnings, ends and intervals. They capture the *moment* of Being in language and how it is organized. The unit provides the space within which phenomena take place and gives them edges. A unit has the power of self-containment. It does not need an external, third-party intelligence to make it work. Self-unpacking by a GP is an illustration. A unit makes the general local. This indeed is the basic reason for having the concept. It bridges general principles such as the dialectic, inhabitance and the dynamic/static dimensions into time, a domain with a host of important linguistic and psychological phenomena. Ideas and utterances have beginnings, middles and ends. Cognitive Being (as opposed to Being as a mode of life) has insights that flash on and off; immediate memory that is truncated both at its beginning and end; attention that shifts and peaks; all correlated with gesture–speech unity. Memory is dynamic over Wundt's awarenesses and changes to something else at their close. All these synchronies with speech require the concept of a unit.

Once you think of units this way, dual semiosis is self-evident and true of the whole; the gesture preparation/stroke/retraction gives the temporal boundaries of simultaneous awareness into which successive awareness sprinkles the linguistic bits. But just laying a gesture and linguistic segment side-by-side is not a unit; it is just two single semiotic elements. The "knot" tying them is the dual semiotic imagery–language form dialectic of opposed semiotic modes, with resolution via unpackings. One takes them all at once.

2.4   "Two tribes"

I add this section with some hesitation. It is speculative and based on personal experience but others say it rings true, and I propose possible tests. From this resonance and potential for testing, I feel justified including it in a discussion of the GP.

I have noticed in conversations with acquaintances and casual encounters two forms of integrating speech and thought: one seemingly fitting the GP, to which I unquestionably belong, and the other more modular—Kita's Information Processing Hypothesis (IPH) (2000), inspired by Levelt's *Speaking* (1989), being a well-developed description of it—that other speakers find more fitting. I summarized the IPH in 2005 and how it differs from the GP as follows:

The IPH addresses what the GP does not, namely, what occurs when a synchronization of co-expressive speech and gesture does not occur– a contextual mismatch, a memory lapse, or some other kind of breakdown. The IPH considers speech and gesture to be independent cognitive streams, running simultaneously and interweaving in time. The concept of independent and interweaving streams gives the theory a way to deal with

---

[6] Based on discussions in spring 2014 with Elena Cuffari (pers. comm.).

speech and gesture asynchronies. When a speech blockage occurs, gesture continues and is able to develop new packages of information suitable for linguistic encoding. The theory thus specifically applies to situations where speech aborts, gesture continues, and speech then resumes, utilizing a new gesture-induced information package.

A further observation in this situation is that once speech and gesture resume, a *second gesture* often takes place, and the second gesture is synchronous and co-expressive with the renewed speech; this gesture-speech combination could be a GP. The two models, IPH and GP, thus might dovetail in time as well as complement each other in function.

In both IPH and GP, imagery is regarded as an integral component of language, but there are also differences:

Minimal unit difference: The GP is a minimal unit in Vygotsky's sense: a unit that retains the essential properties of the whole. Despite its use of 'packaging' the IPH does not have such units. The model envisions speech and gesture modularly, as separate, intertwining streams.

Abstract imagery difference: In the GP, imagery is categorized linguistically. It is thus never purely visuospatial. On the other hand, the IPH appears to regard gesture as visual thinking pure and simple.

Interface differences: Regarding speech and gesture as separate intertwining streams, the IPH requires an image-language interface for the exchange of information between them. The GP does not have an interface—imagery and language combine dialectically. An imagery-language dialectic versus an interface is the single difference that seems to best encapsulate the contrast between the GP and IPH views of language and thought. (McNeill 2005, pp. 129ff.)

What may seem a precursor of the gesture-orchestrated speech concept was pioneered by Robert Krauss (see Krauss et al. 2000) but the resemblance is illusory. It is quite different and has the same limitations as the IPH—modularity that again limits the applicability to only when speech stops. Indeed, Krauss et al. considered resolving speech blockage their problematic—in the model, gesture arises when words fail, applying to silences, the same as the IPH. In both cases, modularity, which is preset and independent of any context, prevents the model from articulating how a language–thought unit absorbs context, this being intrinsic to gesture-orchestrated speech. I wrote of the model:

The key step in this model is the use of gesture to assist lexical retrieval. ... If there is some delay in retrieving a word, drainpipe, say, a gesture with some of the spatial features of a drainpipe (e.g., "verticality," "hollowness") can be fed into the lexical system and prime the word, and thereby aid retrieval. This mechanism will work to fish out missing words but it does not explain [a GP]. The word "drops" had features that matched the downward thrusting gesture (downward, curved, etc.), yet this word was excluded from the gesture stroke via [preparation and] a prestroke hold, the gesture withheld until the word had gone by. Furthermore, the same downward and curved features matched a different set of lexical features, those of the bowling ball (indexed by "it") and the path ("down"). Why did the gesture target these lexical items and exclude "drops"? We know the answer—the contextual contrast of C2 vs. C3. Thus, to achieve its lexical retrieval goals, the gesture system must have access to contextual information at its foundational core. But this content is excluded by the modular design of the Krauss, et al. model. (McNeill 2000, p. 321)

So, although gesture is part of speaking, as the model sees, it cannot explain gesture-orchestrated speech.

Intuitions affect arguments and positions in the field of gesture studies, so it is important to understand this source of differences. I will maintain that the GP is at the core of everyone's linguistic cognition (language evolved so) but for some individuals, a second process arises that shifts thought, language and Being into a kind of third-person mode. In the "GP-tribe," language and thought are non-linear, dialectical and unmodular; while in the "IPH-tribe" they are linear, non-dialectical and modular. Here is the modular scheme:

CONCEPTUALIZER (VERBALIZABLE IDEA)

⇓

FORMULATOR (LINGUISTIC FORM)

⇓

ARTICULATOR (ORCHESTRATION OF
VOCAL TRACT)

The best way to tell which model applies in an individual case is whether the GP or the IPH seems more plausible to a person (assuming they understand both theories). We all rely on our own sense of the nature of language and thought to guide our theoretical ideas, and if these differ in the ways the GP and IPH models suggest, there would be plausible grounds to think that the two kinds of speakers can be identified by what they find natural. While intermediate or mixed cases exist (two are described in the next paragraph), this discussion sketches the differences in stark terms, the better to clarify the distinction.

And extreme cases do exist. I can testify from my own experience that to speak according to *Speaking* is impossible; the required Conception–Formulation–Articulation sequence does not exist, and to impose it causes thought or speech or both to collapse. My experience is to inhabit speech, gesture and context. I have, fortunately, an informant just as purely in the opposite direction. To her the Conceptualizer–Formulator–Articulator sequence is natural, and it is from my discussions with her, in fact, that this section arises. I am told by a second informant (who appears to have both modes) that social interactions seem mediated IPH-style and private thought by the GP—a provocative observation, since it reinforces the intuition that the modes do not blend even if both reside within the same individual, and when they do coexist may gravitate to different contexts of use. Renia Lopez-Ozieblo has been told by a native German speaker with English fluency that he experiences German as an IPHer, English as a GPer. If this does not reflect greater pressure to an IPH style with some languages, it also suggests that when in the same person the GP and IPH may gravitate to different contexts.

Fluency may also differ, with smooth talk a hallmark of modular talkers not necessarily because they use rehearsed speech, but once an idea is conceptualized, formulation/articulation runs off without further intervention; while for a GP talker there is inevitably a further thought-context generation with which to unpack it, and this can break down in various ways. Or, perhaps, the modes are both subject to disfluencies but at characteristically different places—delays of the initiation of idea units for the IPH type; disruptions more midstream for the GP type as fields of equivalents, the GP, unpacking or all are rearranged. Moreover, if the GP is not immediate but itself seems to falter, another form of disruption for the GPer is premature unpacking, which forces the GP to lockjaw as it then is, and this is intuitively distorting. The threat of early closure may be another hallmark of the GP style while withheld speech may mark the IPH.

Another telling aspect of the GP and IPH types is the distribution of effort during speech. As my informant tells me, and from observations of other presumed IPHers, effort comes at the Formulation stage. For a GPer the effort goes into unpacking and can reveal itself anywhere in speech. Effort may reflect distinct GP and IPH styles of inhabitance—the GPer inhabiting in the moment of speech, the IPHer standing outside and observing it.

The two tribes in other words may have different modes of inhabiting cognitive Being. As already characterized, the GP mode is to inhabit gesture and language, more broadly to inhabit imagery with thought and linguistic encoding, and to differentiate the ensemble from the immediate context. The perspective is first-person, inside language. The IPH mode may be less embodied—something more like witnessing one's own performance, where the speaker/thinker adopts an external, third-person perspective towards his/her own thought and language, duly consulting context but not inhabiting it or language or gesture (exactly as Levelt diagrammed in *Speaking*). A tendency of IPHers to load heavily with deixis fits this picture. Disfluencies at the initiation stage of idea units also fit this form of Being: hesitation when the mind contemplates its own speech, but once started there is no further activity (the 'modular' feature).

How can a different mode of cognitive Being—witnessing—arise from the gesture–speech unity framework? They may represent distinct hereditary lines. Are IPHers, like redheads, an inheritable variation of a basic human quality? If so, they would run in families but might have GPer relatives. Or the IPH may be an appended psychological type by the person at some point in their development atop the GP. This explanation seems more likely to me. In this second explanation an IPH utterance begins, as does every utterance, with a GP differentiation of a field of meaningful equivalents, and might even get as far as to be unpacked, but then the IPH speaker steps outside and rather than inhabit gesture and speech, takes a third-person witnessing stance.

The "third person" inspects the GP and its unpacking and only then, only with this license, speech is released. Said Soames Forsyte, a paragon of the type: "I think before I speak; I think again before I act." Introspectively it appears as a Conception–Formulation–Articulation sequence, but actually is a "third-person" appended phase looking at the gesture–speech unit much the way experimenters look at the subjects in their experiments.

The two tribes are not without predicted outcomes. First, as mentioned, IPHer speech delays should appear before speech and not in the middle of utterances. Second, introspectively, IPHers should experience something like the *Speaking* modules but GPers never do.

2.5   Summary of the GP

The GP is the minimal unit of the dynamic dimension of language:

1 The GP is dynamic because it's not stable (the same thought or idea in opposite semiotic modes at the same time, global-synthetic in gesture, analytic-combinatoric in speech).
2 It is dynamic because it cannot exist without the context it differentiates.
3 Differentiation is part of the GP and also changes the context for the next GP.

These are the sources of change in the GP. What changes? Several things, correlated with the sources:

1 The instability of opposite semiotic modes "calls" a construction that stabilizes it.
2 The occurrence of this construction is a further source of change and it explains how the surface utterance occurs, speech pushing communication forward, while cradling the intact GP.

A quick list of GP properties:

1 It is proposed as the minimal unit of gesture–speech unity (Vygotsky).
2 It is a dialectic package that has both linguistic categorial and actional-imagistic components.
3 It is inferred from the totality of communicative events with special focus on speech–gesture synchrony and co-expressivity.
4 It is inseparable from its immediate context, much as a gestalt.
5 It puts the simultaneous and successive awarenesses envisioned by Wundt into an integrated system, as the "it down" sentence again illustrates. "It down" with the gesture was the core idea in simultaneous awareness, covering the whole utterance. It remained intact when unpacked, where it came to the surface. And this process is remarkable for its speech and accuracy; not perfection but when it works it has these qualities to a remarkable degree.
6 It absorbs the context, creating "one meaning is two things," fostering the GP as a particular point in the discourse context.

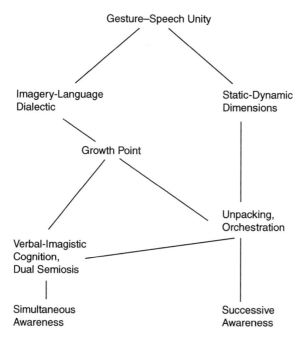

Figure 2.3 Binary oppositions, showing logical relations among terms.

All of this is why we gesture, to answer our original question. Gesture is an integral part of speaking. And language could not have begun without it, as we shall see later. When we turn to phylogenesis, we will find an even deeper answer.

2.5.1   The many binaries

I have made Figure 2.3 to sort out the many binary pairs plus a few other critical terms the preceding has introduced.

3   New forms of human action

3.1   Two kinds of action

The argument of this chapter is that *gesture-orchestrated speech cannot have practical action sources.*[1] This is contrary to a much-taken-for-granted although unconfirmed theory that gestures descend from pragmatic actions. The argument will be that pragmatic actions do not explain *why* we gesture. *When the hands make a gesture, it is one's Being, one's position in the world of meanings that controls them and not a hidden action in relation to the world of objects.* Moreover, the two hypotheses cannot be combined; they conflict at the core. Inhabitance of a gesture is not "done." Whatever its content, it has a different relationship to the person. A pragmatic action relates to the external world. A goal is an intrinsic part of it and cannot be expunged without the action losing an essential part of its significance. Gestures derived from it carry it too (nothing removes it). If Being includes a pragmatic action and goal, it is a separate relationship to speaking (lacking co-expressiveness). The most natural gesture it produces is pantomime, a simulation of action that has the property that it avoids speech, the opposite of gesture-orchestrated speech. Instead, a new form of human action, "new" gesture-action, evolved along with language to perform the gesture-orchestrated speech function. A gesture of wiping something cannot retain the goal of wiping and be co-expressive with "I'm wiping it." This is because speech does not have the goal of wiping something (an external goal). The goal of speech is to communicate that I'm wiping something (a speaker goal). Pragmatic actions have this one defining property that gestures lack, implicit real-world goals. An implicit goal is an unavoidable consequence of a gesture that descends from a pragmatic action; it automatically includes it. Gesture and speech thus each has a goal the other does not; face-to-face co-expression does not exist; and such a gesture therefore cannot

---

[1] This chapter was inspired by an anonymous Cambridge University Press reviewer who vigorously argued to the contrary. The chapter articulates differences I have long sensed between the "trilogy" and the widespread belief that pragmatic actions are the sources of gestures. The differences are profound. Explaining them helps explain the central idea of gesture-orchestrated speech itself.

orchestrate speech. *For this key reason, gesture-orchestrated speech cannot descend from pragmatic actions.*

This chapter also brings further clarification of what is a "gesture," by distinguishing "new" gesture-actions from practical action-actions, the "old" kind (adjectives referring to phylogenesis: "new" in human evolution versus primate "old," and as well to the order of emergence in current-day discussions of gesture). The inhabitance mentioned in Chapter 1 is of "new" gesture-actions. An "old" pragmatic action can be inhabited as it is performed but it then becomes part of one's state of Being. The "new" gesture-action/"old" action-action difference is unbridgeable. An "old" action has a different relationship to the individual, who "performs" it, carrying it out with an implicit goal.

We need to consider three types of goals, only one of which is important for gesture-orchestrated speech but the others of which tend to become entangled with it: (1) *to gesture*, where the goal is to make a gesture with a certain meaning; (2) *to speak*, where the goal is to say something with a certain meaning; and (3) *to perform a pragmatic action*, where the goal is to have a certain effect. Number (2) is the speaker's fundamental goal. The basic hypothesis of *Why We Gesture* is that gestures orchestrate it; accordingly (1), the goal of making a gesture, is irrelevant; it is superfluous. Speakers tend to be unaware of their own gestures because they do not have the goal of making them. Also, while a speaker naturally utters a sentence with the goal of communicating a meaning, orchestration of speech by gesture is not a goal (similarly, to say "pin," "person," "pump," etc. in order to close the lips is not usually a goal). Gesture-orchestrated speech is inherent to language but the gesture is not purposeful. It is a "new" gesture-action, not an "old" action-action. Speech of course may be about a practical action and this action includes its goal, but the vocal movements the gesture is trying to orchestrate have no such goal.

And the main point in this chapter is that gesture-orchestrated speech excludes (3), the goal of practical action. An implicit real-world goal prevents gesture and speech from attaining co-expressiveness. Gestures orchestrate only the speech with which they co-express the same meaning, but speech lacks the "old" action-action goal of a real-world effect; its goal is to communicate meaning, attain rapport, control both intra- and interpersonal coherence, and other effects that occupy one's Being.

Clearly, this differs from Kendon's conclusion that speech and gesture "does not descend from communicative vocalizations and visible displays but from manipulatory activities of a practical sort," like making something flat (Kendon 2009, p. 19).In *Hand and Mind* (McNeill 1992), I described two mathematicians at the Institute for Advanced Study, in Princeton, whom I had videotaped seemingly handing back and forth a brick-like object (standing for a mathematical idea) (Figure 3.1). In 1992, the "new"/"old" difference was not apparent; there was no hypothesis of pragmatic actions as the sources of gestures

(a)   (b)

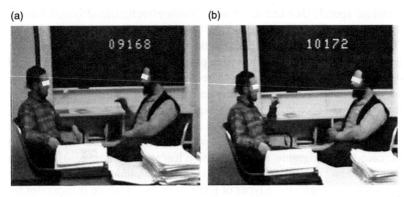

Figure 3.1 Mathematician R seeming to hand an object with mathematical meaning to mathematician L, and L taking it. The second mathematician used his left hand, thus maintaining the side of the gesture space the first mathematician initated (although L was right-handed). The slice of space seems to have taken on a shared non-spatial, mathematical meaning.

of which I was aware and no contrary hypothesis of "new" gesture-actions. Looking at Figure 3.1 now, the gestures may look like "old" action-actions, but were they really actions—one person handing over a mathematical object to another person and the other taking it? Or were they, alternatively, metaphoric gestures, instances of the so-called "conduit" gesture (Reddy 1979; Lakoff and Johnson 1980), in which the hand is not simulating an action but creating an image of what the conduit metaphor presents—an idea experienced as an object in the hand? I choose this second explanation. The first mathematician invoked the conduit metaphor and the second, following the conversation, adopted it, but regardless of this choice the key point is that the two possibilities must be recognized.[2]

Kendon (2004) devised an experiment that unexpectedly illustrates the "new."[3] A video of a New Guinea orator delivering an address in his local language was shown to experimental subjects. They were non-natives, unfamiliar with the culture and had not seen the video before. There was no sound. The subjects replayed the silent tape at their own pace, pausing when necessary as they identified the movements they thought were gestures. A gesture was defined as "part of what the speaker was trying to say," more specifically, a movement that appeared to have been conscious, deliberate and intended. Gestures were to be distinguished from other movements—object manipulations, posture

[2] Thanks to Randall B. McNeill for pointing out this inadvertent ambiguity in *Hand and Mind*.
[3] Müller (2014), in her article celebrating Adam Kendon's achievements, reminded me of this experiment, which Kendon describes in *Gesture* (2004).

adjustments, and nervous tics. The participants did this task with remarkable accuracy, on first exposure. Kendon summarizes his experiment in part as follows: "It seems that participants single out and treat differently some aspects of each other's behaviour as somehow more salient to the immediate communication than other aspects" (2004, p. 12).

The process of gesture-orchestrated speech via "new" gesture-actions explains this ability: the speaker had shaped "new" gesture-actions to orchestrate the speech he was producing. That non-natives could identify them without access to speech (which they could not have deciphered in any case) suggests that these "new" gesture-actions have distinctive kinesic properties, similar enough across languages and cultures for the subjects to detect them. Kendon identified several of these: the movements the participants called gestures had sharp onsets and offsets, and moved against gravity or outward from the body. We can see how "new" gesture-actions could have produced these kinesic properties. They are features not just of movements per se but also what the actualization of a meaning in a speech-orchestrating gesture produces. Meaning does not dawn or dwindle gradually—hence a sharp onset and offset, and it packs energy—hence movement against gravity. A further point, however, is that a gesture need not have any connection with deliberateness or intention (the subjects had to be instructed this way, but it is a mistake to attribute it to the speaker). I submit that the ability to distinguish gestures from other motions shows what this chapter introduces as "new" gesture-actions. The remainder of the chapter develops this concept.

I have the impression that many in the gesture field take for granted that the source of a gesture is an "old" action-action. It seems the default belief. Although his conditional suggests caution, John Haviland (2013) says at one point, "if gestures are practical actions," and Kendon more explicitly says that a gesture of something being flat is like "*making* something flat" (2009, p. 19; the full quote appears in the following text). More generally, alluding to Streeck (2009), Kendon states that "many of the actions [i.e., gestures] understood as meaningful can be understood as being derived from actions of the hands acting in relation to objects in the environment." Müller (2014) has proposed classifications of gesture based on the kinds of practical actions a gesture resembles—drawing, shaping, tracing, etc. The idea always seems to be that gesture stems from practical action. Kendon gives a more complex version:

[Gestures] are "ritualized" versions of grasping, reaching, holding, manipulating, and so forth. Given their intimate connection with speaking, I make a speculative leap, and argue that speaking itself is derived from practical actions. Acts of utterance are to be understood, ultimately, as derived versions of action system ensembles mobilized to achieve practical consequences. The origin of language, that is to say, derives by a process of "symbolic transformation" of forms of action that were not communicatively specialized to begin with. Speech and associated gesturing does not descend from communicative vocalizations and visible displays but from manipulatory activities of a practical sort. (Kendon 2009, p. 19)

Kendon here addresses how "old" action-actions can be refashioned though "ritualization" and "symbolic transformation" to become gestures. But no filter or other means of expunging implicit real-world goals is provided. In terms of this chapter, "ritualization" and "symbolic transformation" are replaced by the "new" gesture-actions that emerged as part of the origin of language, actions that evolved to make gesture-orchestrated speech possible.

The idea that gestures derive from actions is plausible at first glance but there is more (or perhaps less) than meets the eye. A gesture may look like a pragmatic action and to describe it as "outlining" or "shaping" is useful but also to say that such a gesture is a metonym of an "old" action-action (Müller 2014) is to leave something unsaid about what makes it a human sign. The "rising hollowness" gesture (seen first in Figure 1.2) looks like the action of lifting something in the hand, but this gesture is not lifting at all. It is an image of the character rising, of the interior of the pipe through which he rose, and of the direction of his motion upward—all compacted into one symbolic form to differentiate a field of meaningful equivalents having to do with *how to climb a pipe: on the inside*. This complex idea, as a unity, orchestrated the hand shape and movement; it is the same motor response but it is not the same action of lifting up an object.

I do not wish to single out Müller, Kendon or Streeck in this discussion, but they have been the clearest and most articulate advocates of the hypothesis that pragmatic actions are the sources of gesture. That and their stature in the gesture studies field make it inevitable that I am drawn to their writings. I have been told that "old" action-action advocates, in making such proposals, do not assume that gestures have implicit practical goals. Saying they do, I am again told, invents a distinction where none exists. But the admonitions are misdirected. It is not a matter of what an author "assumes" but of what their "old" action-action hypothesis logically includes. Goal-directedness cannot be glossed over or dismissed as "not assumed." As Elena Levy describes the situation, "the argument that gesture-orchestrated speech can't have goal-directedness refers **real-world goals** (as opposed to a progression in speech toward a spoken goal, for example a narrator spelling out a central theme as he creates a complex symbol)" (pers. comm.). I will go so far as to say that *without an implicit goal, the gesture cannot be said to have a practical action source.* "Old" action-action traps its gestures in this logic. To deny that gestures with "old" action-action sources have implicit real-world goals faces a contradiction. The "old" action-action hypothesis cannot remove implicit goal-direction (somehow) from gesture without jeopardizing the very hypothesis it is meant to protect. To posit that the action is of the "old" kind (making something flat) means that a speech-orchestrating gesture of something flat must not have it as its source; and vice versa, if a gesture does have it as a source it cannot orchestrate speech (it will be a pantomime, an action mimicry).

Part of the scope, creativity and distinctiveness of human thought lies precisely in its creation of these new kinds of action—"new" and belonging to a heritage of humans, not apparent in other species. Part of our inhabitance of "new" gesture-action is the freedom it opens from pragmatic action constraints.

One might think that saying something like "over there" with a pointing gesture is a counterexample.[4] The gesture seems capable of orchestrating speech, yet it has a pragmatic goal and speech has the same goal, which is to direct the recipient's attention to a locus. But pointing is not gesticulation. As we saw in Chapter 1, the hand shape in the form of a point relates to speech in a different manner from a gesticulation, more like that of an emblem. The "point of pointing" is to achieve the pragmatic effect of focusing attention on a target. Over this pragmatic range of directing attention, pointing and speech can be co-expressive precisely because they share this goal. Other gestures with pragmatic goals also can orchestrate speech with the same goal; for example, "sit dOWn!" (with a downward, palm-down, gesture). All of this is possible, however, only when speech and gesture share a real-world goal, such as attention-direction. Pointing is unique in other ways—for example, a huge ontogenetic gap opens between the emergences of pointing and the dawn of gesticulation; two or three *years*, strongly suggesting different sources (see Chapter 7).

---

[4] Thanks to Elena Levy.

In summary, I argue that the gestures in gesture-orchestrated speech cannot have implicit goal-directedness in general. Goal-direction prevents the gesture from attaining co-expressiveness with speech (only gestures and speech with shared real-world goals, such as attention-direction, are co-expressive). Gesture-orchestrated speech is speech where synchronous gesture and speech are face-to-face in time and co-express the same meaning; then the gesture can orchestrate the speech. But if each has a goal the other does not, co-expression and gesture-orchestrated speech cannot occur.

3.2   Arguments for "new" gesture-actions

To defend the "new"/"old" distinction I offer five points. First is the very idea that gesture–speech unity and gesture-orchestrated speech are unlikely if the gesture contains the germ of a practical action. The goal-directedness of such a gesture conflicts with the gesture–speech units orchestrating speech.

Second, the case of IW, an individual who had normal actions including gestures until he suffered as an adult a sudden total loss of proprioception and spatial sense (described in Chapter 8). He now performs gestures using vision to guide them. He intuitively calculates the force, speed, direction and extent of movement in advance and monitors its performance. He does the same for pragmatic actions such as picking up or wiping away. In fact his gestures *are* pragmatic actions, goal-directed and made with goals just like other pragmatic actions. The goal is *to make the gesture itself* (goal number 1), thereby to appear "normal" (IW, convinced that gesture is essential to normalcy of self-presentation, explicitly states this goal in almost these words). With vision denied, these steps are impossible and *gestures disappear*. A second kind of gesture, however, which IW calls the "throwaway," has no goal, is unattended and allowed just to happen without preparation or monitoring. When vision is denied, throwaways *do not disappear*. Throwaways continue in exactly the same way, uninterrupted, synchronized with co-expressive speech, for all the world looking like gestures orchestrating speech with normality. Throwaways appear to rely on a thought–language–hand link that survived IW's aproprioception, while his constructed pragmatic gestures do not have access to this link and depend on intuitive calculation and visual monitoring. Thus "new" action-gestures, not goal-directed, survive where action-action gestures, goal-directed, disappear, and this also shows the old/new action distinction (argued in Quaeghebeur et al. 2014).

Third, "temporal gestures" (McNeill 2003) show that when one does act and speak simultaneously, speech and action combine in a fundamentally different way from speech uniting with gesture. Speech, when combined with goal-directed action, is *metapragmatic*; it leaps up a level and refers to (rather than co-expresses with) the action-action. Rather than orchestration of speech, it coordinates with speech to create icons of temporal relations, *a new gesture* made out of the speech and action. It and speech together *are* the gesture. The goal-directedness of the action forces it and speech to split apart into this unique relationship (see Chapter 4 for further discussion).

A fourth argument is that distinguishing "new" and "old" reveals contexts where "old" action-action gestures do occur and what they do when they are there. Without the distinction, this insight is lost. Gestures deriving from pragmatic actions, blocking speech, give metapragmatic status to pauses in speech. The gesture stands out, silence highlighting it. Kendon noticed such gestures with silence some years ago, and the "new"/"old" distinction explains them.

Finally, the pragmatic "old" action-action conception contains no trace of the Vygotsky concepts we have employed in Chapters 1 and 2—the psychological predicate, the minimal gesture–speech unit, the material carrier: all are excluded by sourcing gestures in pragmatic actions. The gesture of "rising hollowness" possesses all the Vygotskian properties, but if it is deemed to have derived from the action of lifting something and this action (including its goal) is part of the gesture, the entire conceptual framework is fenced off. Perhaps this is the most damaging limitation of "old" action-action of all, as it creates a kind of willful narrow mindedness about an entire world of theoretical insights.

To summarize, action-action uses different neural pathways; prevents the entire phylogenesis–ontogenesis–microgenesis parade from starting; blocks more subtle understanding of gestures in silence; and, far from dual semiosis, is worked on by speech metapragmatically to create temporal gestures, a new kind. These are the defenses of "new" gesture-actions that avoid the limits of "old" pragmatic action-actions. While a gesture may engage some of the same movements and tap in part the same motor schemas as an action-action, it has its own circuit in the brain, a thought–language–hand link. In keeping with the unity of speech and gesture, the manual movements of gestures as well as the actions of speech are co-opted and orchestrated by significances other than those of goal-directed action-actions, which again interfere with gesture–speech unity. In the aproprioception case of IW, we observe the action-action and gesture-action difference directly.

3.3   Worldviews and cross-purposes

Whether one takes an "old" or "new" perspective reflects a certain worldview—one to explain the form of given gestures; the other to explain the form of given speech. The first perceives no role for gesture-orchestrated speech. As I construct the "old" action-action worldview, it asks for explanations of the configurations of features of given gestures in semiotic profiles.

The gesture-orchestrated speech worldview, in contrast, aims to explain how gestures orchestrate *given speech*.

Kendon, for example, writes:

> Visible action, for all humans, is a material out of which symbolic forms of expression can be crafted. How this is done, what forms are crafted and when, depends upon whether or not it is used, and how it is used in conjunction with other symbolic systems ... studies must take into consideration what other modalities are available and are being used and what the ecological circumstances are in which these available modalities have been and can be elaborated. In this way, I think, we could work toward a comparative semiotics of kinesic expression. (Kendon 2008, pp. 359–360)

As I understand the thrust of Kendon's aim here and elsewhere, it is to achieve, as he says, a comprehensive explanation of a comparative semiotics of kinesic expression. Rather than "kinesic expression," as such, we are attempting to explain the nature of language when it is understood to include kinesic expression as an integral part, and particularly (since I also argue that gesture was involved in the origin of language) when it includes the kinds of kinesic expressions we define as "new" gesture-action imagery that is inseparable from language and materialized in movement, space and form. A theory of "the comparative semiosis of kinesic expression" that obliterates the special status of language and conceals gesture within the general category of kinesic expressiveness would obscure rather than clarify what we are trying to do, to define the role of "gesture" in the phylogenesis, ontogenesis and microgenesis of language.

To imagine the worldview of the "old" action-action advocates is, of course, speculative, but tackling the problem suggests some reasons why this view has been so widely taken for granted.

The first reason I believe has few advocates today but is still worth mentioning. It is that the action-action view of gesture fits the "yo-he-ho" speech-first scenario—speech emerging out of work chants (M. Müller 1861). Continuity with speech-first may have appeal to those not wishing to join the gesture-first bandwagon but who have not considered the possibility that gesture and speech were equiprimordial (see Chapter 6).

Second and more likely, it may be that the "old" action-action view stems in part from a pre-theoretical commitment to cross-species continuity in evolution—the "everything evolves from something else" assumption. However, in the case of gesture, this something else need not be a goal-directed action. I will propose in Chapter 6 that gesture–speech unity evolved from a quite different source, which primates may someday attain but so far only we have. Liebal et al. (2010), following Kendon (2004), describe what they identify as "gesture families," which in their study are families of chimp gestures based on shared action sources—slapping, pushing, offering, etc. If these gestures are what they seem, miniaturized and ritualized editions of the source actions and not chimp metaphors, they do what human gestures do not, preserve in the gesture the original significance of the action, and would count therefore as yet another morsel of what, on comparison, arose at the origin of language—new kinds of actions of the vocal tract and hands with their own significances. These do not occur with apes. Indeed, the key difference between ape-emblems (if this is what they can be called) and human-emblems is that those of apes are action-stubs, an argument going back to Kendon (1991), while those of humans are conventionalized metaphors—a precision metaphor within "OK," a wiping-off metaphor within "negation," and so forth (see McNeill 2014a, also Chapter 5). It all points to the mode of human cognitive Being that new actions engendered and old actions lack.

In the worldview of this book, the origin of language was a unique event, a moment in human history when gesture–speech unity emerged in which gesture was an essential participant (a "moment" lasting many thousands or hundreds of thousands of years). This "moment" changed everything, including forms of action, and sent human history in new directions. It is the ultimate reply to the old saw that gesture is a mere add-on. Ample evidence exists of chimp symbols and culture, such as one group using sticks and another leaf sponges (*Science Daily* 2010) or monkeys washing potatoes in one group and this spreading to other groups. "New" gesture-action does not mean that symbols and cultures do not arise in non-human primates.[5] Cultural inventiveness is widespread in the biological world. But non-humans are at a level far different from that of every human community as far back as archeological evidence goes (at least one million years, see Goren-Inbar et al. 2004; Boesch and Tomasello 1998).

The third reason is, I believe, the most important. The "old" action-action worldview starts from the multidimensional aspect of gestures kinesically—the complexity of time, space, amplitude, hand-use and configuration over which gestures vary—and reduces them to semiotic profiles. In this way the "old" action-action worldview hovers over the kinesic side rather than the conceptual side of gesture–speech unity. A focus on the kinesic side explains why gesture-orchestrated speech is invisible to the "old" action-action view.

A kinesic starting point, moreover, invites a kind exterior or behavioristic, third-person focus on social practices, compared to the "new" focus on what takes place *within* individuals, including when engaged in social practices. From their writings I identify Kendon more with the kinesic-profile aim and Streeck more with the social-practice aim but the two combine. Streeck, in his *Gesturecraft* (2009), presents gestures from everyday settings such as auto repair shops and architects' offices and regards them as "practices." The entire

---

[5] Not to overlook the gestures of crows and ravens (Pika and Bugnyar 2011).

viewpoint is that of a third-person onlooker. One of the auto shop gestures provides a nice illustration of the "new" gesture-actions, first-person versus "old" action-action, third-person viewpoint difference. The boss, checking on one of his employees, asks, "every•thing you need we got, right?" (the dot indicating the gesture). Streeck (2009, p. 62) describes the gesture as a pointing hand with rapid waving motions, "gathering together the various items [of a car] in a set." This interpretation describes a likely pragmatic effect of the gesture but not necessarily a mental process. For the latter, I would say that the dot-gesture and the boss's words "everything" or " you need" (we don't know the extent of the gesture phrase) were his growth point (GP) differentiating a field of equivalents. It was something like *what you need* (= the field of equivalents, upgraded from immediately preceding "we got all the parts you need?"): *is something we've got* (= the point of differentiation). A different level of reality emerges, centered on the first-person experience of the speaker rather than on the third-person view of an onlooker. It is this onlooker view that strikes me as "behavioristic," and that the third-person perspective brings forth.

Another illustration of "new" gesture-actions and "old" action-actions and the explanations of gesture and speech that contrast between them, what they include and what they do not, is in an example Cornelia Müller presented at the University of Chicago (May 7, 2011). We can look at the example either with an old or new view but with the old gesture–speech unity slips away. The example is interesting, in part, because the new and old seem at first glance just shades of the same explanation, but if you follow what they entail, you see how they differ, not as shades but as different hues altogether.

Müller described a conversation in which a speaker (of Spanish) first outlined an oval shape with a two-handed open palm gesture (the shape of a wall-plaque), and then outlined it again with extended forefingers. Was he tracing an outline of the plaque with his fingers the second time? In speech, he said "lo tenía **con un a marco redondo**" [lit. it he-was holding **with a frame round**].[6]

An action-action interpretation is that the "con un a marco redondo" phrase described the plaque's shape and the extended forefingers gesture traced it, much as in the Kendon quote, *moving the fingers around it*. However, see what this leaves out. Speech and gesture are two tracks referring to the same thing, but there is no organic connection between them; they lie side-by-side and are not unified. This is the inherent limit of an "old" action; it cannot enter gesture–speech unities.

From a gesture–speech unity viewpoint there *is* an organic connection. Synchrony is inherent. The speaker highlighted the roundness of the plaque. The single forefingers are the critical detail. In this gesture-action view, they

---

[6] Thanks to Gale Stam for this translation.

contrasted with the previous full-palm gesture (whereas tracing the fingers around it does not—this relation is in addition to, not in contrast to the planar shape), and what seems to be a tracing shape is not a goal-directed action but imagery of the roundness of the plaque, qua roundness, as this contrasted to the plaque's previously highlighted and now background imagery of a planar surface. The gesture embodied the *idea of roundness*, not moving the fingers around the plaque to trace it. Forefingers contrasted specifically with the size and flatness in the first two-handed open-palm gesture—the total meaning something like *the flat plaque's shape* (field of equivalents from the first GP)*: round* (the new contrast). The stroke was co-expressive with the synchronous speech for this significance and together they formed a GP differentiating the field of equivalents. This, then, is the new gesture-action explanation.

In another example. LeBaron and Streeck (2000, p. 126) describe an architect's gesture that has a semiotic profile with at least three elements—metonymy, iconicity and deixis. The example, from an architecture class, is said to show the source of gesture in practical action. First the action: the professor tracing his finger along the surface of a cardboard model said, "you have uh … uh **long bent**," speech and action redundantly referring to the shape of the model. There is no orchestration, just reflexive word spurts lacking internal structure. The professor then continues with a gesture: the same motion and hand shape, but not touching the model and (from the drawing) moving freely in the space over it. This is more than simply raising the hand. The first and second occurrences are not equivalent. The important difference is in the effect on speech: "and uh uh **linear experience**." In the second version, gesture and speech form a unity, the shape (gesture) merging with the description, the linear experience. It is potentially a GP and raising the hand a *consequence* of gesture-orchestrated speech. The action became "new," that is, lost the goal of tracing the model and took on the function of orchestrating speech ("linear perspective," with internal structure). The "old" action-action worldview emphasizes the temporal and motor continuity of action and gesture in such examples, but a "new" gesture-action, gesture-orchestrated speech viewpoint highlights discontinuity—from the redundancy that suggests no imagery-language dialectic, to a dynamic GP differentiating the context: *what this shape affords: linear perspective* (or some such). The "old" action-action interpretation blinds one to this more subtle and differentiated hypothesis.

Semiotic profiles are not uniquely the province of "old" action-actions. They also can be drawn for "new" gesture-actions. If we do so, we find that gesture–speech unity *explains* the semiotic profile; the profile appears as a result, not a source, as in the "old" action-action worldview. For example, in "it down" the gesture included iconicity (the hand shape), metonymy (pushing down), deixis (the location of the imagined pipe and the direction of the ball's motion) and metaphoricity (the whole experienced as a force for good, the arched hand the agent of it)—all present because the GP was differentiating a field of equivalents *ways to thwart Sylvester: bowling ball down*—far from any single-action reduction. Rather than think of semiotic atoms and the gesture emerging, we see atoms emerging from the whole. The gesture is shaped by an imagery-language dialectic as a part of this differentiation, shaped to carry it out. As it does so it grabs the semiotic bits at hand.

A "new" gesture-action indeed has its own semiotic sources on the conceptual side. Gesture profiles with single semiotic features are possible in theory but most real examples are these mélanges. An interesting point is that speakers bring forth such complexity as in "it down" so easily. That storytelling brought forth more semiotic complexity than the didactic architect gesture may be a clue—genres and their chronotopes (Bakhtin 1981) include hooks based on scenario expectations. A chronotope is how configurations of time and space provide themes in language and discourse. They bring a first-person mental flavor that the concept of a "practice" lacks. Rather than "ways of acting" they are "ways of conceptualizing." For Bakhtin, the chronotope (literally, time-space) was the foundation of literary analysis, using it in his extensive analysis of Dickens's parodic style in *Little Dorrit* for example. For our discussion, the chronotope explains how the psychological predicate acquires the semiotic profile it ends up with, tracing the mélange to its sources in one or more chronotopes. In cartoons, which are cinematic and rich in semiotic types, chronotopes abound, hackneyed and nowhere near Dickens in subtlety yet complex enough, while in a didactic explanation, where the idea is to guide step-by-step, semiotic narrowing results.

To give an illustration of the origin of a semiotic profile in a chronotope, a speaker recalled the moment in our full-length film stimulus, *Blackmail*, he was retelling where a shady character was blackmailing the lead female character. In the film, she has already, in self-defense, killed a sexual attacker and is now anxiously revealing her crime to her boyfriend, who happens to be the very Scotland Yard detective assigned to solve the murder. The blackmailer had secretly observed the crime and now appears, attempting to extort hush money. Her boyfriend-detective decides to pin the crime on the blackmailer instead. In this fraught situation, heroine and hero face an impossible dilemma: submit to blackmail or find some dishonest means to avoid it. In Figure 3.2, the narrator is commenting on this moral quandary. Several chronotopes unfold at once, each with its own space. In (a) he is saying, "everyone's morals are very ambiguous 'cause [they're sup]posed to be the good guys," and gesturally indicates the space to his left (right hand rises and angles left). In (b) he continues with "[but she] really did kill him" and points into his front space. The opposition is continued in (c), with the central space again indicated but now for a different character, the blackmailer, and with

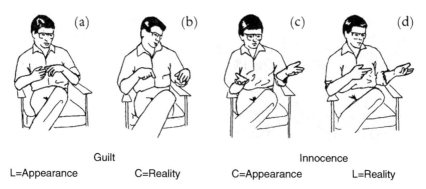

L=Appearance   Guilt   Innocence

               C=Reality   C=Appearance   L=Reality

Figure 3.2 Spatial discourse units during a film retelling. Used with permission of University of Chicago Press.

ascribed rather than actual moral meaning, as he says "and [he's a] bad guy" and then concludes indicating the blackmailer's real morality, "he didn't kill him." The example is of interest because it shows different chronotopes. The speaker had two: Guilt-Innocence, Appearance-Reality. However, Guilt and Appearance took on different spatial values with the Guilt-Innocence chronotope dominating Appearance-Reality. Within each Guilt-Innocence pole, the first mention was always Appearance (reflecting the dilemma – a spatial story about Guilt, the "topic" on which Appearance "comments"). The result is that each chronotope had a spatial contrast of its own, a shifting deictic center for Appearance, and a consistent Appearance-first, Reality-second order. More abstractly, the "new" gesture-action was opposition in space and time, with different semiotic profiles for the chronotopes. There seems to be no other significance for the center-left and first-second distinctions, no metaphoric values than the chronotopes. The concept of a chronotope can apply throughout the "new" gesture-action domain.

Some gestures do ritualize actions. These gestures are of two kinds. Some are pantomimes at their own locus on the gesture continuum. They are unquestionably "old" action-actions, a kind of performance, a replication of the action that may also include posture, spatial location, etc. as well as the manual action; in short, pantomimes. Others are "character viewpoint" (C-VPT) gestures, gesticulations with the viewpoint of the character who is being recounted. Unlike pantomimes C-VPTs are co-expressive with speech. Their viewpoint is part of the semiotic with which they oppose linguistic form in a dialectic—a C-VPT is, among other things, *not* an "observer viewpoint" (O-VPT), a contrast that it has but that a pantomime does not. Pantomime is simulated action and has no contrastive value. In the "it down" example, the speaker's hands were Tweety's hands, the space his space, her body his, and so forth—the speaker stepped into Tweety's shoes and incorporated this into the utterance itself. It was part of the caused-motion unpacking, making Tweety the agent and the C-VPT perspective was shaped by this significance. The most telling difference from a replicated action is that the hands thrust the ball down, in contrast to the release of it in the cartoon stimulus. All of this could happen because the gesture was a "new" action, formed over the thought–language–hand link.

Other gestures, not pantomimes, do ritualize actions through fetishism. They create "magic." They don't orchestrate speech but have an independent pragmatic existence. "**Magic**" results when gestures appear to take on new powers by which the gesture itself, when made, seems to cause a change in something else—"magical powers," the making of it changing something in the world, granting approbation, gaining authority, etc. To produce "magic" is the reason for the gesture. Morris et al. (1979) show photographs of obscene gestures in live contexts being made not for self-expression but as weapons. We regularly use emblems that are many thousands of years old. No spoken language has survived so long, including the ancient Greek and Latin with which many emblems originally occurred (if they did not predate even them)—"dead languages," "live gestures." This very disparity is one reason why gestures appear to possess magic. And because of it emblems can be read for deeply held values that may differ across cultures and epochs, such as approbation in North America—which may be recent—versus authority in Naples—which seems ancient (see Section 5.6 "The emblem as metaphor" in Chapter 5).

Magic is fetishism, giving the form of a gesture the sense of a pragmatic power beyond its normal semiotic role. The "OK" sign can mollify; the Neapolitan ring can assure the speaker that she knows whereof she speaks. Fetishism also explains the hold ancient theories have on the modern mind, like vision via eyebeams: gestures, fortified as fetishes, recreate the beams in one's own experience.

Presumably all emblems participate in fetishism to some extent but the "finger" is an exceptionally clear if disreputable example. A belief in its magical power appears to be the main reason it is raised nowadays. It exists not merely as an expression of outrage: it is meant to inflict damage. In Rome it was called the "indecent finger," was an insult and may even have been used propositionally (Caligula wagging it).[7] It has become, on American roadways at least, purely illocutionary, a generic insult, the approbation theme absorbing it to inflict, in inverted logic and "as if by magic," the incompetence and unworthiness of existence of another driver. Its origin in a graphic depiction of sexual acts is lost and new powers to diminish if not efface the other are created. I have seen the gesture aimed at

---

[7] Thanks to R.B. McNeill.

targets for extended intervals, as if extra time increases the effect (visibility not being a problem), and at inanimate objects. Also, sculpted models posed on tables are a kind of talisman. Performers of a certain kind display it to audiences to gain control.

Whence this feeling of magic? There can be no doubt it exists, and not only with this gesture but with every emblem. Even those (most of us) who think of "magic" in quotes can feel it. Pick an emblem and you feel its power in your hand (it must be an emblem you personally inhabit). I can only guess the causes but suggest two. One is a sense that emblems are ancient. The past and its mysteries often possess an aura of magic. Many emblems are, in fact, ancient and in this respect are like myths—micro-myths—in which we touch ancient truths. The other is the feeling—described in this book and arising from our daily speech—that gestures fuel speech by orchestrating it. Gestures orchestrate speech and seem to push it forward. Making the gesture you sense this power, the gesture "fueling" something—but what? You are not speaking but are making the gesture. Nothing is there, yet your hand is filled with energy. This could be what we feel, power on the loose, without speech to absorb it, and this, combined with the sense that we are touching the ancient, is "magic."

3.4   Conclusion

To summarize, I have argued in this chapter that the gestures in gesture-orchestrated speech cannot have implicit goal-directedness. An "old" action-action prevents the gesture from attaining co-expressiveness with speech. A "new" gesture-action replaces the implicit goal-directedness of "old" action-action with significances of any kind, extended without limit through gesture metaphor. They are actions with new significances, not those of the actions themselves; the example of "rising hollowness" illustrates the novelty. Gesture-orchestrated speech is speech where synchronous gesture and speech are face-to-face in time and co-express the same meaning; then the gesture can orchestrate the speech. But if each has a goal the other does not, co-expression does not exist. The "new"/"old" distinction places limits on what "old" action-action proposals can assert.

The concept of "worldview" sums up this chapter. The two theories of gesture we have compared, the "old" action-action and the "new" gesture-action, differ in worldview. *Why We Gesture* belongs to the millennia-long effort to explain the "gift of language," and language in this worldview is unique, the pivot from which everything else spun outward. Gesture in particular was a key step in building the entire edifice. In this worldview, our understanding of what is language itself warps if gesture is ignored. It is then lopsided.

4 Orchestration and unpacking

This chapter explains the concept of gesture-orchestrated speech in full. Our arguments so far have been that gesture–speech unity embodies the core meaning of a sentence, a meaning that takes the form of "one meaning is two things," and occupies both simultaneous and successive awareness. The core meaning, cast in different semiotic modes at the same time—a dual semiosis and an imagery–language dialectic—is unstable and seeks stability through unpacking. Unpacking parcels the growth point (GP) and its context into a construction (or approximately one).The more discontinuous an utterance from the context, the greater its communicative dynamism ("communicative dynamism" is the extent to which a given spoken or gestured form "pushes the communication forward," Firbas 1971), and the more probable a gesture, the more internally complex it will be, and the more complex the synchronous co-expressive speech as well (see Figure 1.3). The GP and its unpacking "absorbs" the immediate context, and this also shapes gesture-orchestrated speech. In narrative discourse, the communicative dynamism push comes with a sense of "ongoingness." All of this can go into one gesture–speech unit, and is the packaging of gesture-orchestrated speech.

4.1 Orchestration and unpacking

Orchestration is the action of the vocal tract organized around manual gestures. A surface reflection of orchestration is the amount of time speakers take to utter sentences. This is remarkably constant, between one and two seconds regardless of the number of embedded sentences (up to five or six, from 1970s notes). One to two seconds is also the duration of a gesture typically, and the constancy is explained if gestures orchestrated them. Second, when a listener indicates he does not understand, the speaker's gestures tend to increase in frequency but not change in form, suggesting increased effort with more gesture–speech units while the gesture-orchestrated speech within each unit stays the same (Hoetjes et al. 2015). Having more gesture–speech units, the overall speech rate slows (each new gesture–speech unit adding another one or two seconds), and this Hoetjes et al. also found—2.1 down to 1.7 words per

(a)   (b)   (c)

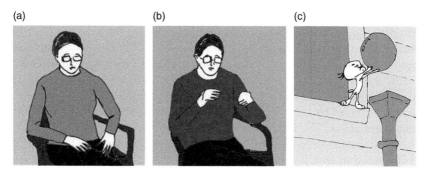

Figure 4.1 The bowling ball as a downward thrusting force was embodied in the downward hand positions at the start of preparation; also the 'hands', being shaped over the bowling ball, were those of an agent launching it. The transformation of imagery from that of the cartoon stimulus, where there was no downward thrust but a release with gravity doing the rest, was complete. Computer art by Fey Parrill. Used with permission of University of Chicago Press.

second over repetitions. Third, languages differ in prosodic/rhythmic patterning and flows of words, and fluent bilinguals tell me they experience changes of muscular organization of the vocal tract when switching languages (for example, from English to French). The hypothesis is that gestures orchestrate these experiences, and indeed (informally but consistently) I observe equal changes in gesture, so much so that I can tell, without sound and by sight alone, when the bilingual shifts from one language to the other (not because of "French" emblems but because her individual style changes at the shift).

How does it all occur? The gesture is a "new" gesture-action (spanning the whole *preparation–holds–stroke–retraction* phrase). It is also in successive awareness (*stroke and poststroke hold*), reflecting the dual temporal awareness of the GP. We can use the words "it down" and thrusting-down-gesture in Figure 4.1 to demonstrate the process. The gesture was made with two symmetrical hands—the palms loosely cupped and facing downward as if placed over a spherical object moving down, then holding during the "-wn" portion of "it down."

The inferred GP is this image of downward movement plus the linguistic content of the "it" (indexing the bowling ball) and the path particle "down." The poststroke hold continued the shape and position of the gesture until "down" was fully uttered; then the stroke entered its retraction, bringing the simultaneous awareness of the GP to an end (the next GP immediately commencing). With simultaneous and successive awareness we have:

(4.1)   "and Tweety Bird runs and gets a bowling ba[*simultaneous awareness of GP starts*ll and Øtw drops*GP enters successive awareness* **itdown**$\underline{\text{}}$*GP leaves successive awareness* the drainpipe*simultaneous awareness of GP ends*]"

The GP **unpacked itself** into this linguistic form (how will be explained shortly). The causative "drops" construction provided the template. What is striking and why the example is illustrative, is that "it down" was divided into different constituents of the construction ("it" with "drops," "down" with "the drainpipe"), yet the word pair as orchestrated by the stroke and poststroke hold remained a unit in successive awareness. The GP was alive and not effaced by the construction. Both dimensions, static and dynamic, thus were active. The GP orchestrated the "it down" word pair and with its static dimension unpacking brought the whole to dynamic life. The result is a construction with a gesture at the right place, a static *langue* entity given new (temporary) dynamic life.

Unpacking articulates the GP into a communicable, socioculturally mandated construction that (a) stabilizes the imagery–language dialectic, without (b) disrupting the GP, its field of equivalents and how it is differentiated. A GP and its unpacking can arise together or in sequence with potential effects on fluency. Either way, it is what the speaker's *langue*-feeling provides.

Self-unpacking. From its start the "it down" GP had Tweety as the agent of change. In this case the GP and its unpacking template arose together. The telltale is the shape of the hands (Figure 4.1, left panel). At the start of preparation and simultaneous awareness they were arched and turned down, already in the agentive role. So, from its start, the gesture included the significance that Tweety was the agent both of Sylvester's thwarting and the bowling ball's motion. Had the speaker begun differently, with "and Tweety sees him," for example, we would expect a different gesture and GP/unpacking, something like "and stops him with a bowling ball," and a gesture without agency. With caused-motion came a slot for a verb that could affect the change of the bowling ball's location, and "drops" was the choice over other possibilities such as "throws" or "thrusts," which do not leave an opening for the role of gravity Tweety actually deployed (Figure 4.1, right panel). This winnowing zeroed in on caused-motion and the verb "drops." Table 4.1 shows how it could have worked.

To complete the analysis, the GP's on-flash was during the first mention of "ball," from which speech continued smoothly and without interruption, implying that the GP came to life and called the construction at the same time. This was the dawn of the simultaneous awareness of the sentence. The GP in successive awareness awaited its turn after the verb that unpacking provided.

Gesture phrases therefore do not always honor linguistic boundaries. They do not in the "it down" GP's successive awareness, spanning two constituents, and also at its simultaneous awareness onset, which took place in the preceding clause. In other cases, multiple gestures orchestrate single sentences: "I guess [**swa**llows][it **'n' he comes** _out_]" is an example from a different speaker and

Table 4.1 Unpacking: a growth point calls for caused-motion, winnowing a "Making Something Happen" cohort.

		Subject	Verb	Object	Complement
GROWTH POINT imagery includes agent thrusting down, plus "it down"					
TEMPLATE	FORM	Subject	Verb	Object	Complement
	SPEECH	Ø = Tweety	drops	it = b-ball	down
	ROLE	Agent	Causes-change	Thing changed	Other info

again simultaneous awareness does not conform to syntax. This lack of alignment is understandable if the construction is dependent upon the gesture, not the gesture on the construction. Further richness hidden behind linguistic structure comes forth when multiple fields of equivalents infiltrate one sentence. "It down" shows this as well. Its full discourse stretch is in Figure 4.2. The "it down" GP is in panel (b).

4.2   The catchment

We, however, first need a new concept, that of the **catchment**. A catchment is when space, trajectory, hand shape, etc. recur in two or more (not necessarily consecutive) gestures. The catchment conveys a discourse theme. An ingenious illustration of a catchment appears in Furuyama and Sekine (2007). They noted a systematic avoidance of gestures with referentially correct spatial content precisely where this content would have disrupted an ongoing catchment. A catchment was the force that blocked it, attesting to its functioning reality.

To define a catchment:

- A catchment is recognized from recurrences of gesture form features over a stretch of discourse.
- A catchment is a kind of thread of consistent dynamic visuospatial imagery running through the discourse and provides a gesture-based window into discourse cohesion.
- The logic of the catchment is that discourse themes produce gestures with recurring features; these recurrences give rise to the catchment.

Thus, reasoning in reverse, the catchment offers clues to the cohesive linkages in the text with which it co-occurs. The "catchment" metaphor comes from the land area, a catchment (= "*the field of meaningful equivalents*") that drains into (= "*is absorbed by*") a body of water (= "*a GP*"). The metaphor's flaw is that it makes the GP seem a static entity while in reality it is a dynamic process, but it captures the GP's absorbing context.

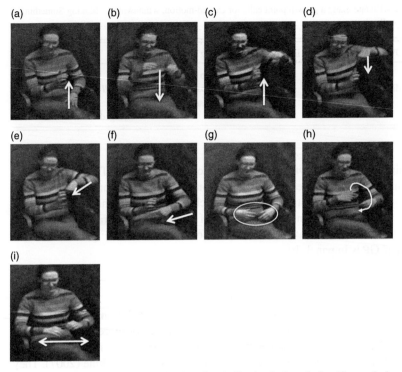

Figure 4.2 Catchments in a bowling ball episode description. Transcription by Susan Duncan. Used with permission of Cambridge Univerity Press.

The first point to notice, as mentioned, is that the timing of the gesture stroke (boldface) is somewhat off if we think that gestures should line up with synchronically definable linguistic constituents. The stroke excluded the verb "drops" and coincided instead with "it down," and in this way combined two constituents, the Figure and Satellite (using Talmy's 2000 categories), but excluded another, the Activating Process, to which the Figure, "it," is actually more tightly coupled. However, grammatical structure comes from unpacking and is not necessarily part of the GP ("it" and "down" have combinatoric potential with other words but not with each other).

This exclusion of "drops" was no accident. First, the preparation phase of the "it down" gesture has two features that skip over the verb. Preparation began at the first mention of the bowling ball, in the preceding clause (also indicated in Figure 4.2b), which suggests that the bowling ball was in discourse focus at that moment. Second, preparation continued right through the verb, suggesting that the verb was not part of this focus. Further, a brief prestroke hold may have preceded "it down" (although coding varies), which, if present,

Table 4.2 Catchment themes.

Catchments	Utterances
C1 One-handed gestures—items (a) and (f)—ties together references to Sylvester as a solo force.	(a) he tries going up the inside of the drainpipe and (f) and he comes out the bottom of the drainpipe
C2 Two-handed *symmetrical* gestures—items (b), (g), (h) and (i)—groups descriptions where the bowling ball is the antagonist, the dominant force. The two-handed symmetric gesture form highlights the shape of the bowling ball.	(b) Tweety Bird runs and gets a bowling ball and drops it down the drainpipe (g) and he's got this big bowling ball inside him (h) and he rolls on down into a bowling alley (i) and then you hear a strike
C3 Two-handed *asymmetrical* gestures—items (c), (d) and (e)– groups items in which the bowling ball (LH) and Sylvester (RH) are equals differing only in position and direction of motion.	(c) and as he's coming up (d) and the bowling ball's coming down (e) he swallows it

suggests that the stroke, fully cocked, waited for "it down." Finally, the unmistakable poststroke hold lasted exactly as long as it took to complete the spoken "down." This hold preserved the semantic synchrony of the gesture stroke with the complete articulation of "it down." So the stroke fully and exactly timed with just these two words, and actively excluded a third, "drops," which happens to be the closest lexical approximation to it.

Table 4.2 reveals three catchments, recognizable from hand shape and position. The following thematic values are apparent when we coordinate gestures with the accompanying verbal descriptions:

C1—one hand = Sylvester as a solo force.

C2—two similar hands = the bowling ball as an antagonistic force.

C3—two different hands = the relative spatial positions of the bowling ball and Sylvester inside the pipe.

Each of the gesture hand shape/position features embodies a bit of thematic content and this content is what motivates the catchment; the catchment as a whole is a cohesive discourse segment: **C1** is a about a single moving entity and its recurring gesture feature is a single moving hand; **C2** is about the bowling ball and what it does, and its recurring feature is a rounded shape (in gesture transcription terms, "two similar hands"); **C3** is about the relative positions of two entities in the drainpipe and its recurring feature is two hands in the appropriate spatial configurations ("two different hands").

With these catchments, we can analyze the real-time origin of the utterance and gesture in (b). We do it in a way that incorporates context as a fundamental component. The surfacing of (b) in the symmetrical catchment shows that one of the factors comprising its field of equivalents in its role of an antagonist. This catchment set the bowling ball apart from its role in **C3**, where the bowling ball was on a par with Sylvester. The significant contrast in (b) was the downward motion of the bowling ball as an antagonist. Because of the field of equivalents at this point, this downward motion had significance as an antagonistic force against Sylvester. We can write this "two-things" meaning as

Field of Equivalents: Point of Differentiation, or:
Antagonistic Force: Bowling Ball Downward.

This was the context and contrast. Thus, "it down," an unlikely unit from a grammatical point of view, was the cognitive core of the utterance in (b)—the "it" indexing the bowling ball, and the "down" indexing the significant contrast itself in the field of equivalents. The verb "drops," therefore, was *excluded* from this GP. As noted earlier, exclusion is evidenced in the fact that the stroke did not synchronize with the verb; in fact, it was withheld from the verb by continued preparation and a possible brief prestroke hold. The verb describes what Tweety did, not what the bowling ball did (it went down), and thus was not a significant contrast in the field of equivalents involving the bowling ball. The core idea at (b) was the bowling ball and its action, not Tweety and his. Line (f) is simultaneously C1 and C3, a fusion that captures the only-in-a-cartoon concept that Sylvester has turned into living bowling ball. The gesture is made with a single hand, which in C1 was associated with Sylvester in motion, but it is the *left* hand, which in C3 was associated with the bowling ball; here the gesture belongs to both catchments, Sylvester as a solo force and the bowling ball heading down.

4.3   Multiple contexts

A sentence can absorb more than one context. That "drops" was excluded from the GP yet was included in the sentence points to a second context at play in the origins of (b). Although a single grammatical construction, simultaneous awareness of the sentence grew out of two distinct contexts and gained oppositional meaning from each. Only when taking the dynamic dimension of the utterance in (b) into account is this evident, showing clearly what taking into account this dimension adds.

The first context we have already analyzed; it was the C2 theme in which the bowling ball was an antagonistic force. The second context can be seen in the two-handed gesture at (b) that also contrasted with C1—the preceding one-handed gesture in (a), depicting Sylvester as a solo force. Utterances (a) and (b) comprised a paradigm of opposed forces. This contrast led to (b) via a partial repetition of the utterance structure of (a), a poetic framework within which the new contrasts were formed (cf. Jakobson 1960). Contrasting verbal elements appeared in close to equivalent slots (the match is as close as possible given that the verb in (b) is transitive while that in (a) is intransitive):

(a')	(Sylvester)	up	in "he tries going up the inside of the drainpipe"
(b')	Tweety)	down	in "and (Tweety) drops it down the drainpipe"

The theme can be summarized as an opposition of counterforces—Tweety-down versus Sylvester-up. This was the field of equivalents, and the "it down" GP differentiated it. Our feeling that the paradigm is slightly ajar is due to the shift from spontaneous to caused motion with "drops." This verb does not alter the counterforces paradigm but transfers the counterforce from Tweety to the bowling ball, as required for the objective content of the episode.

The parallel antagonistic forces in (a') and (b') made Tweety the subject of (b'), matching Sylvester as subject of (a'). Gesture-orchestrated speech included both agent and the subject slot it filled. The contrast of (b') with (a') thus had two effects. It was the source of the verb, "drops," and was also why the subject was "Tweety," rather than "bowling ball." The subject slot expressed Tweety's role in the contrast and the verb shifted the downward force theme to the bowling ball. The identity of subjects, and the similar syntactic frames, expressed the antagonistic forces paradigm itself. The prestroke hold over "drops" is thus also explained: the verb and stroke absorbing different contexts, and the stroke waiting until the other context had been fulfilled.

Unpacking completed and stabilized the paradigm. Unpacking had to meet all these requirements: the GP was "it down" plus the downward gesture in (b); they had to be kept together in successive awareness; the GP differentiated a field of equivalents of Antagonistic Forces; the verb was "drops"; the subject was "Tweety"—all of this was provided by unpacking of the GP into a caused-motion construction.

Let's summarize how Figure 4.2b came into being:

1 A field of equivalents in which the significance of the downward motion of the bowling ball was that of an antagonistic force gave the growth point a core meaning centered on "it down." It's noteworthy that the preparation for the gesture in 4.2b began in the preceding clause, concurrent with mentioning the bowling ball for the first time ("Tweety Bird runs and gets a bowling ba[ll and drops it down the drai]npipe"). That is, the new growth point embodying the idea of the bowling ball in its role as the antagonist to Sylvester began to take form as soon as the bowling ball itself entered into the discourse.

2 A field of equivalents in which the significance was the counterforces of Sylvester-up versus Tweety-down. This gave a sentence schema that included the words "drops," "down," "drainpipe" and the repetition of the sentence structure with Tweety in the subject slot.

The choice of verb in 4.2b was "drops," rather than "throws," "thrusts" or some other caused-motion option for a downward trajectory from a manual launch, possibly because it, among these options, corresponds most closely to the force-dynamics of how Tweety made use of gravity to launch the bowling ball. Thus, a further aspect of the context of 4.2b is this force-dynamics.[1] If this is the case, we have further support for the analysis in which "drops" and "it down" belong to different contexts. This comes from the hand shape of the gesture in (b). The speaker made the gesture with her hands facing *down*, in a thrusting position (Figure 4.1, middle). They were not a simulation of Tweety's hands when he exploited gravity to launch the bowling ball. In the cartoon stimulus, Tweety held the bowling ball from the bottom and chucked it into the pipe, allowing gravity to do the rest (Figure 4.1, right). The GP image altered this force-dynamics by making the launch into a thrust. The verb "drops," meanwhile, captured the role of gravity (hence was favored over "thrust" itself). So the two contexts—the "drops" context captured the objective content of gravity doing the work, and the opposition of forces of which Tweety was a source; a different context shaped the GP, in which the bowling ball and its direction of movement, not Tweety and his action, was the significant element. The gesture and sentence, that is, reflected the speaker's conceptualizing of the cartoon as much as the objective cartoon content. The new force dynamics is not appropriate to Tweety, but it does fit the field of equivalents that concentrated on the force-dynamics of the bowling ball in its persona as antagonist.

3 It is important to emphasize that the GP calls for its own unpacking. It does not require a third-party or agent; it is a kind of self-unpacking done by the GP itself and arises out of the imagery–langue dialectic. The GP evokes, on its own, a construction that does the job (usually). A GP and its unpacking-construction can arise together (as in the example) or in sequence. The situation with caused-motion in unpacking the "it down" GP is a good model of the selective forces that emanate from GPs. The "it down" GP was not formed "out of" a gesture for thrusting down plus the linguistic segments, "it" and "down." This inverts the dependencies. The gesture was thrusting and the linguistic categorization "it down" because the GP was the basic unit of thinking for speaking; it was differentiating a field of meaningful equivalents, *ways of countering Sylvester*, with a

---

[1] Pointed out by Karl-Erik McCullough (personal communication).

psychological predicate, *bowling ball down*. The gesture and speech segments did not exist outside this GP. They were shaped to do its job and descended from it. We can be sure the dependency ran in this direction for two reasons. First, the **gesture** was not an iconic depiction but was an image altered precisely to make Tweety into the agent of the bowling ball's motion. Second, the **speech** of the GP was not a grammatical combination, a V plus an Object, as would be expected if speech were the independent "atom," but instead "drops" was cut off by the gesture stroke from its object, "it," creating the non-grammatical yet co-expressive segment, "it down." Both speech and gesture, in other words, were products of the GP and not the other way around.

The combination of contexts in "it down" thus enabled the GP to call the caused-motion construction where Tweety was agent, occupied the same subject slot the conflict paradigm gave to Sylvester, and provided a location for "drops" with which to shift the antagonistic force from Tweety to the bowling ball. We will see later how the speaker's simultaneous awareness of these aspects of the GP would very quickly winnow a field of possible unpackings to just one.

4.4   The "strong prediction"

GPs in successive awareness remain intact no matter the constructions that unpack them. Belonging to different syntactic constituents—the "it" with "drops" and the "down" with "the drainpipe"—did not break apart the "it down" GP. Syntactic form adapted to the gesture. The example shows that gesture is the force shaping speech not the speech shaping gesture. This follows from the expectation that unpacking will not disrupt a field of equivalents or its differentiation. Gesture–speech unity means that speech and gesture are equals, and in gesture-orchestrated speech the dynamic dimension enters from the gesture side. In a second version of the "strong prediction," *speech stops when continuing would break the GP apart.* The absolute need to preserve the GP in successive awareness then puts a brake on speech flow. The following from another speaker illustrates this outcome (Example 4.2, simplified Susan Duncan transcript):

(4.2) a [he tries **climb**ing up the rai]n barrel [and]
       b [**Twe**]ety Bird <uh> sees him coming
       c and [[drops a bow**lingbal**][**l down the** rain b][arrel so it **hits** him on][**the head**]]
       d [and he winds up ro**lling down** the str**e**][et

(a)   (b)

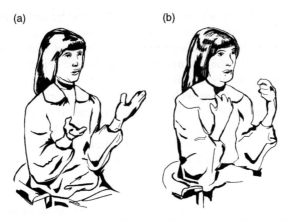

Figure 4.3 Gesture at line (e) with two fields of equivalents. Drawings by Dusty Hope.

e   because it* th* <uh> wel'ac][tually what happens is he*
     I* you assume that he **swa**llows this bowling b][[all
f   and he **comes rolling out** of the bottom of the rain bar][rel
g   and **rolls down the**]][street

The shut-down was at line (e). The illustration is complex because of the speaker's confusion in navigating the sentence, including a mid-stream change in simultaneous awareness. For this very reason, however, we can verify the strong prediction that speech halts when continuing would break the GP apart.

In line (e), the speaker seems to have had two fields of meaningful equivalents in mind at once, not in a dialectic but a mix-up, *what happened next* as well as *what one supposes*. It is the first that shuts down; the second then takes over, despite being less co-expressive with the ongoing gesture (a co-expressive "swallows" gesture has the downward motion near the neck, not at the chest as in Figure 4.3, as indeed some narrators display). We start with the grammatical subjects, "it," "the" (bowling ball), each immediately dropped. They belong to the first field. Had their sentence continued, it would have been something like "it/the bowling ball *I/you assume* goes into him," with the second "I/you assume" field intruding. This would not have been simply two added words but an entire "two-things, one-meaning" ensemble. The unpacking thus stopped because *continuing would have broken the GP apart*. The prestroke and poststroke holds show the "swallows" GP where it surfaced in successive awareness. The speaker might have returned to "it/the bowling ball" with "I/you assume" at the start, but this would already have been the second field. Instead, she took up the second in full strength with "you assume he swallows," and here unpacking did not interrupt the GP.

In all this discussion, the gesture phrase, from the onset of preparation to the end of retraction is the orchestrating force. We see this in the misalignment of syntactic boundaries with gesture boundaries and in the cessation of unpacking if continuing with it threatens the GP's integrity, all of which is explained if the gesture has "called" the construction, which then drops into it to provide the unpacking. The gesture finds its place in the successive awareness of the construction, but still it is dominant.

4.5   Metapragmatic orchestration

One last layer to the selection of the (b) caused-motion construction brings us into the realm of metapragmatic orchestration, the framework that guides and oversees the discourse as a whole, such questions as the speaker's intentions and sense of discourse direction. These areas have always been a gap in the growth point story—areas of obvious importance and self-evident activity but not captured (so far) in our way of discovering psychological predicates and GPs as they emerge. I propose an approach based on the work of my Chicago colleague, Michael Silverstein, which I dub "metapragmatic orchestration." Metapragmatic orchestration reveals aspects of this level of the discourse framework (cf. Silverstein 2003). It identifies the intended effects of the speaker's uttered speech ("intended" in sense two, to communicate), as well as her sense of overall direction in the discourse as it focuses on the moment of speaking. Like its field of meaningful equivalents, the GP absorbs what is indicated metapragmatically and also shoehorns this larger framework into each conceptual instant. In our example we see that metapragmatic orchestration zeroed in onto caused-motion in (b).

Importantly, it was the metapragmatics of the situation that required incorporating the bowling ball into the narrative (it had to be mentioned); also, given the speaker's characterization of the cartoon as a paradigm of opposed forces, it created a field of good/bad equivalents and spotted the necessity of shifting the good force to an instrument, the bowling ball. This was the selection pressure that summoned caused-motion itself, and was a force from the beginning of the GP, as we have seen. Moreover, metapragmatic selection accounts for the verb, "drops" over alternatives such as "throws" or "thrusts." All fit caused-motion, but this verb attributes the motion of the bowling ball to the force of gravity, as was depicted in the original cartoon.

Combining catchments and metapragmatic indexicals gives a fairly complete picture of how the utterance emerged. All of the factors—GPs, psychological predicates, unpacking with constructions, syntagmatic values, context and metapragmatic orchestration—were aroused at once. The speed with which this is accomplished is a "mystery" we unravel later in the chapter.

4.5.1   Orchestration by cohesion

Holds

Karl-Erik McCullough (2005) and Mischa Park-Doob (2010) have found a form of catchment in which holds cover multiple GPs. A hold over several GPs embodies discourse continuity: one or both hands motionless in space indicating the continuing relevance of whatever significance the discourse has attached to the location and/or the gesture form they occupy. The hold provides cover for gesture-orchestrated speech. While McCullough and Park-Doob perceive extended holds as different from catchments, only one difference seems important. The hold is continuous while the catchment allows breaks and interpolations. Whether a discourse segment runs continuously over some stretch of discourse or recurs intermittently may find prominence in different speech styles ("paragraphs" versus "episodes") but gesture-orchestrated speech is possible with both.

Ongoingness via cataphora

A second form of metapragmatic cohesion is what Elena Levy and I called "ongoingnesss" (Levy and McNeil 2015). At least four varieties of cohesion can be discerned in gesture-orchestrated speech—the catchment, multiple contexts, gesture-holds and what Karl-Erik McCullough (2003) has termed "assemblages." Here we take up numbers three and four under the heading of "ongoingness." Along with the first two, they show speech being orchestrated as gestures form cohesive linkages.

Ongoingness is cohesion with a feeling of forward motion. It is when gesture-orchestrated speech carries a sense of direction as part of cohesion. At its strongest, ongoingness takes on a new character, becoming storytelling with its own conventions and traditions, but weaker levels permeate nearly everything—the very ordinariness of someone asking "what's your point?" suggests its pervasiveness, reaching into every corner of gesture-orchestrated speech.

Cataphora is the anticipation of a future reference, as distinguished from recalling a past reference, which is anaphora. It is a force for ongoingness and seeking its resolution itself a form of orchestration. Classic examples, found on Wikipedia, are "after *he* received his orders, *the soldier* left the barracks" for cataphora, "after *the soldier* received his orders, *he* left the barracks" for anaphora, the first a pronoun co-referring with a later noun and pushing forward to meet it; the second a later pronoun co-referring with an earlier noun and looking back to recall it, recollection rather than progression. Cataphora and anaphora both register cohesive links beyond the sentences in which they occur. The examples show single words, but more complex versions also appear. Levy and I in our work (not published) focused on cataphora, since this compels ongoingness.

Ongoingness in satellite- and verb-framed languages
We were greatly aided by an insightful but never published essay by Karl-Erik McCullough, written we believe around 2003, *Gaze, Gesture, and the Construction of Meaning*. The ongoingness motif appears in the following statement, especially in "coherent, extra-temporal assemblages" and what they imply:

[O]ne might characterize story narratives as existing both as expository structures unfolding in time, that can be observed, recorded, and studied, but also as the *coherent, extra-temporal assemblages* that can be inferred, like event structures, to exist as such in the minds of storytellers. As storytellers translate this global structure into a linear narrative, the bundles of narrative information thus revealed progressively transform their mental representation of the remaining, as yet unspoken story structure. The notion of "discharge" … characterizing the transformation of the speaker's sense of the story structure, as the speaker is speaking. Here, we seem to be seeing hierarchically distinct units of information emerging together with anticipatory gestures indicating overarching hierarchical structure unpacked downstream, as it were. (Karl-Erik McCullough, 2003, p. 7, emphasis added)

"Coherent, extra-temporal assemblages" can be revealed cross-linguistically, by drawing on Leonard Talmy's (2000) distinction between two broad types of language differing in how they package information about motion ("satellite-framed," "verb-framed"). These motion-event packages open up contrasting assemblages, forms of cataphora, and hence of ongoingness—what propels discourse forward in one language is less likely in the other. Dan Slobin (e.g., 1996) has extensively applied the satellite-/verb-framed distinction in psycholinguistics studies. The distinction provides a dynamic version of the Whorfian hypothesis. Whorf himself (1956) took a typically static view, seeking the effects of language form on "habitual thought," itself a static conception of thought divorced from both context and ongoing speech. Here, however, our view is dynamic, and a dynamic version of the Whorf hypothesis seems not only possible but desirable—in contrast to the difficult and controversial efforts to demonstrate a static linguistic impact on "habitual thought" (see Pinker 1994 for colorful pooh-poohing) gesture-orchestrated speech effects on thinking are obvious, and easily revealed (McNeill 2009). Speakers organize information to fit the motion-event packagings of the language they are speaking (realizing Slobin's 1987 "thinking for speaking" as "imagery for speaking").

One Talmy language type, the "satellite-framed" (English is an instance), puts the manner of motion into the verb and the path into a separate "satellite" ("rolls out" has "rolls" for manner, "out" for path). The second type, the "verb-framed," has path in the verb and manner in a separate adverb (Spanish "sale *volando*"—"exits flyingly"— "flies out"). English is our satellite-framed example, Turkish our verb-framed one (for which we have a striking illustration of contrasting ongoingness, thanks to a narrative example provided by Asli Özyürek and Sotaro Kita, pers. comm.).

Satellite-framed (English)

The assemblage in Figure 4.4 at (e), (f) and (g) shows a typical satellite-framed package (McNeill and Duncan 2000): path, the information in the extra-verb satellite, stands out and cataphora projects it. McCullough analyzed an extended series of gestures (Figure 4.4) from the subject described earlier in the "strong prediction" (Figure 4.3), as she described, with lingering confusion, the bowling ball scene. Figure 4.3 was her second description of the same event, and immediately followed her description here. McCullough (2003, p. 7) found anticipatory gestures, "agglomerations of partially (gesturally) discharged information. ... anticipatory information ... [which] becomes a living index of ongoing exposition—a sort of cataphor, in effect, of the realized and referentially anchored expression that ensues." These agglomerations and assemblages are our interest—how a speaker forms a totality and then with it develops a coherent linear discourse with forward propulsion. It is a process whereby a whole is dissected and the parts arranged in time, without losing cohesion. After demonstrating this aspect of cataphora, we will consider how it meshes with the imagery–language dialectic and fits the two awarenesses, simultaneous and successive.

Several noteworthy features having to do with the speaker's assemblage are seen in Figure 4.4a through 4.4i (for this catchment with cataphora I am using McCullough's term, "assemblage," rather than "catchment," although I see them as catchments). The assemblage/catchment in Figure 4.4 had the field of equivalents of *how to stop Sylvester*. Frames (a) through (d) cover multiple events, each with a gesture—hand rising for Sylvester's entrance into the pipe (a), Tweety's reaction (b), and the hand moving down for Tweety's launch of the bowling ball (c, d). They cohere given the assemblage; they are not just steps in a sequence, but a sequence stripping off pieces of an assemblage. Frames (i) and (j) are Sylvester's trajectory after his encounter with (and swallowing of) the bowling ball, the gestures timed with "rolling down the street" and are also part of the Sylvester-stopping assemblage.

The two gestures spanning (e)/(f) and (g)/(h) are another exception that proves the rule. They show Sylvester's living bowling-ball trajectory but apparently too soon—with "it hits him on the head." But this is not

(a)	(b)
he tries **climbing up**the rain barrel	and **Tweety Bird**ah sees him coming and drops a

(c)	(d)	(e)	(f)
bow<u>ling</u> ball **down** the rain barrel		<u>so</u> it **hits** him	

(g)	(h)	(i)	(j)
on the head		and he winds up **rolling down the street**	

Figure 4.4 Ongoingness in English. Boldface indicates a gesture stroke. Drawings by Dusty Hope.

anomalous in the assemblage—within it they are meaningful (bowling ball hits head, has stopping-effect). In fact, as McCullough points out, it is a gestural cataphora, creating cohesion by foreseeing, a moment later, at (g) and (h), the gesture repeated, now with its co-referential speech, to provide the denouement of Sylvester's rolling down the street. All of this is part of the assemblage, of stopping Sylvester by making him into a living bowling ball.

McCullough points out another detail that also shows the assemblage. For all the gestures, the speaker's hand is on the same vertical axis. Those for vertical paths (Sylvester's ascent, the bowling ball's descent) occur in the same place, and those for horizontal paths (down the street) start from it. This *axis is the location* of the HOW TO STOP SYLVESTER assemblage. Each gesture is performed in relation to it and tells us that even Sylvester's ascent is meaningful, not in terms of getting at Tweety but in relation to how Tweety stops him.

McCullough notes a further telling detail. The hand in (c) and (d) faces down. Then, in (e), (f), (g), (h) and (i), it turns up. It shifts from being Tweety's hand launching the bowling ball (facing down) to the edge of the bowling ball as it meets Sylvester (facing up, the hand-backside becoming the active face). The two orientations again cohere within the stopping assemblage. The force of stopping Sylvester has moved from Tweety to the bowling ball (as indeed we saw in the "it down" description as well, in Table 4.1), and the transformation of the gestures, down to up, tracks the movement of this force. Given the assemblage, the downward-facing palm is a cataphor for the later upward-facing palm, the palm being the cohesive link here.

As our italicized HOW TO STOP SYLVESTER notation suggests, we propose that assemblages are fields of equivalents—catchments—but of a special kind with stable, multiple gesture cross-linkages rather than the one-by-one differentiations of the-bowling-ball-as-an-antagonistic-force catchment in Figure 4.2. They are fields that GPs differentiate as the story progresses with a sense of a forward motion as part of the orchestration.

Awareness is an important feature and so is communicative dynamism. At the moment of cataphora, the communicative dynamism includes a tension that later events resolve. The tension is pushing not just "forward" but forward to a specific future reference that fulfills the push. Those events, the speaker is aware (explicitly or not), are also part of the assemblage. The anticipation of the stopping-Sylvester theme gave meaning to the too-early arm sweep over (g)/(h). This tension is experienced in successive awareness; it looks forward to a later successive awareness; and this is possible because of *a simultaneous* awareness that is not just of the sentence but of the whole assemblage. As the GP has a double temporal reference, cataphora and anaphora in assemblages do also. These hierarchies of awareness are of the field of equivalents that the GPs differentiate. A field that is ongoing, one field with successive differentiations, possibly is a defining feature of the assemblage.

Verb-framed (Turkish)

What stands out with verb-framed cataphora? If the languages are equal in their opposite ways, the stand-out should be *manner*; and so it is. In 1999, at the Max Planck Institute in Nijmegen, Asli Özyürek and Sotaro Kita showed me a compelling example of a gesture speech-gesture *temporal mismatch* in the speech of a Turkish language speaker. Turkish is also verb-framed (see Özyürek 2001a, 2001b). Again, a gesture is "too soon," and this seems to be another case of gestural cataphora. The speaker was describing the bowling ball scene and produced a series of phrases, each with a gesture. However—here was the surprise—the gestures appeared to correspond to the spoken phrases that *immediately followed* the gesture, not to the phrases with which they timed (see Figure 4.5; recording, transcription and English translation by Asli Özyürek):[2]

(4.3.1) [top bi sekil-<u>de</u>] *ball in one way*
hands hopping in place. See Fig. 4.3.3a.

(4.3.2) [zipla-ya zipla-ya] *while hopping*
hands hopping and moving right. See Fig. 4.3.3b.

(4.3.3) [yuvar-lan-a <u>yuvar-lan-a</u>] *while rolling itself*
hand moves right. See Fig. 4.3.3c.

(4.3.4) [sokak-tan] *on the street*
hands again move right without hopping = path alone

(4.3.5) [gid-iyo] *goes*
hands again move right without hopping = path alone

The key to explaining these seeming asynchronies is the two occurrences of the adverbial "while," in (4.3.2) and (4.3.3). They do two things. First, they referentially link their speech to the gesture of the preceding phrase, fulfilling the gestural cataphors:

Gesture	Speech
(4.3.1) hands hop	"ball somehow"
(4.3.2) hands roll	"while hopping"
(4.3.3) hands move to right	"while rolling"
(4.3.4) hands move to right	"on the street"

Second, they form gesture–speech units. The gesture at (4.3.1) showed hopping in place with speech describing the bowling ball, not motion. The phrase that followed, at (4.3.2) ("while hopping"), was co-expressive with this gesture at (4.3.1) but not with the gesture it synchronized with. The gesture at (4.3.2) with "while hopping" in turn showed rolling (hopping and moving to the right at the same time) and was co-expressive with the utterance at (4.3.3), "while rolling itself." This in turn was accompanied by a gesture showing pure path, corresponding possibly to the phrase at (4.3.4), "on the street." The cataphors and the speech co-expressive with them are the gesture–speech units. From (4.3.4) onward, speech and gesture line up in the usual one-to-one way.

With each gesture the speaker was creating a field of equivalents, then categorizing it in the next gesture–speech unit with the adverb "while." In a verb-framed language, the manner of the motion event is the stand-out. Like

---

[2] Shuichi Nobe (pers. comm.) added to this discussion.

(a)   Hands hop in place = manner without path

(b)   Hands hop and move to right = manner with path

(c)   Hand moves to right without hopping = path alone

Figure 4.5 Ongoingness in Turkish: (a) with "ball somehow," (b) with "while hopping," (c) with "while rolling itself." Translation by Asli Özyürek. Computer art by Fey Parrill. Used with permission of University of Chicago Press.

path in the satellite-framed paradigm, manner in the verb-framed package receives special status; it stands outside the basic fact of motion. Thus, we can see that the English example in Figure 4.4 and the Turkish in Figure 4.5 reveal the same phenomenon, cataphora riding on the "outside" semantic information. Such is perhaps a "Whorfian" effect. This exploits their respective separations from the basic motion event in each language. Satellite- and verb-framed languages differ in what this is but both are able to achieve gesture-orchestrated speech through cohesion, and do so with the aspects of a motion events their respective languages regard as "outside." The "theory" of motion built into English verb structure is that it is inextricably a *manner* of moving—rolling, running, etc. Path is the extra added to the fundamental of manner of motion. The "theory" in Turkish and other verb-framed languages is that motion is fundamentally *motion on a given path*, and manner of motion is the extra. Speakers of both languages project the "extra" information in gestural cataphora (of course, since this is dynamic, each language can project a cataphor with its built-in component instead (see McNeill 2009 for all combinations).

4.5.2   Orchestration by temporal gestures

"Temporal gestures" were described in Chapter 3 to show a difference between "new" gesture-actions and "old" action-actions. The demonstration was that when one does act and speak simultaneously, speech and action combine in a fundamentally different way from speech unifying with gesture. When combined with goal-directed action, speech but not the action is *metapragmatic*; speech leaps up a level and refers to (rather than co-expresses with) the action. Rather than orchestration of speech, speech coordinates with the action to create icons of temporal relations, *a new gesture* made out of the speech and the action. It and speech together *are* the gesture. Moreover, it is of the "new" gesture-action type. In this section, I describe temporal gestures, give examples and explain how the temporal gesture, as a kind of "new" gesture-action, orchestrates speech and the "old" action-action too. The "old" action-action is both carried out, as an action, and becomes part of the "new" temporal gesture-action, expunging the "old" action-action's goal-directedness.

We separate (a) the pragmatic action and (b) the same action as part of the temporal gesture. The action (a) has a real-world goal. In (b) it is referred to metapragmatically and this temporal gesture does not have the real-world goal. Its goal instead is to take a certain view of the "old" action-action. The metapragmatic reference indicates how the action is being viewed, either internally (imperfective view) or externally (perfective view). The real-world goal is expunged. The goal of the temporal gesture is the same as speech, to create a meaning, inside the action or outside it, not to effect a change in the world, which is goal of the action-action. The action in this new state is part of a "new" temporal gesture-action and takes part in orchestrating speech. In the orchestration, speech and action will often be modified to fit the gesture; this is part of the orchestration. I give examples in the following text.

Extensions of actions with non-functional movements are an important clue to what is involved. The following illustrates one speaker's adjustments of speech and action to form temporal gestures (from McNeill 2003). He was placing a small window-style aquarium's water filter—a tube—inside its container and (as requested) describing his actions as he performed them:

> (4.4)
> [well] [...] I'm picking this up with my left
> *(1)   (2)*
> *(1) Left hand rises. (2) Left hand grasps tube and lifts.*
> [...and I] ['m]
>   *(3)   (4)*
> *(3) Right hand opens. (4) Right hand grasps container and lifts.*
> grasping this with my right hand ... and holding it [...]
>   *(5)*
> *(5) Left hand moves tube over container.*
> [and then I'm plac] [ing] this
>   *(6)*   *(7)*
> *(6) Suspends tube vertically over container.*
> *(7) Left hand drops tube down partially, an inch.*
> [...] I'm placing the ... tube ... the other thing which I'm holding
> steady with my right
> *(8)*
> *(8) Rotates tube back and forth.*
> hand [...] [and] I'm [just] drop[ ]ping it in ...
>   *(9) (10)*   *(11)*   *(12)*
> *(9) Left hand drops tube into container. (10) Lifts index finger*
> *to push down tube. (11) Pushes down. (12) Maximum extent of*
> *the push down.*
> leaving [] go with my left hand
>   *(13)*
> *(13) Lifts left hand away from tube.*

The excerpt illustrates a number of important features. The logical type of the verb varies: some are "activities" (Vendler 1967), such as *holding it*, while others are "accomplishments," such as *dropping it*. Verbs of the first kind are logically unbounded, while those of the second kind have, as part of their meaning, the attainment of a logical endpoint. "Achievements" such as "release" are instantaneous accomplishments. A second important distinction is between progressive and non-progressive verb forms. Progressive marking, such as "I'm picking it up," is one of the few formal devices in English for indicating imperfective aspect. Non-progressive on verbs, although not reliably indicating perfective aspect can be used that way, usually in the past perfect tense ("I've picked the part up").

Figure 4.6 diagrams the alterations in the flow of speech and movement produced by temporal gestures; this is part of the gesture-orchestrated speech by

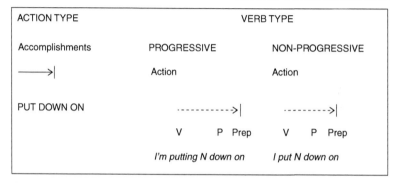

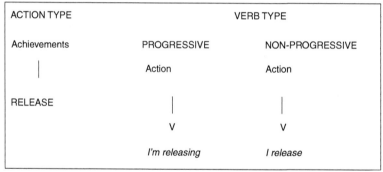

Figure 4.6 Temporal gestures formed from action-speech metapragmatic combinations with different aspects and logical action types. Used with permission of John Benjamins Publishing Company.

this gesture and is seen for example at (3) and (4), where speech was interrupted while the hand opened and grasped the container. Conversely, at (8), downward movement was interrupted and replaced by a symbolic rocking when the speaker groped for the appropriate words to refer to the tube and container. At other times the action was extended to line up with various parts of the utterance, as in (10) through (13). Similarly, at (5) through (7), the action of dropping the tube into the container was performed in little spurts each timed with a different linguistic segment. At (7), the action of dropping was suspended as the speaker sensed that he wouldn't be able to find a word to identify the container (as we see from the elaborate clausal reference to the container that follows). In all of these cases the speaker seems driven to keep speech and gesture temporally together. At other times speech and movement alternated. At (2) the subject picked up the tube in silence, then described what he had done, "I'm picking this up with my left hand," while his left hand froze in midair.

What do these alterations tell us about temporal gestures and their role in gesture-orchestrated speech? To take one example,

> (4.5) "[and then I'm plac][ing] this [...]
>   *(6)*   *(7)*   *(8)*
> *(6) Suspends tube vertically over container.*
> *(7) Left hand drops tube down partially, an inch.*
> *(8) Rotates tube back and forth.*
> I'm placing the ... tube ... the other thing which I'm
> holding steady with my right hand [...]"
>   *(9)*
> *(9) Left hand drops tube into container.*

the added movement at (8), rotation, extended the action of placing the tube in the container so that the "–ing" verb would occur before the action was fully accomplished. The conceptualization at (7) included this imperfective *langue*-feeling of "–ing." However, this does not explain how speech was orchestrated. The speaker's hands were not experiencing a "new" gesture-action. It was an "old" action-action and with it came a conflict of action-to-speech purposes. The addition of a metapragmatic view however changed the field of equivalents and GP into a reference to the "old" action-action, something like, PLACING TUBE: *HOLDING STEADY TO GET INSIDE THE ACTION* (metapragmatic in bold). This was the temporal gesture. The GP was *about* the pragmatic action, about getting inside *it*, and this imperfective-inside-view temporal gesture was a "new" gesture-action, not reaching the goal but forming an imperfective view, and this "new" gesture-action was capable of gesture-orchestrated speech. The "old" action-action, not capable of it, became removed from its own pragmatic goal in the temporal gesture (while continuing as the pragmatic "old" action-action of inserting the tube). As it were, the "old" action-action slid into speech. In terms of Wundt awarenesses, the "new" gesture-action was the simultaneous awareness of looking inside the action, and the metapragmatic reference to the "old" action-action of actually inserting the tube was a temporal gesture within successive awareness.

4.6   Inner speech and Vygotskian internalization

"Inner speech" is a hallowed topic for psycholinguistics, and occupied an important place in Vygotsky's psychology of language (1987). However, it is not exactly clear how it should be understood. It is not just talking to oneself or unspoken speech but speech that is "a function in itself. It still remains speech, that is, thought connected with words. But while in external speech thought is embodied in words, in inner speech words die as they bring forth thought. Inner speech is to a large extent thinking in pure meanings. It is a dynamic, shifting, unstable thing, fluttering between word and thought, the two more or less stable, more or less firmly delineated components of verbal thought" (Vygotsky, 1987, p. 149). Inner speech in fact resembles a *non-unpacked GP and its dialectic of imagery and linguistic form.* Being non-unpacked, the speaker would experience the GP and inner speech in simultaneous but not in successive awareness, and would not be able to orchestrate external speech or could do it only partially, as "at each moment it is present in consciousness as a totality" but not as a "configuration chang[ing] from moment to moment in its cognitive condition" (quoting Wundt, Chapter 2); all of this is *inner* speech and explains the dynamic instability Vygotsky so vividly describes.

Whether Vygotsky considered inner speech to be **intermittent** or **continuous** is unclear. Both can be supported with arguments, but the linkage to non-unpacked GPs favors intermittency. Non-unpacked GPs are intermittent, as Vygotsky envisioned, when the individual engages in thought for oneself or some blockage or imposed silence occurs, but Vygotsky also equates inner speech with the psychological predicate, of which every GP, unpacked or non-unpacked, is comprised. Vygotsky was not concerned with gesture-orchestrated speech, and so did not encounter this ambiguity, but insofar as inner speech is experienced as a unique cognitive mode, the intermittent non-unpacked GP is the model—the mode of cognition of which he wrote, "words die as they bring forth thought." For the purposes of the following example that is the understanding of inner speech, at least.

Vygotsky emphasized that inner speech develops because **interactional content** appears on two planes, with different functions on each. The link is "internalization." A GP likewise describes how thinking internalizes content from the "interactionally effected" plane to create idea units that support discourse coherence on the other plane. This is the key to their interfacing and their distinctiveness. The snippet of a dialogue in Table 4.3 between two graduate students instructed to "have a conversation" while being

Table 4.3 Mr. A probes Mr. B.

Mr. A	Mr. B
Q_{A7} did you [go to school thére] or uh *points to shared space*	
	$R_{B7.1}$ I did go to school [there] *points to shared space* $R_{B7.2}$ [I went to school hére] *points to left* $R_{B7.3}$ [álso] *circles left*
uh-huh	
	$R_{B7.4}$ [I] *points to shared space* $R_{B7.5}$ [/ um] *points to left* $R_{B7.6}$ so I [came back] *points to **shared space***
oh, uh-huh	
	$R_{B7.7}$ [kind of /] *points to **right***
Q_{A8} an' [you wént to under-graduate hére or *points to shared space*..........*	......(A's gesture hold)] R_{B8} [in Chicágo] át, uh, Loyola *points to **shared space***
óhóhóhóhóh I'm an óld Jésuit Boy mysélf // unfórtunately	

Speech transcription by Silverstein (1997), gesture transcription by author.

videotaped illustrates internalization and the formation of inner speech. Mr. A (so named by Silverstein 1997) probes Mr. B's educational history, while Mr. B dodges his queries. Mr. B finally gives in and reveals his secret. The example comes from a larger investigation of face-to-face interaction (Duncan and Fiske 1977). The participants were previously unacquainted male graduate students at the University of Chicago, "Mr. A" a law student, "Mr. B" a social work student. A and B were introduced, placed in front of a video camera, and told simply to "have a conversation." As might be expected in such a situation Mr. A and Mr. B sought topics about which to talk, starting with their respective academic biographies. They already knew that each was a graduate student at the university and knew the schools within the university to which they were attached but did not know anything

Table 4.4 Meanings attributed to the right, center, and left spaces, and Mr. B's inner speech.

Utterance	Right	Shared	Left
QA7 did you go to …		Iowa-then	
RB7.1 I did go to …		Iowa-then	
RB7.2 I went here			c/uChicago-then
RB7.3 also			c/uChicago-then
RB7.4 I		??	
RB7.5 /um			??
RB7.6 so I came back RB7.7 kind of	uChicago-now	cChicago-now	**Mr. B's inner speech:** Non-unpacked GP: *BE POLITE, TELL THE TRUTH: THE UNIVERSITY*
QA8 you went to undergraduate here		uChicago-now	**Mr. A's external speech** *The University: undergraduate*
RB8 in Chicago at Loyola		cChicago-now	**Mr. B's external speech** *the two Chicago's: the city*

of each other's prior history. And this unknown history created up the situation we shall examine.

Table 4.3 picks up at the end of what has been Mr. A's by then already extended effort to uncover Mr. B's academic history. Mr. A had pursued this line for a number of turns and had earlier asked, "Where did you come from before?" and Mr. B had offered, "Mm, Iowa. I lived in Iowa." However, this led Mr. A down the garden path since Mr. B was unwilling to take up Iowa as a topic. The theme, however, is relevant since it led directly to the exchanges in Table 4.3. After Iowa petered out, Mr. A resumed his quest for Mr. B's biography (Q means a question, R means a reply, A or B means the speaker, superscript C means the city, U the university, C/U Mr. B's ambiguous reference to "Chicago," and the number of the question or reply the ordinal position of the item in the snippet; notation by Silverstein, 1997).

The most visible manifestation of functional differentiation occurred at $R_{B7.7}$ where both Mr. B and Mr. A simultaneously pointed at the shared space with opposite intended meanings and incompatible fields of equivalents (see Table 4.4 for the meanings attached to the gesture spaces). Then Mr. B moved into the right space, the only use of this space in the dialogue. Here is a new GP with its own imagery but not unpacked. His speech is fragmentary, as expected if his GP is non-unpacked and awareness is partial. *Inter*psychically, this was a tussle over the meaning of the space. *Intra*psychically, the tussling had the further significance that it embodied Mr. B's dilemma, whether to lie or tell the truth. On this *intra-* plane, the tussle was part of Mr. B's personal mental Being and was subject to autochthonous forces of his own (his wish to camouflage his past, his rejection of lying), while on the *inter-* plane it was subject to the social forces of the interaction between Mr. A and Mr. B (politeness especially; cf. Brown and Levinson, 1990). The point is, both planes are sources of representations running through Mr. B's mind at this moment, as evidenced in the precise form of his utterance. In this plane Mr. B's inner speech, as non-unpacked GPs, had come to full life.

The very construction of Mr. B's meaning—his Chicago past—as a deictic field with entities, an origo (see Bühler 1982) and a perspective is a snapshot of significant relationships translated from the inter- to the intra-plane, there becoming inner speech. The GP is the point where these various factors came together. At the moment of capitulation his GP (awareness of his contradiction with Mr. A., the moral dilemma of whether to lie or come clean) is intrapsychic in the Vygotskian social-mental dichotomy. Internalization refers to the movement of significances from the interpsychic plane to the intrapsychic. While the GP itself is intra-, it ties together forces on thought and action that scatter over both the interpsychic and intrapsychic planes. Vygotsky said that everything appears in development twice, first on the social plane, then on the individual.[3] The same logic applies to the GP. Vygotsky also saw the necessity of a unit that encompasses this transformation, invoking the concepts of psychological predicates and inner speech to express this unity in the minds of socially embedded individuals. The GP model merges seamlessly with his insights.

4.7   The mystery of speed

With the concepts introduced—awareness, feeling, gesture–speech unity, inhabitance—we can propose a solution to the mystery of how words and structures pop up so quickly during the unpacking of GPs. The information load—all things considered (sounds, words, constructions, gestures)—is high, as noted. Hesitations and errors reflect the burden, so it is wrong to say the emergence is flawless, but there is, on the whole, a remarkable speed and accuracy to this memory process. Speaking is the living demonstration of it. **Winnowing a cohort** zeroes in on an object in *langue*—a "construction" (from Goldberg (1995), following Fillmore et al. (1988) who present it as a dynamic

---

[3] This assertion is occasionally suffers an 'intraectomy' at the hands of unnamed authors—Vygotsky turning into a kind of sociologist than a semiotician of mind.

concept) with built-in units and syntagmatic values, slots for words and other constructions and internal combinatoric potential (fulfilled or not), deployed as a whole). The effect is complex, including multiple contexts and different parts of the construction stemming from various aspects of the whole. The "it down" GP again offers an illustration, now of this complexity factoring in different contexts.

With such complexity, how does winnowing work quickly? The answer I propose is in terms of "feeling." The word evokes apprehensions of vagueness but I am using it narrowly. I will call it "*langue*-feeling." James (1890) spoke of feeling's fringes and overtones. He wrote of the feeling of "and" (roughly, more to come) and "but" (contrariness). These are not the systematic *langue* features of the words but a channel into them via one's own inhabitance. *Langue*-feelings apply to gesture–speech units, not just words or constructions. They are part of the speaker's simultaneous awareness of the GP. *Langue*-feelings and inhabitance open the very fast winnowing and meshing that fill speech with words and constructions.

A discovery by William Marslen-Wilson (1987), who introduced the "cohort effect" concept, suggests a solution. Just as words are recognized as they are experienced, in a very fast winnowing of a cohort of known words compatible with the sequential left-to-right phonetic input up to that moment ("captain" triggers a cohort of some seven words up through the "capt–", all simultaneously active, as experiments show), could not something like this take place when speaking? What would be the cohort? Here we turn to Saussure. As we know, he considered the synchronic approach a methodological axiom of *langue*—to see the system of language, in which only differences matter, it is necessary to see it laid out all at once—but could it not also be a psycholinguistic axiom? The parts of *langue* a feeling inhabits is the "cohort" on a given occasion. This cohort is not accessed, as is speech input, in left-to-right temporal order but all at once—all of the axis of selection alternatives of a given feeling alive and accessible at a single instant. This use of the cohort differs from Marslen-Wilson's in several ways but it retains his idea that a single state is reached by winnowing a cohort of viable candidates. For example, a feeling of Making Something Happen winnows *langue* down to the causative construction with slots for the Agent, Cause, Object and Goal to articulate the GP's unpacking:

Construction:	Agent	Cause	Object	Goal
Output:	*Øtw*	*drops*	*it/the b-ball*	*down the pipe*

And words? They are summoned by *langue*-feelings as well, in productions evoked all at once (the left-to-right readout, if it commences immediately, will not affect this speed). The cohort effect has been defined for phonetic elements but words are thicker. The concept of a "lemma" applies (Levelt

1989)—*langue*-feelings attach to lemmas, sound patterns and grammatical potentials (both the axis of selection and the axis of combination) as well as intentions and presuppositions.

A memory in which *langue* is available all at once is also involved. This memory need not be large. Context, prior speech, presuppositions and indexical indicators narrow the areas of *langue* the speaker has to hold in memory at any moment (cf. Van Petten, et al. 1999). It can be of credible size but when these sorts of factors do not narrow it sufficiently, speech may cease. Most speakers are familiar with the effects of being temporarily overwhelmed by their own speech process.

Moreover, the constructions and words accessed in these ways work on each other in the winnowing of both, further speeding things. We see this in "it down"—the verb, "drops," part of the construction, won against alternatives such as "thrusts" or "pushes," because it added something the construction needed but did not have on its own, that in the cartoon story Tweety had released the bowling ball, letting gravity do the rest; "thrust" and "push" contradict this, "drops" permits it.

4.8   The micro-level

So far we have seen that gestures orchestrate speech at the level of words and constructions. Gestures also orchestrate operations at the **micro-level**. The gesture shapes them, resets parameters and reorders steps. A hint of gesture-orchestration at the micro-level is the (more or less) constant two seconds that speakers take to utter sentences over a range of embedded clauses, matching the duration of gestures.

Evolution of the micro-level

MacNeilage in his 2008 book traces speech evolution to jaw movements during the ingestion of food. With phonation, the basic mandible closing-opening maneuver creates CV (consonant–vowel) syllables. The child's acquisition of the speech of his community includes specific tunings of how, to what extent, for how long, etc. the closing/opening movements occur (at this point called "frames with content"). Language-specific timing is a good example of a micro-level step, and here gesture–speech orchestration is expected to shape things.

Experiments

Careful experiments by Sahin et al. (2009) reveal some of the micro-level features that gestures could reshape. The experimenters, thinking in reductive terms, however, did not tap gesture-orchestrated speech (they carefully removed or neutralized all except word inputs, supposing it gets at fundamental processes), but we can see how gesture-orchestrated speech could alter this micro-level. Sahin et al. recorded directly from brain areas of patients undergoing open skull surgery and, taking clues from Levelt et al. (1999), found that lexical, grammatical and phonological steps occurred with distinctive delays of about 200ms, 320ms and 450ms respectively. We hypothesize that gesture should affect this timing for the one or two seconds the orchestration lasts. That the brain falls back upon a lexical → grammatical → phonological sequence when receiving isolated words without fields of meaningful equivalents does not mean the sequence will remain the same when it has this information. If the idea unit differentiating a past time in a field of meaningful equivalents begins with an inflected verb plus imagery, does the GP's onflashing wait 320 or 450ms? Delay seems unlikely (although would be fascinating to find). It may be no faster (and perhaps slower) to say "bounced" in an experiment where a subject is told to make the root word into a past tense than to differentiate a field of equivalents with past time gesturally spatialized and the gesture in this space. A difference or equality would show imagery orchestrating speech at the micro-level. Experimenters have not asked these questions but this effect of gesture is predictable.

Browman and Goldstein (1990) developed a "gestural" (in the articulatory sense) phonology in which the production of speech is represented as an orchestral "score" (their term) of the moving parts of the vocal tract. We expect that (manual) gesture speech-orchestration can alter the score's timing. Armstrong et al. (1995) made a similar proposal. Figure 4.7, from Browman and Goldstein (1990, p. 361), is a hypothetical score for uttering the fragment "must be" in two versions—(a) citation form (without gesture-orchestration) and (b) fluent speech (with it). Fluent speech compresses actions, and this is what we would expect of gesture-orchestrated speech also. As in Armstrong et al., meaning (on several levels) intervenes, and how this intervention takes place under the guidance of gesture (the hands) is the process we have described. Actions occur in an order specified by the score but timing shifts. This is how the Sahin effect could shift and with an order inversions as well. Wu and Coulson (2010) observed what could be a perceptual counterpart of the production effect envisioned in Figure 4.7: "Gestures modulated event-related potentials to content words co-timed with the first gesture in a discourse segment" (from the abstract).

Considering the micro-level and how the gesture-orchestration of speech can affect it helps dispel mysteries, such as the seemingly longer processing time the production of speech takes, compared to that of comprehension (e.g., Levinson and Torreira 2015). This comparison considers the intake of speeded-speech to picture-naming latency, with a large discrepancy in favor of the first over the second. However, producing six clauses in two seconds is indeed fast and brings the two directions closer together. Picture-naming is just the kind of process that assumes speech production is a bottom-up "assembly," the "Information Processing Hypothesis (IPH)" style (described in Chapter 3),

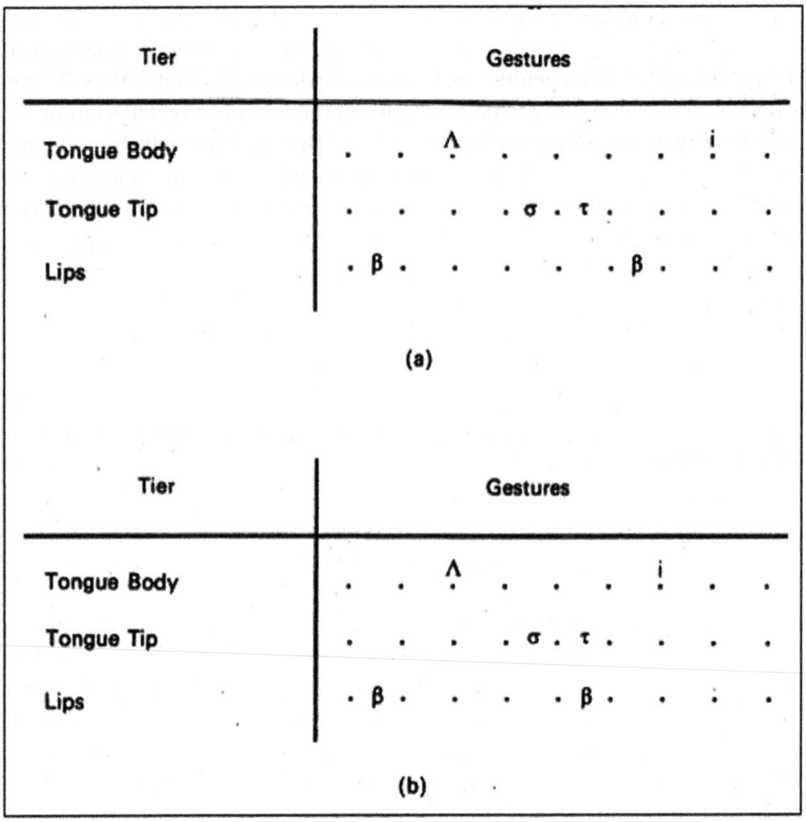

Tier	Gestures
Tongue Body	. . Λ . . . . i .
Tongue Tip	. . . . σ . τ . . . .
Lips	. β . . . . . β . . .

(a)

Tier	Gestures
Tongue Body	. . Λ . . . i . .
Tongue Tip	. . . . σ . τ . . . .
Lips	. β . . . . β . . : .

(b)

Figure 4.7 Micro-level phonological "score" from Browman and Goldstein (1990) for the utterance fragment "must be" in citation form (a) and fluent speech (b). Gestural metaphor would modify (a) in various directions of which (b) is one. In Browman and Goldstein's notation, Λ is a back vowel; i is a front vowel; σ is a sibilant; τ is dental contact; and β is bilabial contact. Used with permission of Cambridge University Press.

and that does not tap the main features of the gesture-orchestrated speech process; it leaves out the GP and its differentiation of in-built contexts or psychological predicates; in other words, everything that could speed the micro-level to degrees the isolated naming of pictures cannot approximate.

Kröger et al. (2010, p. 202) have developed a computational model with a role for "the activation of the course of a temporal scheme for coordinating all elementary movement actions." If such a model could be steered in the direction of gesture-orchestrated speech, it could turn the "temporal scheme" into a picture of how gesture shapes micro-level events as envisioned here.

4.9   Codability

How does the speaker apportion information to gesture and speech? The aspects of a gesture–speech unit, when different, that end up as gesture and in speech seem largely a matter of codability. This concept was originally formulated for color words—a color that could be accurately and communicatively named with a single word ("red") is more codable than one requiring modification ("reddish"), and this more codable than one requiring a descriptive phrase ("kind of red, like the color of your socks") (Brown and Lenneberg 1954). For our purpose, the concept is applied to conceptualizations. In the gesture–speech unit high codability seems to flow to speech, low to gesture. We can see this in Figure 2.1, where "rising hollowness," a paragon of low codability for English, appeared in gesture and not in speech (which had interiority, upward motion, etc.—analytic versions of "rising hollowness" but not the low codability concept itself).

4.10   Overall summary

The overall lesson of this chapter is the complete penetration of language and thought by the context of speaking. This is more than the cliché that context is important. Gesture–speech unity cannot exist without it. Its absorption is constitutive. When action and speech cannot merge, as in self-description, speech rises to metapragmatic reference, and forms a new temporal gesture that orchestrates speech.

5   Mimicry and metaphor

Two further aspects of gesture-orchestrated speech are: (a) its social dimension, actuated in mimicry (the psychological predicates of one person appearing in another person); and (b) metaphoricity, bringing imagery to what is not imagery so that abstract, non-imagistic meanings can orchestrate speech. The chapter extends gesture-orchestrated speech in these directions. The conclusion I reach is that mimicry and metaphoricity are found in the very act of speaking itself, intrinsic to "new" gesture-actions, and are not add-ons.

5.1   Why mimicry?

Mimicry is perhaps the aspect of gesture-orchestrated speech least expected but it is frequent in human interaction: it is *the orchestration of one's own speech by the gestures and speech of another*. Mimicry gives new meaning to the old saw that language is social.

Voluntary mimicry can be socially aggressive, a kind of taunt, but involuntary mimicry marks rapport and is surprisingly frequent, especially when rapport is close (Kimbara 2006).[1] It is important to emphasize that the mimicry we are considering is unconscious and involuntary. It need not be conspicuous. Micro-movements suffice. With it *the mimic absorbs the other's growth point (GP), including the field of equivalents it differentiates*. The mimicked GP follows the same path as one's own GP, having a gesture–speech unity, the GP itself, its differentiation of a field of equivalents, its unpacking and the speech it orchestrates. Such mimicry is a powerful instrument of social engagement or entrainment. Materialization through involuntary mimicry explains a frequently experienced but never remarked upon phenomenon: **tip of the tongue contagion**—when someone unexpectedly cannot recall a common word whose meaning is known and clear to everyone, often the interlocutors are also suddenly unable to recall it. "Mind merging" can include "tip-of-the-tongue merging" through involuntary mimicry (suggested by Liesbet Quaeghebeur,

---

[1] This paper and conversations with Kimbara during her PhD student days at the University of Chicago triggered my appreciation of mimicry as a living force.

personal communication). Involuntary mimicry could be a product of the evolution of social thinking-for(-while)-speaking in small groups, possibly the bands described by Dunbar (1996), where it would have had adaptive value.

I was drawn to noticing it by seeing gesture-coders in our lab spontaneously mimicking gestures and speech in videos to clarify meanings. By replicating another person's gesture and speech, the mimic imports a gesture–speech unit. It is a tool for the coder to absorb and materialize an absent speaker's thought and speech and is also widespread in human interaction generally. We posed self-discovery examples utilizing mimicry in Chapter 1.

5.1.1   Mimicry cases

We consider next the mimicry of gesture-orchestrated speech in conversations and narratives with a range of natural (not evoked) examples. Such mimicry shows every sign of being involuntary and unconscious. In terms of speech, **person A orchestrates person B's speech**. In terms of awareness of the sentence, **A's awareness becomes B's** (the awareness at which coders also aim). The result is two persons sharing gesture-orchestrated speech and awareness. Quaeghebeur (2010) connects the phenomenon to "intercorporeity":

This exemplifies well Merleau-Ponty's (2007) concept of "intercorporeity": in social or linguistic interaction our bodies become aspects of a shared dynamic system; we "share a body" because it has been formed the same way (we speak the same verbal and nonverbal language) and because we find ourselves in this concrete situation together, i.e. a shared framework for making reference to … A full multimodal analysis shows that when engaged in conversation, we are at all times immediately attuned to each other's meaningful behavior, so that it is better to say that we think, speak and listen "along." (Quaeghebeur 2010, p. 119)

Embodiment in two bodies

In accord with intercorporeity, there exist spontaneous **two-body GPs** (Figure 5.1, from an experiment devised by Nobuhiro Furuyama 2000). In Figure 5.1a, one person's speech is orchestrated by another's gesture. The setting was person R teaching L, a stranger, how to create an origami figure. The learner on the left mimics the teacher's gesture and the mimicry has social-interactive effect. It occurred without the learner speaking but synchronized with the *tutor's* speech. As the tutor said, "[pull down] the corner," the learner performed the gesture during the bracketed portion. The learner thus appropriated the other's speech, combining it with her mimicked gesture, as if learner and tutor were jointly creating a single GP. The similarities to what Gill (2007) calls "entrainment" are notable.

(a)   (b)

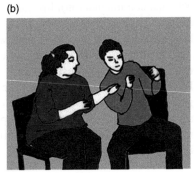

Figure 5.1 Embodiment in two bodies.
Panel (a): Silent involuntary mimicry of gesture by learner (on left) synchronized with teacher's speech.
Panel (b): While speaking, learner (left) appropriates teacher's gesture, nullifying usual prohibition of physical contact by strangers. As Furuyama (2000) observed, the teacher invited contact by turning his body away, giving to his gesture space the same left-right orientation as the learner's. Computer art by Fey Parrill. Used with permission of University of Chicago Press.

The reverse appropriation also occurs. In Figure 5.1b, the learner appropriates the *tutor's gesture* by combining it with *her speech*. Again, there is inhabitance, this time of gesture, and there is again a kind of joint GP. The learner says, "[you bend this down?]," and during the bracketed speech moves the tutor's hand down. As Furuyama observes, the tutor had turned in his chair so that the same left–right gesture space was available both to him and the learner, a maneuver that invited the learner to enter his gesture space. It is striking that the American taboo normally prohibiting strangers from non-accidental physical contact was overridden, possibly because the hands had become shared symbols, no longer body-parts belonging to another person.

Mimicked gesture–novel speech
Like (b) in Figure 5.1, Person L in Figure 5.2 orchestrates her own speech with Person R's gesture. The unusual aspect is that the speech is a confabulation, an alteration of her own memory of the cartoon as a result of her mimicry of the other's gesture; through mimicry, her memory acquired an error. L is recounting the bowling ball episode and, in (a), has started to describe Sylvester's ascent ("he's climbing the drainpipe") making a left-hand gesture curved around a vertical space, her imagery of the pipe's interior (circled in figure—the palm, the "interior" of the gesture, being the active part as usual). Person R, who remains silent throughout, is at the same time preparing to make

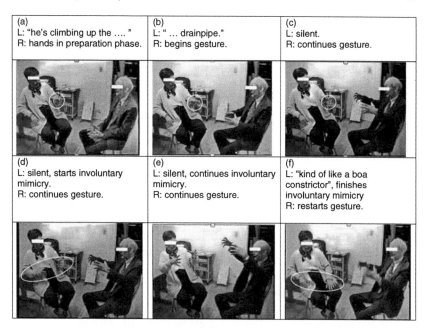

(a) L: "he's climbing up the .... " R: hands in preparation phase.	(b) L: " ... drainpipe." R: begins gesture.	(c) L: silent. R: continues gesture.
(d) L: silent, starts involuntary mimicry. R: continues gesture.	(e) L: silent, continues involuntary mimicry. R: continues gesture.	(f) L: "kind of like a boa constrictor", finishes involuntary mimicry R: restarts gesture.

Figure 5.2 L mimics R's gesture and incorporates it into her GP with "boa constrictor" (not uttered by R, not in the cartoon). L was the narrator; R did not speak. Example from Susan Duncan.

a gesture of his own—hands energized, fingers extended, but still at lap level, not yet a stroke. He exemplifies the same appropriation of the other's speech we saw in Figure 5.1a. Figure 5.2, Panels (b) and (c), a second later, show his stroke starting. Person L now has become silent, left hand frozen in the pipe position, watching R's gesture. In this gesture both hands rise in unison, moving in and out as they go, an upward-traveling bulge. His gesture continues in (d). L remains silent, still watching, her left hand still held, but now her right hand comes into action. Panel (e) shows L's mimicry of R's bulge in full swing, her former pipe gesture gone, replaced by one side of the traveling bulge. Panel (f) is the end of her mimicry, her left hand now at rest and she resumes speaking, saying "kind of like a boa constrictor," the speech the mimicked gesture has orchestrated. The speech was original, not mimicked. It was orchestrated by the mimicked gesture (the cartoon, which she was retelling, doesn't mention boa constrictors nor show the pipe swelling). This was one person (L) taking over another's (R's) momentary cognitive being, not unlike (b) in Figure 5.1, and in addition evoking a false memory (the possibilities for false testimony in legal contexts of interrogators' taking over someone else's speech are noteworthy).

Figure 5.3 Seat assignments for USAFIT war-game exercise. Used with permission of John Benjamins Publishing Company.

Turn-taking

The example that follows was recorded during a roundtable meeting of US Air Force officers taking part in military gaming exercise at the Air Force Institute of Technology (see McNeill et al. 2010). The commanding officer for the session is in position E (Figure 5.3). The goal of this particular meeting was to figure out how a captured "alien missile head" (actually a coffee thermos with fins glued on) functioned. The session lasted approximately 42 minutes. The example that follows is from the latter half of this period.

The speech is as follows (E in charge, G current speaker, F next speaker):

1 E: "okay. u-"
2 G: "So it's going to make it a little tough."
3 F: "It was my understanding that the– the whole head pivoted to provide the aerodynamic uh moment. But uh I could be wrong on. That uh ... "
4 G: "that would be a different design from-"
5 F: "From what–"
6 G: "from– from the way we do it."
7 F: "Okay."
8 E: "Okay so if we–"
9 G: "But we can look into that."
10 E: "If we're making that assumption ((unintel.)) as a high fidelity test"
11 F: "Yeah."

An obvious case of a **GP starting with one speaker and moving to the next speaker** appears at line 5, where F says "from what" and G, at 6, takes over with "from– from the way we do it." G's speech is being orchestrated by F's. We propose this is the psychology of one participant predicting the end of another participant's turn in a conversion, the "projection" of the turn-end in the conversation-analytic sense (Sacks et al. 1974). The joint inhabitance is seen in the deployment of gaze and gesture:

F begins with a glance at E, then gestures interactively toward G, followed immediately by gaze at G and an iconic gesture depicting the alien coffee mug.

The turn-exchange here is a multimodal unit within which dimensions of gesture and gaze exchange places in creating a GP comprised of imagery that depicts the object and a linguistic component asserting that this procedure is "the way we do it" vis-à-vis the object. Thus, at the turn exchange, there was a synchronizing of inhabitances by F (the next speaker) with G (the current speaker) via joint gaze with the dominant figure at the roundtable, E. Purely static analyses, as in most **conversation analysis,** can be seen in this light as arranging for these sorts of synchronized inhabitances to occur. F's GP included the idea of his collaboration with G, their joint clearance with E whose authorization was being checked, and with this their cognitive states lock-stepped. F's GP was in fact a continuation of G's. The details appear in how gaze and gesture deployed around the table:

1 Dominant E continues to gaze at designated speaker G when G gestures at object and others apparently look at the object.
2 G gazes at the dominant participant, and makes deictic/conduit gestures in his direction. G then shifts his gaze to the object, and then quickly shifts back to E. Non-speaker D doesn't shift to E when G shifts but keeps gaze at G—suggesting that what we see is the speaker affirming the dominant status of E, but the overhearers are free to respond to the speaker's new turn.
3 Also, when F takes turn from G he waits until G finishes his ongoing sentence, but first turns to look at E in the middle of the sentence, and then starts his turn while still looking at E (only after this shifting to G).

Mimicry is a constant and turn-taking is conveyed by it. Once more, we see the dynamic dimension at play. Many of the turn-construction and turn-completion dynamics discovered in conversation analysis (see Sacks et al. 1974) can be viewed from this angle as the adaptations a culture makes to foster gesture-orchestrated speech mimicry.

Coalitions
The same process of synchronized inhabitance can build coalitions. Gaze is crucial. C tries to secure G, but his gaze is not reciprocated, then he secures D's gaze, and finally E's (arrows show direction of gazes).

1 C→G
2 C↔D
3 C↔E

A shared co-referential chain with C was created when D and E returned his gaze, a form of mimicry; G did not, and was not part of the coalition, and loomed instead as a point of conflict. The important point is the alignment of the coalition around a shared field of equivalents, making possible the merging GPs we saw with turn-taking—a kind of turn-taking without taking the turn.

5.2   Mimicry of author-GPs

Involuntary mimicry is not limited to face-to-face or face-to-video observations. Written prose often contains hidden gestures that can be mimicked. Written prose does not necessarily mean that imagery is lacking; rather, it is possible that we write in such a way that gestures are incorporated into the written text. A reader, reading out loud, will often restore the gestures that are in the written text implicitly. We cannot tell if they are reproductions of the author's gestures, but they are readily evoked and seem to the reader to fit the text. Written prose may thus contain hidden gestures. Part of learning to write (not forming letters but composing prose) is discovering how to incorporate them. Much of what we sense as the rhythm of written prose, descriptive as well as dialogue, seems gestural. If you read this small bit from a letter by the character Jane in *Pride and Prejudice* aloud with hand movements, you readily spatialize the text gesturally:

something has occurred of a most unexpected and serious nature; but I am afraid of alarming you—be assured that we are all well ... what I have to say relates to poor Lydia.

On the other hand, a verbatim transcript of actual spoken speech, its original gestures lost, is notoriously unrhythmic and nearly unintelligible, even though it was fully comprehensible in its original face-to-face form with gestures (if you read such a transcript and force yourself to form gestures, the gestures seem to be repeated beats, hitting stress peaks, which alone remain of the original gestures; see Tuite 1993, who proposed that rhythmical pulses underlie every gesture).

HALDEMAN: Pat does want to. He doesn't know how to, and he doesn't have, he doesn't have any basis for doing it. Given this, he will then have the basis. He'll call Mark Felt in, and the two of them ... and Mark Felt wants to cooperate because ...

Writing is traditionally described as decontextualized, as standing on its own. However this tradition may have missed something. If the origin of language was in fact the origin of language and gesture, a unified system, there may be gestures hidden in written prose as a matter of its own history. Writing systems that engage the sounds of speech would encounter the gesture imagery that orchestrates speech actions, the moment the writing goes beyond a mere phoneme notation to actual prose.

Literal transcripts, on the other hand, are famously lacking in fluid qualities, and this could be precisely because the manual gestures that originally occurred have been stripped away, and nothing like the hidden gestures of well-constructed prose have taken their place.

Alphabetical writing aims to depict the sounds of speech. Ideographs, Chinese and Japanese characters specifically, relate to conceptual content more than to sound. Nonetheless, ideographs also depict aspects of speech (see Daniels and Bright 1996), and the order of characters on the page exactly matches the sequence of speech, and this is in the realm of gestures. So there too, fluent "scannable" writing may be gestural.

5.3   Mimicry in performance

Mimicry of the gestures hidden in written prose can be a factor in theatrical performance. Mimicking them recovers GPs and fields of meaningful oppositions built in by an author even centuries before, which can guide the actor and be transmitted to the audience. Taking *Pride and Prejudice* again, at one point Lizzie, touring Pemberley and believing that no one of the family is at home, suddenly finds herself face-to-face with Darcy. For both characters it is a moment of surprise and awkwardness. Austen describes Darcy's reaction as a full start. I first tried a gesture that would go with just this line ("a full start"), without considering the preceding context of Lizzie's dawning new relation with Darcy. It was a sharp upward jerk of one hand (described by one observer as looking like a seizure)—a "full start" gesture, tied closely to the text. However, considering Austen's likely field of meaningful equivalents this gesture would not be what she had built into the "full start" as part of her GP. An altogether different gesture appears when the immediate context is considered (in which the Pemberley housekeeper, to Lizzie's astonishment, has delivered an enthusiastic recommendation of Darcy's character—generous, amiable, fair, "the best master"). My two hands form an open space and rock upward and forward. This fits a field of meaningful equivalents in which the Lizzie–Darcy relationship is in focus and is transforming. The gesture "presents" this dawning relationship and moves it forward in a future direction. It is the first encounter after Lizzie's revelation and the turning point at which Lizzie comes to see Darcy in a new way. Austen's own GP as she wrote would surely have had some such meaning beyond surprise, and plausibly it was in part this opening up (and beyond, in the following narrative, Darcy's own transformed demeanor). Unlike his character, the actor knows the context of Darcy's full start. The scene has been played in films. How does a professional actor do it? A full start is certainly present but at the same time there was a slight movement forward, against the natural withdrawal of a full start, the same direction as my mimicked metaphoric movement. So perhaps the actor was mimicking Austen's GP as well.

5.4   Metaphors and metaphoricity

Returning to the "new actions" of gesture and speech, we see that they include metaphoricity (yet another contrast to "old" action-actions, which are pantomimes and literal). From this inherent metaphoricity, metaphors naturally spring up. It is one reason why metaphor is so widespread in human thinking. Within thc realm of gesture–speech unity, *metaphor controls iconicity*. This follows from metaphor's role in gesture-orchestrated speech, for iconicity provides the imagery with which the metaphor orchestrates the speech. The abstract significance of "the good" cannot orchestrate speech, but a shoving-bowling-ball-down metaphor provides imagery. This analysis applies to impromptu gestures such as "it down" as well as to established metaphors like the conduit hand "holding" a discursive object, and explains why they occur at all. In impromptu metaphors, the speaker thinks one thing and finds her own image that presents it as something else. "Literal" and "metaphoric" occur together, not when one (the literal) is abandoned and the other (metaphor) steps in, as has been proposed by some psycholinguists (see review in Glucksberg and Keysar 1990). Moreover, *metaphoricity recruits iconicity*—a metaphor of a discursive "object" recruits an iconic gesture that depicts a container for it, a metaphor of an agent for the good recruits an iconic gesture of hands pushing down on a bowling ball, etc. The reason that speakers follow this seemingly round-about method is, again, gesture-orchestrated speech, because it supplies the gesture imagery with which to orchestrate speech.

Metaphoricity is experiencing, or being one thing in terms of another thing (as argued by Müller 2008). A **metaphor** is a gesture or linguistic package relying on this semiotic. Metaphoricity, the semiotic, comes about when the orchestration of the vocal tract and hands is undertaken by something other than their native actions, by meaningful gesture. The motions of the vocal tract in gesture-orchestrated speech are experienced as the imagery of a manual gesture. Actions of the hands likewise move from "old" action-actions to "new" gesture-actions. In the semiotic of metaphoricity one thing (voice, hand motion) gains significance in terms of something else that it is not, enabling "it down" to be experienced not as a sequence of vocal movements, and not (only) as a concrete event, but as the image of a character in a battle of good versus evil, and for the hand motion of thrusting down to have the same significance.

Metaphor, the package using metaphoricity, arises in gesture-orchestrated speech in two ways. First, the very fact that a gesture orchestrates speech movements has the semiotic of metaphoricity. At this basic level we find it. Second, gestures are themselves often metaphors, packages with the semiotic of experiencing or being something else. The extension of metaphor gives abstract meaning its reach into the world of gesture-orchestrated speech. The "it down" gesture depicted not just the bowling ball going down, a concrete event, but also a force for good, an abstraction. Metaphor enables abstract meanings to orchestrate speech, bringing into it the imagery they lack. Via metaphor the meanings that gesture can orchestrate are unlimited.

(a) (b) (c)

Figure 5.4 Two concurrent gesture metaphors for processes during an academic lecture using whole body ("process as motion") and arms ("process as rotation"). From McNeill (2005). Computer art by Fey Parrill. Used with permission of University of Chicago Press. Example from Eve Sweetser.

5.4.1 Examples

I give here examples of gesture metaphors—one using motion, one space, the third shape and space on a meta-level—that make gesture-orchestrated speech possible with abstract conceptualizations. Many other gestures could be cited, but these give a good picture.

The first is two gestures performed simultaneously during an academic lecture for the operation of a computer program (Figure 5.4, example from Eve Sweetser, pers. comm.). The first displays it as the speaker's own self in motion. This metaphor is joined by another, where the computational process is portrayed as a rotation. The metaphors together orchestrated "the dynamics of how you get through the—right?" on the speech side ("right" revealing a second impinging context, the social dynamics of speaking to an audience). The gestures unpacked into an embedded sentence, different clauses for each gesture—"the dynamics" orchestrated by the forward-motion gesture; "how you get through" by the rotation. It is a straightforward case of gesture-orchestrated speech, the unusual aspect being that it used two gestures, simultaneously orchestrating speech segments that were successive. The two do not combine into a higher gesture but merge to bring the two aspects of the computer's operation into one portrayal. The whole-body motion summoned the embedding construction, while the arms, moving "within" the body's motion, called the embedded one. The compound sentence thus echoed the large and small gestures.

Next, Figure 5.5 illustrates space as a metaphor. It shows the same instance presented earlier (Figure 3.2) depicting what the speaker took to be a moral ambiguity in the Hitchcock film *Blackmail* we used as a narrative stimulus, which he was recounting. In panel (a) he is saying "everyone's morals are very ambiguous 'cause [they're sup]posed to be the good guys," and indicates the space to the left (right hand pointing). The guilt-innocence chronotope in Chapter 3 is also a source of metaphors. The metaphor in this case used the center versus left space distinction to orchestrate speech around the abstract

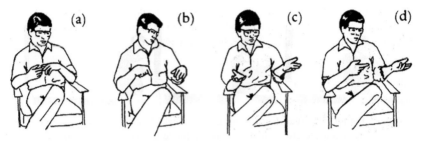

Figure 5.5 Spatial metaphors during a film retelling (Hitchcock's *Blackmail*). See text for explanation. Repeats Figure 3.2. Drawings by Laura Pedelty, now on the faculty of University of Illinois Medical School. Used with permission of University of Chicago Press.

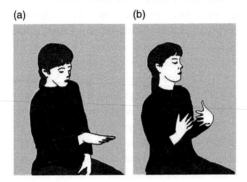

Figure 5.6 Front doors as metaphor for restarting a house tour. From McNeill (2005). Computer art by Fey Parrill. Used with permission of University of Chicago Press.

conception of a character chronotope, guilt (left side) versus innocence (center). With a metaphor of space, the moral values sorted out. Space was not space. The unimageable became imageable and gained power to orchestrate speech.

In the third example (Figure 5.6), reference is on a meta-discourse level, conveying information about the structure of the discourse itself, that the main storyline was being interrupted to interpolate a restart (Susan Duncan transcript):

> (5.1) [I **forgot to say**] [when you come **through** the*][a**nnd you**<ou>**openn** the doors with t][he*][/ **the glas**][s **inn them #**]

Several gestures occur, first with "I forgot to say," then with five two-similar hands that show opening the front doors of a house—this is their iconic aspect. As metaphors they convey the idea of restarting a part of the speaker's description—a discourse portal experienced as an architectural one. The two-hands catchment had this restart theme and the gestures bridged it to individual growth points and thence orchestrated speech.

5.5 Phonetic symbolism

Gesture-orchestration of speech also produces "phonetic symbolism," the pairing of referential dimensions with phonetic dimensions. Orchestration of speech with phonetic symbolism is of the simplest kind, iconic replications of the imagery of gestures ("large"→ large vocal space, "small"→ small vocal space). Which is the better name for a large table—"mal" or "mil"? Sapir (1929) found that nearly 90 percent of respondents chose "mal." No doubt the same holds today. The effect can be explained as a vocal maneuver orchestrated by a gesture. The imagery of something large gives meaning to the vocal tract maneuvers of a large vocal space (open [a]). We are saying that "mal" has meaning in the form of something else, the imagery of something large. Although this appears the reverse of Sapir's explanation it follows from the dynamic conceptions of this book. Rather than saying that in the phonetic symbolism of a "mal" versus "mil" mouth shape (open versus closed) determines meaning ("large" versus "small"), we are saying that meaning (imagery) determines (orchestrates) mouth shape (directing it to open for large imagery).[2] This explanation also fits better with Diffloth's (1994) description and explanation of the exact opposite direction of phonetic symbolism in Bahnar, a Mon-Khmer language of Vietnam: "the iconic values of the vowels are … High [i, u] = Big and Low [ɛ, ɔ]= Small [are] exactly opposite to the English" (1994, p. 112, transcription symbols and one word added), a difference he relates to the "rich sensation package of the articulator movements involved." In high vowels, the tongue both closes the space at the top of the mouth and also opens space at the back; one language (English)seizes on the closure, the other (Bahnar) on the opening for equally iconic images of small and large respectively. They are however *the same metaphor*: spaces in the mouth being experienced as something else. Thinking in terms of gesture-orchestrated speech, the metaphoricity of Smallness and Largeness also has this choice of realizing imagery, and the existence of the opposite directions thus fits the analysis that begins with metaphor and ends with the iconicity to realize it. Diffloth emphasizes that phonetic symbols remain within the phonetic system of their language, so we would expect the languages to differ at this level as well.[3]

---

[2] See Rhodes and Lawler (1981) for a pioneering linguistic study of such words, at www-personal .umich.edu/~jlawler (under heading of "phonosemantics," accessed May 1, 2015) for more recent work, including extensive word lists.

[3] The "sn-" nasal words, "snot," "sniff," "sneeze" and others may also be gesture-orchestrated phonetic symbols. When air is actually expelled through the nose, a reflex action occurs of

5.6   The emblem as metaphor[4]

Emblems are codified gestures of the kinds found in dictionaries. It is not customary to think of them as metaphors but that will be our analysis here. While they are the most sign-language-like of gestures, only one step on the gesture continuum from true sign languages (see Figure 1.1), emblems contain inner metaphors. From the inner metaphor the emblem gains the ability to orchestrate speech that otherwise it would not have. Figure 1.1 showed lines between emblems (and points) to gesticulation, suggesting a link. We can see now that metaphoricity is this link. Emblems are in other words extensions of gesture-orchestrated speech. Not a "gesture language," but the logical end-result of regular spoken language. They emerge from speaking itself. The intrinsic metaphoricity of gesture–speech unity here reaches its zenith in the realm of the culturally codified.

Cultures historically pick metaphors, codify them with standards of form and function, ensure social standardization and intergenerational transmission, yet never lose contact with them. No emblem or "quotable gesture" in Kendon's (2004) study of Neapolitan emblems reverses or contradicts its inner metaphor.[5]

The "**ring**," the "OK" sign in North America, typifies this process. North America and Naples both use the ring as a metaphor of precision, but differ in the use they make of it. If what a culture chooses to do with a metaphor, here the ring for precision, reflects possibly deeply held values, we can compare the American and Neapolitan cultures on this limited front. The ring is approbation in North America; the same metaphor is authorization in Naples.

In the metaphor precision is experienced as contact or a narrowed space between surfaces. It is called "the ring" but it is not the ring shape but the forefinger-thumb contact that is the metaphor. The shape is abundant in the Neapolitan gesture code and covers a range of meanings, all of which have some connection to the idea of precision. It forms what Kendon calls a *gesture family*. It is also a *metaphor family*. However, the one meaning the Neapolitan code ring family apparently does

---

closing the vocal tract at the alveolar ridge and crimping it at the palate but this reflex can also be experienced as something else, as one of these "snout" meanings, and this is gesture-orchestrated phonetic symbolism. "Snooty" is a metaphor on this metaphor-based phonetic symbol, a lifted snout cartoonishly depicting someone "supercilious, haughty, conceited; affecting superiority, snobbish; 'highbrow', 'stuck-up'" (*Oxford English Dictionary*).

[4] Based on McNeill (2014a).

[5] Dropping a bowling ball does not seem a likely starting point of an emblem, but somewhat absurdly we can envision a society of slapstick comedians valorizing Figure 4.1, "The good is dropping a bowling ball," and making the shoving-down gesture into an emblem, with standards of form, codified meanings and the rest, as it bounces off Curly's iron-clad head. (A deeper question is why this is amusing at all, if it is.)

not include is approbation, the "OK" meaning. In Naples, the ring has stabilized around other foci (based on Kendon 2004):

1 Ring first, then open hand: a topic-comment sequence, the ring coloring speech with an aura "in which something quite specific is being mentioned."
2 Hand raised, ring forms and is held before interlocutor: clarifying or giving exact information. Again, the ring colors the accompanying speech with an aura of precision. The effect is metalinguistic: what I am saying is "precisely so."
3 Hand in ring held vertically, palm facing interlocutor's midline: a specific point in contrast to some other point or position.

Far from dispensing or requesting approbation, like the American "OK," the Neapolitan ring thus signals *authority*—the *speaker's authority for* giving a topic with a comment, for having information that is precise, and to contrast it with other information, all stemming from a codification of the same metaphor of precision as in "OK" but with the opposite pragmatic effect—authority rather than approval. We see two contrasting cultural valuations. Where one anxiously seeks or comfortably administers approval, the other derives authority. Why is it called "OK"? While the ring is metaphorizing precision the hand shape can be read pun-like as the letters, "O" and "K." "OK" as a pun is one explanation at least.

"**Thumbs up or down**," like "OK," conveys approbation (or its opposite) but has a different metaphor source: better is higher, "up on top" (Lakoff and Johnson 1980), to which the upturned thumb points. Equally, "thumb-down" indicates a locus at the bottom, the reverse metaphor, lower is worse. The difference explains how the two emblems, "OK" and thumbs up/down, differ while both signaling approbation. The thumb's ancient uses, at least in Hollywood versions, involved the same metaphor: "up is better (= survival)"/"down is worse (= death)." This conceit, however, is thoroughly debunked by Morris et al. (1979). The actual Roman gesture was the thumb extended in an unspecified direction = death; the thumb retracted under the fingers = survival. Morris et al. suggest the thumb was an iconic sign for the sword that would perform the deed. I have been told that the thumb was also connected in ancient Rome with concepts of power and authority,[6] echoes of which may also exist in the Neapolitan ring today. A further possibility is that the thumb-sword was also deictic, pointing at the gesturer's neck, showing where the sword would plunge—a deictic/iconic gesture similar to a forefinger across the neck for us. With time, the higher = better/lower = worse metaphor took over.

What raises a metaphor to emblem status lies in environment, culture and history. For Neapolitan emblems, Kendon emphasizes the noisy open-air life

---

[6] Thanks to R.B. McNeill of the Lawrence University Department of Classics for this and the next observation.

of Naples where value accrues to ways of communicating meanings without speech. In this environment, speaking was subject not just to interference from a noisy environment but to cultural forces such as the valorization of authority through precision shaped the gestures arising in gesture-orchestrated speech, eventually to become in the noisy environment the ring emblem. In this case and others, emblems have deep historical roots—ancient and except in the form of gesture long hidden (the "OK" sign seems a newcomer as emblems go, the ring emerging with this use in only the last few hundred years, but has been following a similar trajectory starting from the precision metaphor). All extant emblems seem to embody culturally significant metaphors (precision, etc.) with which to orchestrate speech but impromptu metaphors can do it also, and in their potential we see how emblems could have begun their careers.

The very possibility of an emblem can thus be considered another effect of gesture-orchestrated speech. Cultures imbue gestures, metaphors, with standards of form that carry them from gesticulation to other locations on the gesture continuum.

The *grappolo* is another Neapolitan emblem with a hidden metaphor, as Kendon (2004) illustrates. As a speaker introduces a discourse topic, he forms a gesture with the fingers in a bunch (shaped by standards of form), then opens his hand to present the comment (also shaped by standards of form—both shapings attested by Kendon (pers. comm.); one of a family of *grappolo* usages Kendon describes (see Kendon 2004, Figure 11.3).

The *grappolo* in this example appears to hold a discursive object; the hand then opens but continues to support it. Where the ring is a cultural codification of a precision metaphor, the *grappolo* codifies a different metaphor, the so-called "conduit," originally identified by Reddy (1979) and Lakoff and Johnson (1980) with linguistic examples. Following a suggestion by Lakoff (pers. comm.), I extended it to gesture in my 1985 paper, "So you think gestures are nonverbal?" Both steps in the example embody the imagery of a surface (first curled, then opened) with a substance in or on it. Gesturally the conduit depicts "content" "in" or "on" the hand, which may be open or closed, partly or totally, as in the *grappolo*. In its raw (non-emblemized) form it appears in at least Asia, Northern Europe and North America. But as a conduit it lacks the Neapolitan stabilization of how it should be formed and the discourse effects it should have. Nonetheless, like the *grappolo*, the conduit metaphor defines a container or surface that supports a discursive object. We have an early (possibly emblematic, perhaps even the *grappolo* itself) use of the conduit in a quote from Montaigne (sixteenth century), who attributes a series of conduits for degrees of epistemological certainty to Zeno of Elea (sixth century BC). The *grappolo*, in its topic-comment use, appears as part of this series (boldface):

Figure 5.7 English speaker's "conduit" gesture with "the final scene was ... " Palm "holds" the object—the "final scene" of the cartoon. Computer drawing by Fey Parrill. Used with permission of University of Chicago Press.

Zeno pictured in a gesture his conception of this division of the faculties of the soul: **the hand spread and open was appearance**; the hand half shut and the fingers a little hooked, consent; **the closed fist, comprehension**; when with his left hand he closed his fist still tighter, knowledge. (Montaigne1958, p. 372)[7]

As with Zeno, the *grappolo*'s closed version is a bounded container that conveys a sense of certainty; in its second, open version, the certainty is less, corresponding to the Neapolitan codification of a comment.

Finally, the open hand part of the gesture also included deixis, pointing. Multiple dimensions converged. Although in this example the deixis was to a concrete locus, deixis can readily take on metaphoric value, pointing to a space whose meaning is non-spatial and is established or recaptured by the deixis.

The non-emblemized conduit metaphors of English also include the hand "holding" discursive objects (in Figure 5.7, "the final scene," the "object"). The gesture is like the open-hand version of the *grappolo* but is also different from it. It is not held to standards of form. It arises exclusively out of the conduit image, the only constraint on its form. The metaphor of a discursive object recruited an icon of a container to hold it. There is no history or culture of gesture form behind it and the gesture has no standards other than to iconically depict the conduit's container but, like the *grappolo*, can orchestrate speech ("the final scene ... ").

The open hand, in addition to being the less certain end of the Zeno and *grappolo* conduit sequence, conveys its own metaphor of openness—the idea

---

[7] Thanks to Josef Stern of the University of Chicago Department of Philosophy.

of a discursive object that is "open" to discussion, dispute, etc., as is appropriate for the second half of topic-comment. Again, Neapolitan culture has codified form and use, so that the open hand zeros in from conveying something "open" to something where "the object being indicated is not the primary focus or topic of the discourse but is something that is linked to the topic" (Kendon 2004, p. 208).

The open hand in this second kind of emblem takes two forms in the Neapolitan code, prone or palm-down (including away) and supine or palm-up. They comprise a gesture family of shared forms but, unlike the ring, not a metaphor family. Kendon emphasizes that the orientations have different contexts of use, and this is our clue. Two unlike metaphors are involved that do not combine. Palm-down denies, negates, interrupts, or stops something—metaphorized as an incoming force, a beam, with the **palm as a barrier**. Palm-up is the conduit and offers, shows or requests something—metaphorized as an object, the palm a surface or container. From a metaphoricity viewpoint, the two types are different, not opposites but unconnected. Thus how one regards a gesture, as form qua form (as in Kendon) or as a metaphor (again, the "kinesis" worldview versus the "meaning" worldview described in Chapter 3), affects whether they resemble each other or not. From a form angle they go together as a family, but from a metaphoricity viewpoint, palm-down belongs with the other beam emblems while palm-up belongs with the *grappolo* and other conduits.

A third metaphor family thus involves **beams and obstacles**. They appear in both emblem and spontaneous gestures. In both, palms are the active site of force, energy and action (presumably derived from the orientation of the hand in contact with objects). This is why the palms face the danger in warding-off emblems, widespread also in spontaneous gestures and a fixed feature in the Neapolitan code: the palm as obstacle. In the examples Kendon presents, the palms face outward but in spontaneous gestures the palms present their faces both outward and inward. The code apparently has chosen one direction, outward, from a variety in spontaneous cases, the palm facing in various directions depending on the semantics of the situation, to ego, sideways and outward.

Beams and obstacles imagery appears in a host of spontaneous gestures. In Figure 5.8 for example (from a second *Blackmail* retelling), the left hand is a wall, the right hand an emanation of eyebeams moving outward through a superimposed (translucent) crowd that the wall hand represents to contact the main character. The ancient theory that vision is like touch by beams out of the eyes was brought to life in the gesture while attempting to describe translucent imagery. In Figure 5.9 shadows are conceptualized as beams, "cast out" from the body onto a wall, the surface of which the right hand depicts (palm upright, facing the shadow).

What of **canned metaphors**? For example, "a sea of grief—How and where does one come across a sea that is filled not with water, but with

Figure 5.8 Beam and obstacle metaphor A. "People are walking by her and you can see though the people into her" where left hand is "the people" and right hand for "seeing" moves past it. Art by Laura Pedelty. Used with permission of University of Chicago Press.

grief?" asks the author of an online article (http://examples.yourdictionary.com/metaphor-examples.html, accessed November 7, 2014). "A sea of grief" and other canned metaphors may be like emblems, bits of gesture-orchestrated speech that have been culturally codified and stabilized, but on the speech side of the gesture–speech unit. If so, they also may contain original orchestrating metaphors. How to tell? I turned to mimicry and tried a waving "surface of the sea" gesture, and got an unexpected image of a slapstick-mustachioed, snake-oil performer (why is unclear, but the image was vivid). Making a "sea" gesture embodying depth (both hands, palms upward, moving down and slightly arcing as they did) brought forth an impression of vast grief, from which I infer in "sea of grief" a hidden metaphor of depth, not a surface, which the gesture had awakened (Müller 2008). From this bit of evidence, canned metaphors may also participate in gesture-orchestrated speech, using awakened hidden metaphoric images, not unlike emblems.

Figure 5.9 Beam and obstacle metaphor B. A shadow being cast off to contact a surface. Left hand is the shadow, right hand the surface. Speaker is saying (in Georgian), "you see a shadow ... the shadow of a man in a top hat." Translated from Georgian by Kevin Tuite. Art by Laura Pedelty. Used with permission of University of Chicago Press.

5.7   Musical growth points

Another possibility stemming from the intrinsic metaphoricity of gesture-orchestrated speech is that there can be **musical GPs**—only now *gesture-orchestrated musical performance* (not only singing and conducting but also instrumental performance). In this extension of metaphoricity, musical performance is experienced as gesture.

A musical GP would require a semiotic opposition of musical forms to gestural imagery, but it would not be language. I am thinking that musical GPs can be found in the performing musician organizing actions (performances on an instrument) via imagery, combined with an awareness of music as structure, to create units of meaningful musical (performance) actions. Crucial to this possibility is that performers gesture as they perform. Conductors are obvious instances and I have observed gestures seeming to throw out bits of sound (which the orchestra was producing) but instrumentalists also gesture with their instruments where possible. Even pianists can gesture with torso and head movements. A flutist we were shown used her instrument deictically while playing on it, making pointing gestures not to physical locations, including not to the printed page of music she was reading, but to metaphoric spaces similar to those that speakers create as a routine necessity.[8] Perhaps it was equally a necessity for the musician. She appeared to be organizing two material carriers simultaneously, one the performance itself (a highly structured sequence of actions), the other pointing gestures within a meaningful and non-concrete space. This seems not unlike the dynamic dimension of language but pertaining to musical thought. Not words, but the kind of thinking that—in its linguistic form—fuels language, but in this case fuels a performance of music. I think it is safe to say that musical ideas are a force in structuring a performance. What are the fields of equivalents? Zbikowski (2011) lays out this kind of analysis, revealing something that can be taken as both "static dimension" musical content and "dynamic dimension" torso-formed catchments and fields of oppositions.

An informant has described to me her experiences with language when she was intensely practicing the Beethoven piano repertoire six or seven hours at a stretch. During these stints she entirely resided in the world of his music and did not engage in any other kind of activity. To her astonishment, after these long musical sessions, she found that she *could not speak*. It was as if speech had switched off. She is a fluent, highly spontaneous and engaged speaker of multiple languages, so this was quite contrary to her normal self. Could my informant have bundled all her GP resources into the musical mode, with speech becoming, literally, speechless?

What of the non-musician listener? For untrained listeners, music can be a borrowed form of Being. One may absorb the performer and composer and become, for the moment, someone or something else, shaped by the music, the performer and composer. In this respect it equals the cognitive Being of speech and gesture but without speech of any sort. For this listener, the music is experienced as a body motion. It is not a musical GP, lacking the dual semiosis of static and dynamic in a dialectic, but it could have a primitive metaphoricity—music experienced as body motion, the motion having no significance other than itself. A listener, non-musically trained, does not have bundles of significant musical equivalents, but still hears melody, tempo, rhythm, volume, etc. that derive from general experiences with sounds, including music, and esthetic responses from who knows where, and these, plus perceptions across time may be experiences of pure speechless thought. They are not the musical GPs of a musician but still they can be a form of Being. Gesture

---

[8] This draws on a seminar on music and gesture at the University of Chicago at which Lawrence Zbikowski and Ric Ashley, music theorists and performers in their own right, presented eye-popping examples of spontaneous, unrehearsed gestures by instrumentalists as they proceeded with their performances.

exists in foot-tapping, hand-waving, torso bobbing back and forth. These and other reflex-like movements while listening to music provide material carriers that embody the music heard in something like gestures. I have been struck by how non-musicians, listening to music, move in these reflex-like ways far more than musicians, who move little—possibly because they create full musical GPs, to which the non-musician's reflex movements may be the stumbling approximations. Levitin and Menon (2003) recorded different fMRI responses in Broca's Area to music and to scrambled versions of the same music (keeping acoustic parameters constant), concluding that the response to music is in part a motor reaction in the brain affecting temporal coherence; such coherence could be orchestrated by imagery and gesture in the listener.

This whole line of thinking gives fresh meaning to the catchphrase, "the language of music." Mithen (2006) has put forth the idea that singing was a precursor to speech. Music may now be in a condition of alternation with speech for infiltrating the GP, as our informant's story of speechlessness after intense musical performance suggests. Singing seems special, since it combines linguistic and musical motor orchestrations, and the instrument is the same vocal system as in speech. It could be organized by imagery similarly. Logically, the speech control mechanism had to be orchestrated by meanings other than the meanings of vocal actions themselves. Humming and other musical efforts meet this requirement and could have been in place along with speech, but not before. The oldest discovered musical instrument (a flute), pointing to "second language" instruction, dates back 35,000 years, according to news reports (*WSJ*, 2009), but that would be nowhere near the dawn of music if it co-evolved with speech. That would have been 1–2 million years ago, according to indications of organized communal life.

Also, children who from exposure and native ability have knowledge of significant musical oppositions and perform one or more instruments while very young would be interesting to observe from a musical GP point of view. Is their music acquisition anything like their own speech acquisition, the beginning of musical thinking being timed, as with the GPs of language, to the dawn of self-aware agency, around age three or four, and developing from there? This could show itself in the kind of musical gestures that we have been identifying suddenly surging upward. I am not aware of any evidence pertaining to this question, but such a correlation would be convincing evidence in itself of musical GPs.

Part II

Phylogenesis, ontogenesis, brain

6   Phylogenesis

How language began provides the ultimate explanation of gesture–speech unity, the final answer to why we gesture, its dynamic dimension, that gesture is an integral part of language, that language gives inhabitance and how gestures orchestrate speech.

Theories of the origin language differ but basically there are only three. Many today posit gesture-first, a language of gestures or signs that speech eventually emerged to supplant. In earlier years, the choice was speech-first, theories mentioned earlier and absurdly named bow-wow or yo-he-ho among others (speech evolving out of onomatopoeia or work-chants, M. Müller 1861). Speech-first is equally derailed by the arguments that undo gesture-first and I concentrate on the latter. Even though we are referring to events hundreds of thousands of years ago, origin theories can be tested. We ask: can the theory explain how gesture–speech unity evolved? Also, can it explain speech–gesture synchrony? If it cannot, that is one kind of falsification. Does it also positively predict that these things did not evolve? That is another kind. We shall see that gesture-first (and speech-first) fails both tests. The theory here takes the third position. It posits *gesture–speech equiprimordiality* (a term of art coined by Liesbet Quaeghebeur, personal communication). I propose later in the chapter a mechanism called "Mead's Loop" that assumes gesture and speech evolved jointly. Unlike gesture- or speech-first, it produces gesture–speech unity, dual semiosis, an imagery–language dialectic, psychological predicates absorbing context and gesture-orchestrated speech, and thus passes the tests they fail.

6.1   Gesture-first

The gesture-first theory, going back centuries (see Levelt 2013) and popular again today in many books and articles, says that the first steps toward language phylogenetically were not speech, nor speech with gesture, but were gestures alone. Vocalizations in non-human primates, the presumed precursors of speech without gesture's assistance, are too rigid and restricted in their functions to offer a plausible platform for language, but primate gestures appear to offer the desired flexibility. Thus, the argument goes, gestures could have been the linguistic launching pad (speech evolving later). The gestures in this theory are regarded as the mimicry of real actions. They are in fact "old" action-actions, a kind of pantomime, hence the appeal of mirror neurons as the mechanism (Rizzolatti and Arbib 1998). Current chimps show this kind of action mimicry, but as a possible starting point non-human primate gestures would have to lead to the human ending point, gesture–speech unity. One might think that adding speech via a separate evolution creates gesture–speech units, but the gestures themselves also must change, becoming "new" gesture-actions, and this change is also an aspect of the origin of language.

6.1.1   Problems with pantomime

I do not deny that gesture-first may once have existed, but if it did exist it could not have led to human language. It would have created pantomime, an "old" action-action that does not synchronize with co-expressive speech, and thus would fail one of the tests for a possible theory of language origin. If gesture-first once existed, it either extinguished or branched off into a dead-end. In fact, early current-day children's language offers clues that it possibly did once exist and entered a dead-end (this will be described).

There are several distinguishing marks of pantomime compared to gesticulation. One is that gesticulation integrates with speech; it is an aspect of speaking itself. Pantomime separates from speech. There is no co-construction, no co-expressiveness; timing is different (if there is speech at all), and no dual semiotic modes. Pantomime, if it relates to speaking at all, does so, as Susan Duncan (pers. comm.) points out, as a "gap filler"—appearing where speech does not, the "language-slotted" position of the Gesture Continuum, for example completing a sentence ("the parents were OK but the kids were [pantomime of knocking things over]"). It is also a "gap-producer." If one performs a pantomime while speaking, it punches a hole in the speech, orchestrating a burst of silence rather than speech.

A second distinction is that a pantomime, as an "old" action-action, is made with a purpose, to re-enact an action, entity or event. Gesticulation lacks purpose; it is part of thought and speech; it is experienced, not "done." How is a gesticulation identified? The only certain method I know is to carry out a growth point (GP) analysis. We ask: does the gesture combine with speech to differentiate a field of meaningful equivalents? If yes, it is gesticulation; if no, it is potentially a pantomime. It can relate to speech as a "language-slotted" completion but not as a co-expressive partner in a gesture–speech unit.

There is also a movement signature that follows from pantomime's single semiosis. *Pantomimes do not have gesture phases*; lacking dual semiosis it has no speech–gesture synchrony, no sudden onset and offset that Kendon (2004) emphasized, no preparation, hold, stroke and retraction. Pantomimes are mimicked actions and events and lack the temporal structure built around a gesture–speech unit.

Given its pantomime commitment, gesture-first portrays the initial communicative actions as symbolic replications of actions of self, others and entities. It was these replications it supposes that scaffolded the eventual emergence of speech. The process appeals because it so clearly taps the mirror neuron response. Arbib (2012) gives pantomime, via mirror neurons, a central role. Donald (1991) likewise posited mimesis as an early stage in the evolution of human intelligence. It is likely that pantomime is something an apelike brain is capable of and was already in place in the last common chimp–human ancestor, some eight million years back. Contemporary bonobos are capable of it, supporting this idea (Pollick 2006; see Figure 6.2).

The problem is not a lack of pantomime precursors but that *pantomime repels speech. It does not unify with it.* If we surmise that an old pantomime/sign system did scaffold speech and then withered away, this leaves us unable to explain how gesticulation emerged and unified with speech. We conclude that scaffolding by pantomime, even if it occurred, would not have led to current-day speech–gesticulation linkages.

Michael Arbib (2005, 2012) envisions an " 'expanding spiral' of increasingly sophisticated protosign and protospeech," a spiral moving from gesture to speech, with pantomime the bridge in the center. He writes:

the path to language went through protosign, rather than building speech directly from vocalizations. It shows how praxic hand movements could have evolved from the communicative gestures of apes and then, along the hominid line, *via pantomime* to protosign. (Arbib 2012, p. 229, emphasis added)

The spiral indeed introduces gradual change. The problem is that with each turn of the spiral two codes, sign and speech, meet; this is the mechanism and, as we will see later in models of codes coming into contact, the existing gesture-first code's *gestures repel the newly coded speech and/or divide the labor of sentence formation between themselves and speech.* In neither case does gesture–speech unity evolve.

The spiral might work however by *exchange*: as gesture and speech move around the spiral, bits of co-expressive gesture and speech trade places, a gesture (a bit of sign language up till now) giving structure to a bit of speech (a vocal gesture till now) and the speech (vocal gesture till now) giving global-synthetic semiosis to the bit of gesture. Something like an exchange may be the intended mechanism. Arbib writes, "Protospeech builds on protosign in an expanding spiral: Neural mechanisms that evolved for the control of protosign production came to also control the vocal apparatus with increasing flexibility, yielding protospeech as, initially, an adjunct to protosign" (Arbib 2012, p. 231,), which seems close to an exchange. But note what this exchange does. It supplants gesture by speech, yes; but it also supplants speech by gesture. Each bit of gesture, formerly a bit of language, ceases to be language. Gesture–speech unity is again impossible and, worse, sign languages cannot arise from it. The former gesture-first language cannot be a language again unless the whole exchange reverses. The existence of deaf sign languages, especially the "home signs" invented by deaf children growing up isolated from any usable language experience (Goldin-Meadow 2003a), is a counterexample to the exchange. The spiral has to evoke some different process to explain them. In any case, an exchange process does not lead to gesture–speech unity; dual semiosis is not simply the two semiotic modes an exchange process creates lying side-by-side, but *two in one unit*, co-expressively covering one idea.

So the spiral hypothesis either produces mutually repellent gestures and speech, contrary to fact; forces sign languages to be based on different principles from spoken language, also contrary to fact; and does not result in gesture–speech unity, again contrary to fact.

Michael Corballis (2002, 2011, 2014) likewise continues to advocate gesture-first in recent work. Gesture-first seems less essential in his larger project, which has as its central theme a posited universal, recursion, the embedding of like things into like. This ability Corballis proposes is part of the psychological foundation of human culture, "providing the creative potential for such diverse activities as reconstructing past episodes or imagining future ones, telling stories, creating music or art, and manufacturing edifices and complicated machines" (Corballis 2011, p. 181). This far-reaching idea has great appeal, but *the gesture-first creature would have been incapable of it*. The problem is that like other aspects of gesture-orchestrated speech, recursion has dual semiosis, it enters into gesture–speech unities, placing it in a realm that the gesture-first creature, supplanting gesture with speech, could not have entered (see Figure 6.1).

6.1.2   *Problems with supplantation*

Gesture-first claims that speech, once it evolved, supplanted the original gesture/sign language; gesture then withered. Why does gesture-first say gesture withered when speech emerged? The logic of gesture-first, at its very core, means that the supplantation of gesture by speech, overt or hidden, is inescapable. This is why every advocate automatically posits it (see examples in Table 6.1). Empirically, there is a perfect correlation of those advocating gesture-first and the supplantation step. This logical position is inescapable and in fact is the undoing of every gesture-first theory.

There is this conceptual point that explains it; namely, supplantation is built into the gesture-first theory. It is important to see that gesture-first is a theory about the origin of *speech* (not gesture). Given that aim, it must logically

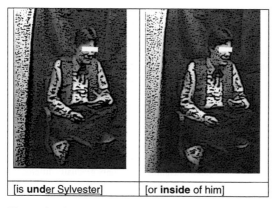

| [is **under** Sylvester] | [or **inside** of him] |

Figure 6.1 Gesture–speech unity with recursion. The speaker has outlined what she took to be an ambiguity in the bowling ball episode. She first states the ambiguity ("you can't tell if the bowling ball") and then, recursively, states the alternatives ("is under Sylvester or inside of him"); concurrently and co-expressively, she moves her left hand to a certain space for the ambiguity itself (the first gesture—actually two gestures in the same space with "you can't tell … " etc.), and then opposes two spaces within it for the poles of the ambiguity (two further gestures in the "ambiguity" space—first the hand moves inward with "is under," then forward with "or inside of him"); so there is recursion on both sides of the dialectic. The recursions, spoken and gestured, partake of the usual dialectic semiotic oppositions: while speech is codified, comprised of recurrent elements with constraints of meaning and form, gesture is global and synthetic and the meaning of the whole (ambiguity) determines the meanings of the parts (the two poles, the "under" pole, in particular, being anti-iconic). Transcriptions by Susan Duncan.

consider that from gesture one gets to speech; and here supplantation enters: it is unavoidable logically.

6.1.3   Models of gesture–speech crossover

The effects of bringing two codes into contact as supplantation requires can be seen with bilingual speakers of contemporary encoded gesture systems. I have picked two examples, the Warlpiri sign language and American Sign Language (ASL) signs with speech, in each case performed by hearing sign-speech bilinguals. The codes do not combine. Speech and sign mutually repel each other in time, so breaking synchrony, or if simultaneous are not co-expressive: either way these language-like coded gestures do not form gesture–speech unities. The conclusion is that juxtaposing two codes does not pose semiotic opposites; in fact, they are semiotically similar and an imagery–language dialectic cannot form.

Table 6.1 Gesture-first advocates and supplantation of gesture by speech.

Source	Statement (supplanted gestures in boldface)
Henry Sweet (and presumably Henry Higgins):	Sweet imagined a gesture language with signs like "point at teeth" for teeth, bite, eat, etc. Later, a "sympathetic lingual gesture" was formed when the signer would sound a signal to draw the interlocutor's attention—an audible vowel with the tongue contacting the teeth. This "would then accompany the hand gesture **which later would be dropped as superfluous** so that ADA or more emphatically ATA would mean 'teeth' or 'tooth' and 'bite' or 'eat', these different meanings being only gradually differentiated" (Sweet 1971 [1900], pp. 3–4, emphasis added). (Thanks to Bencie Woll for bringing this passage to my attention.) Used with permission of Oxford University Press.
Rizzolatti and Arbib:	"Manual gestures progressively lost their importance, whereas, by contrast, vocalization acquired autonomy, until the relation between gestural and vocal communication inverted and **gesture became purely an accessory factor to sound communication**" (Rizzolatti and Arbib, 1998, p. 193, emphasis added). Used with permission of Elsevier Press.
Stefanini et al. (referring to Gentilucci and others):	"[T]he primitive mechanism that might have been used to **transfer a primitive arm gesture communicative system from the arm to the mouth** … " (Stefanini et al. 2007, p. 218, emphasis added). Used with permission of Elsevier Press.
Tomasello thinking in terms of primates and very young (one-year and less) human infants but with the suggestion that something similar took place in phylogenesis:	"Infants' iconic gestures emerge on the heels of their first pointing … **they are quickly replaced by conventional language** … because both iconic gestures and linguistic conventions represent symbolic ways of indicating referents" (Tomasello 2008, p. 323, emphasis added). Used with permission of MIT Press.

1 **Warlpiri sign language**. Women use the Warlpiri sign language of Aboriginal Australia when they are under (apparently quite frequent) speech bans and also, casually, when speech is not prohibited. When this latter happens, signs and speech co-occur and we see what might have occurred at the hypothetical gesture or sign-speech crossover. The example is from Kendon (1988, graphic based on Kendon's description, pp. 306–307):

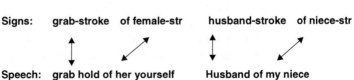

(Used with permission of Cambridge University Press.)

The spacing is meant to show relative durations, not that signs and speech were performed with temporal gaps (they were performed continuously). Speech and sign start out together at the beginning of each phrase but, since signing is slower, they immediately fall out of step. Each on a track of its own, they do not unify. Speech does not slow down to keep pace with gesture as would be expected if speech and gesture were unified (and as IW accomplishes with his "throw-aways," illustrated in Chapter 8, Figure 8.6). Sign and speech then reset (there is one reset in the example) and immediately separate again. So, according to this model, co-expressive speech–gesture synchrony would be systematically interrupted at the crossover point of gesture and speech codes. Yet synchrony of co-expressive speech and gesture is what evolved.

2   **ASL/English bilinguals**. The second model is Emmorey et al.'s (2005) observation of the pairings of signs and speech by hearing ASL/English bilinguals. While 94 percent of such pairings are signs and words translating each other, 6 percent are not mutual translations. In the latter, sign and speech collaborate to form sentences, half in speech, half in sign. For example, a bilingual says, "all of a sudden [LOOKS-AT-ME]" (from a Sylvester and Tweety narration; capitals signifying signs simultaneous with speech). This could be "scaffolding" but it does not create the combinations of unlike semiotic modes at co-expressive points that we are looking for. First, signs and words are of the same semiotic type—segmented, analytic, repeatable, listable and so on. Second, there is no global-synthetic component, no built-in merging of analytic/combinatoric forms with global synthesis. Third, the spoken and gestured elements are not co-expressive but are the different constituents of a sentence. Of course ASL/English bilinguals have the ability to form GP-style cognitive units; but if we imagine a transitional species evolving this ability, the bilingual ASL-spoken English model suggests that scaffolding did not lead to GP-style cognition; on the contrary, it implies two analytic/combinatoric codes dividing the work.

Gesture-first says that language began as non-spoken gestures and signs. Despite a legion of supporters, however, this theory is faulty in two respects. It *predicts what did not evolve* (that gesture was supplanted by speech) and *does not predict what did evolve* (gesture–speech unity). A theory that predicts what did not occur and does not predict what did occur is unlikely to be correct, to say the least.

6.1.4   *Early child language development ("Acquisition 1")*

Nonetheless, gesture-first may have existed once but then underwent extinction. Of all indicators it is **early child language** that suggests gesture-first existed in human history. This is because something like a recapitulation of it, what I am calling "Acquisition 1," arises in ontogenesis and performs a scaffolding function much like that envisioned by the gesture-first advocates in Table 6.1. It then dies out in a kind of extinction roughly from two to three years (the "dark age"). GPs finally emerge with multiple indications of dual semiosis across a wide front "late," at age three or four years ("Acquisition 2"). All of this suggests that gesture-first once existed but went extinct and a new form of language followed, where speech and gesture imagery merged into the unified packages inhabited by thought and Being that we see in ourselves.

This style of argument—an ontogeny-recapitulating-phylogeny argument—has been often derided but there has been a recent revival of interest in it (see MacNeilage 2008). It can be useful and heuristic for sorting out steps in phylogenesis. The acquisition gesture-first provides is limited, much as Bannard et al. (2009) describe:

children's speech for at least the first 2 years of multiword speech is remarkably restricted, with constructions being seen with only a small set of frequent verbs ... and many utterances being built from lexically-specific frames.

In Acquisition 1, children's first gestures consist of pointing, and appear a month or two before the first birthday. Indexicality seems to be the cognitive mode at this time—connecting oneself to interesting events and objects, possibly by way of the interrupted grasping that is shared with other primates (Vygotsky 1987). These steps are a single semiotic and prior to the GP. Some cultural emblems (waving bye-bye and the like) arise around the same time (Acredolo and Goodwyn 1990). That pointing and emblems emerge together suggests an underlying similarity (which could be a shared indexicality—being directed at others—as a child displays interesting events and objects).

Next to appear, still in Acquisition 1, are the gesture "names" described by Goldin-Meadow (2003a, 2003b) and Goldin-Meadow and Butcher (2003). An example is placing a cup pantomimically to the mouth, not to drink, but to label the action of drinking (Bates and Dick 2002). There are gesture–speech combinations (mostly pantomime and pointing) that foreshadow word–word combinations a few weeks later with the same semantic relationships. Something like scaffolding is taking place in which, as with gesture-first, gestures and speech, while not co-expressive, supplement each other. The gesture seems an "old" action-action, with implicit pragmatic goals (a gesture of drinking is *having* a drink, truncated). A child who pointed at an object (a pragmatic action with the goal of getting attention) and said "go" would, a couple of weeks later, produce word–word combinations with "go" plus object names, and the "old" action-action gesture drops away, now superfluous, just as gesture-first envisions. These also are all still single semiotic.

The full story of the second year of development thus seems to be, first, speech and gesture occurring in rough vicinity of each other but not yet synchronizing;

Table 6.2 Pivot grammar with "want" (Braine 1963, p. 5). Prototype of gesture-first "syntax."

Want +	
	Baby
	Cat
	Do
	Get
	Glasses
	Hand
	High (= "put it up there")
	Horsie
	Jeep
	More
	Page
	'pon (= "put on"/"up on")
	Purse
	Up
	Byebye car

then synchrony of speech and gesture in supplemented, non-co-expressive semantic relations; and last, the same relations in word–word combinations, showing supplantation as "old" action-action gestures drop away. This is the gesture-first style origin of language recapitulated in early child language.

The highest achievement of this gesture-first language is possibly what Martin Braine (1963) called "pivot grammars" and Elena Lieven et al. (2009) called "templates." The example in Table 6.2 is from Braine. The word "want" anchors other words to form simple Pivot + (Other) Word "constructions." Each pivot word like "want" is a grammar unto itself. There are as many grammars as pivots, possibly in the hundreds or thousands for gesture-first creatures (such grammars would not have the infinite productivity of human language, in which there is no last sentence: in a pivot grammar there is always a "last sentence," when the Other words run out).

In other words, the first steps that children take toward language may not lead to language, but to something coming from a long-extinct creature; then a second origin yields the language we take for granted (Acquisition 2), but by then the first has extinguished or is in the process of doing so. The gestures of the Acquisition 1 phase—pointing, pantomime, emblems, action-stubs, motor responses loosely linked with speech or produced alone—although they linger on are unlike those of the last—dual semiotic and unified with speech.

It is during this "dark age" that the gesture-first of Acquisition 1 disappears, replicating extinction as well. The next chapter provides examples of the two origins, gesture-first and gesture–speech unity, surfacing in the same sentences, alternating but not influencing each other, as if the two curves, in and out, were crossing without interacting.

The dual semiotic, gesture–speech unity dynamic launches simultaneously and suddenly across a wide front around three or four years—motion event decomposition, a gesture explosion, tailoring fields of meaningful equivalents to make differentiations possible, meaningful gesture perspectives and the onset of self-aware agency, this last underpinning the rest. Each possesses dual semiosis and gesture–speech unity, and heralds the extinction of the gesture-first style Acquisition 1 as well as the dawn of Acquisition 2.

The upshot is that gesture-first has little light to shed on the origin of language as we know it; at best it explains the evolution of pantomime as a stage of phylogenesis that, if it occurred, went extinct as a code and landed at a different point on the continuum of gestures. See Levy and McNeill (2015) for extensive discussion of this entire process.

6.2   Mead's Loop

This section details the alternative, the gesture–speech–equiprimordiality theory of language origin. Human language drew for its origin on many sources, a number of which are outlined later. The hypothesis of this section is that a unique trigger also existed. This gave us gesture–speech unity, and vast changes in human life followed from this. Non-human primates show steps toward culture and communication but not this trigger. Such is the "gift of language." Setting aside gesture-first and speech-first as incapable of achieving gesture–speech unity, I take up the third option. Speech and gesture were equiprimordial. Natural selection favored gesture and speech together. The "trigger," named after the early twentieth-century philosopher, George Herbert Mead, is called "Mead's Loop." Mead's Loop is a hypothesis of what emerged in the evolution of the human brain. There emerged, it says, a thought–language–hand link, localized in part in the anterior left hemisphere area that became Broca's Area, as well as looping though other brain areas, including the prefrontal cortex, the right hemisphere and Wernicke's Area (see Chapter 8 for details of this hypothesis). It is the inheritance of this brain link that emerges as gesture–speech unity today.

In Broca's Area the link included a new kind of mirror neuron, "inverted" or "twisted." Mirror neurons have been directly recorded in monkeys and reside supposedly in all primate brains, including ours. I call these mirror neurons "straight," to distinguish them from the Mead's Loop "twist." To quote Wikipedia: "A mirror neuron is a neuron that fires both when an animal acts and when the animal observes the same action performed by another."[1] *The action of another is repeated and becomes as one's own.* If the straight mirror neuron circuit produces a gesture, it will be a mimicked

---

[1] http://en.wikipedia.org/wiki/Mirror_neuron (accessed April 12, 2015).

action, a pantomime, an "old" action-action. The significance the response has for the speaker is that of the action she mimics. We have seen what this provides. Pantomime repels speech. Its timing vis-à-vis speech is loose; often there is no speech at all or if there is, it comes out only in disjointed spurts.

In the Mead's Loop "twist," in contrast, *one's own gesture is responded to as by another*. The brain not only produces a gesture but also a response to it. In so doing, it gives a social/public reference to the gesture. A social/public reference fits into the interactive contexts of the small tribes where humans first lived (see Dunbar 1996) and is the foundation of much else—for example, the mimicry we examined in Chapter 4 and experienced in Chapter 1. It also explains why, even today, gestures require a social presence (we gesture on the phone but not alone in a room to a tape recorder; see Cohen 1977).

The self-response is not a second gesture. A gesture has reality on two levels; the self-response is part of the gesture intrinsically. The word "response" sounds sequential, but think of it not as a stimulus–response sequence but, all at once, as a gesture that has self-response as an integral aspect. This is no different than self-awareness of any action (you don't act and then, in a second step, recognize that you are the one doing it). With a self-response, awareness has a public reference, awareness of self as by another.

Here is the twist: Mead said that a gesture is meaningful when it evokes the same response in the one making it as it evokes in the one receiving it (emphasis added):

The gesture which indicates the object indicates the object both to the other and to the individual himself. In so far as this takes place the gesture is called significant. The meaning of significance is that the individual, in indicating the object or a part of the object to another and *by this same process to one's self, takes the role of the other and the indication of the object involves one's tending to act upon this gesture, as the other.* The gesture is said then to signify the action, and comes therefore to stand for this character of the object. It stands for the reactions to the object, or for its meaning.[2]

The twist (1) created a new selection pressure: Mead's Loop was adaptive where it was advantageous for gesture to have a public/social reference. It also (2) created conditions for gesture–speech unity. Through the self-response the gesture comes face-to-face with and orchestrates speech. The self-response "sees" co-expressiveness. Mead's Loop thus also (3) created conditions for gesture-orchestrated speech. Finally, since gesture-orchestrated speech occurs only where gesture and speech are co-expressive, Mead's Loop (4) created

---

[2] In University of Chicago Special Collections Research Center, G. H. Mead. Box 13, Folder 21, top page, "The gesture which indicates the object."

"new" gesture-actions without extraneous pragmatic goals; they too are products of the natural selection of Mead's Loop. Other properties of the dynamic dimension fell out as well—gesture-orchestrated speech came from the face-to-face presence of the self-response and speech; psychological predicates became possible; GPs likewise; and the dual awareness of the sentence arose. Mead's Loop ushered in the entire dynamic side of language.

Conventionally, one begins a book sketching the ideas and theories to which it relates, the better to situate it and highlight what it adds. Indeed, some ideas have been discussed to make the arguments clear, but the portrait convention demands is absent. This book is meant as a capstone of ideas wending their way through the three earlier books and focusing, where I gather there was progress, on what is new, especially the two central concepts of "new" gesture-actions and gesture-orchestrated speech. My approach most naturally fits the embodiment conception of mind – the upending of Cartesian dualism that has attracted much current attention (two examples: Andy Clark 1997 and Shaun Gallagher 2005). I can also say however where the idea of embodiment we have now after Mead's Loop and self-response appears to differ. Language is embodied, yes; but it is also unique among embodied cognitive realms. I focus on the uniqueness, at what I believe is a fundamental level, including the evolution that produced it. The uniqueness is captured in the idea of gesture-orchestrated speech. It is this which sets us apart. No other animal species has experienced it. For our primate neighbors gesture and vocalization, far from forming a unity, are at odds. We did spring from that. This book aims to explain, if explanation is possible, the "gift" of language, not the divine benefaction traditionally believed but the result of human evolution. I do not deny that other animal species may be on the same path, but they have not reached it yet. Electronic devices seem unlikely ever to reach it. They aim in a different direction (cf. Simon 1996) – to simulate but not to recover our "gift" (why I say so I explain at the end of the chapter).

Mead's Loop and self-response unexpectedly have a place in the literary effect of the indirect free style; they produce co-expressive gestures that are able to orchestrate it. Kamala Russell (pers. comm. 2012) points to an indirect free style in gesture, much like that in literary writing, which C-VPT produces – a "new look" in this section. Indirect free style reports thought and subjectivity rather than words: "now she had got to be bothered by that beast of a woman" (D.H. Lawrence, quoted by Russell). Contrast this to direct and indirect quotes – "she said: 'I'll be bothered by … etc.'" or "she said she would be bothered by … etc."(which also may have their gesture counterparts). Indirect free style in speech can be orchestrated by gestures and self-response. For example,

(6.1) and₁[he **grabs**Tweetie Bird #and as] ₂[he **comes back down**] ₃[he **lands** on the ground] ₄[and he **starts running**] away [and at this time the five hundred pound weight comes down **and lands**on him] [and **Tweetie** Bird] gets away #

Some gestures combine perspectives, one part in O-VPT, another part in C-VPT, and this happens here. These have been termed "dual viewpoint gestures" (McNeill 1992). Now we see a connection of them to Mead's Loop and its self-response, and from there to indirect free style. The narrator, Viv, is describing a complicated scene in which Sylvester stands on aseesawand catapults himself up to Tweety by throwing a weight on the other end. Shooting up exactly the right height, he grabs Tweety, falls down again on the see saw, and relaunches the weight. As he runs off, prize in hand, the weight, arcing through the air, lands on him. In gestures, as Sylvester comes down, Viv's hand is Sylvester's, grasping Tweety – C-VPT. At the same time the hand is moving down, Sylvester as a whole moving down – O-VPT. The effect is a kind of gestural irony. Russell points out a similarity of this dual viewpoint gesture to the indirect free style. The C-VPT portrays Sylvester's subjectivity, his satisfaction with his catapult method. However, it is also externally observed. The O-VPT trajectory displays (unbeknownst to Sylvester) the unfolding disaster – the weight arcing overhead to land on him, the essential step in Viv's ironic take.

Why did Viv continue with a C-VPT when she took on O-VPT for the trajectory? We see that it is a Mead's Loop self-response that created the indirect free style in gesture: each O-VPT at 2, 3 and 4 opened this avenue. All Viv. needed to do was ride her C-VPT (Sylvester's grip) on the observer perspective self-responses as by another (Sylvester's running off) to obtain the indirect free style. Thedual viewpoints then could orchestrate co-expressive indirect free style speech (or, more accurately, gesture–speech unity) – what Sylvester was complacently thinking as the weight came crashing down.

But not theory of mind. Mead's Loop, however, is not a theory of mind (Wimmer and Perner 1983). In a sense, theory of mind is the opposite. The Mead's Loop adaptation brings awareness of one's own behavior as social, not a theory of the cognitions and intentions of another (a theory of mind ability could evolve from straight mirror neurons in any case).

And not imitation. Neither is Mead's Loop imitation. A controversy among primatologists has concerned whether non-human primates learn through imitation (the consensus being that they do), but Mead's Loop is not this. In a learning situation, imitation and Mead's Loop function collaboratively but each in a different role; the Loop fortifies the "instructor" with the sense that her own gestures are social entities. Imitation provides a mechanism for the learner. Thus Loop and imitation can work together but are not the same.

6.2.1   How Mead's Loop launched the dynamic dimension

I list here the chief properties of the dynamic dimension as launched by Mead's Loop.

- First, **gesture-orchestrated speech**. A Mead's Loop self-response brings a gesture, with social reference, face-to-face with speech. When they are co-expressive Mead's Loop provides the ground for gesture-orchestrated speech. It is inherent to Mead's Loop and creates "new" gesture-actions. The micro-level processes illustrated in Chapter 3—lexical, grammatical and phonological steps occurring with distinctive delays—adjust themselves to fit the encompassing gesture.
- **The growth point**—the merger of two semiotic modes (gesture and language form), a minimal unit differentiating and absorbing a context—is a direct result of the Mead's Loop self-response. The self-response brings the gesture semiotic face-to-face with the language semiotic where gesture and speech are co-expressive. From this, the other properties follow.
- **Dual semiotic dialectic**. The new form of mirror neuron response laid the ground for the imagery–language dialectic, by bringing co-expressive gesture and speech together. A dialectic is the natural response when one meaning is simultaneously cast in opposite semiotic modes.
- **Psychological predicates**, the differentiations of the newsworthy in immediate contexts, were inherent to Mead's Loop by virtue of how it brought in gesture as a speech-orchestrating force. From this came "one meaning is two things"—a differentiation and a field of equivalents, the psychological predicate. Because a psychological predicate is not portable from context to context, absorbing context is intrinsic to it. Moreover, the psychological predicate naturally carries a social framework from the Mead's Loop self-response.
- **Catchments**. Given gesture–speech unity, a series of similar gestures brings similar meanings. The recurring theme is constant while details vary. These are catchments. Adding communicative dynamism we also trace "assemblages"/"ongoingness" to the Mead's Loop self-response, as each new gesture–speech unit pushes toward a future co-referent.
- **The two awarenesses**. The *simultaneous* is that of dual semiosis and dialectic. As Mead's Loop puts gesture and co-expressive speech together, the speaker becomes aware of the whole. The *successive* is linked to communicative dynamism and inhabitance. It is the awareness of speech as it moves.

Gesture is the material carrier of the GP, and it and its unpacking by a construction is experienced in both kinds of awareness.

- **Social reference**. Without Mead's Loop, gestures have social reference only if directed at an interlocutor. But gesticulations are not usually aimed at someone. Gestures with Mead's Loop are intrinsically social/public entities. "Language is social" but in a way the old saw barely suggests.

- **"New" actions**. Mead's Loop established new gesture-actions, a gesture with (a) no goal-directedness and (b) speech co-expressiveness. The co-expressiveness is incompatible with goal-direction and expels or absorbs it into specialized "temporal gestures," and all this sets the gesture apart as "new."

- **Mimicry of GPs**. The mimicry of another's gesture is via one's own self-response. The gesture and speech of the other are brought face-to-face in the mimic's Mead's Loop. It then forms a GP and with it a field of equivalents it can sensibly differentiate. A psychological predicate results, the other's now a one's own. This is what gesture coders do instinctively, the reader did in the self-demonstrations of Chapter 1, and actors accomplish with the gestures hidden in lines written even centuries ago.

- When speech is blocked, **sign languages** are natural outcomes of a gesture–speech unity. Unity gives the modes equality for codification. Sign languages thus arise as naturally as speech. That they are far outnumbered by spoken languages in the world we propose (Goldin-Meadow et al. 1996) has to do with the superiority of gesture for the global-synthetic imagery semiotic side of dual semiosis and dialectic. In keeping with this unity (now, gesture–sign unity), signs in a sign language should also have their own spontaneous gesticulations *with the hands*. Susan Duncan (2005) observed co-expressive manual gestures in Taiwanese sign language. The gestures were iconic distortions of canonical sign forms and thus were perfectly synchronous with the signs. The distortions incorporated context and differentiated interiority in Canary Row narrations when the signer had just before described Sylvester's climbing the pipe on the outside, exactly as gestures by hearing speakers did in the natural experiment and in Figure 1.2.

- **Equiprimordiality**. Finally, to select Mead's Loop, speech and gesture had to be equiprimordial. One could not come first and the other later. The logic of Mead's Loop required it. This is perhaps the one step, if we try to name one, that sets human evolution apart. Some avian species (crows, ravens) have evolved surprisingly elaborate vocal and gestural repertoires (Pika and Bugnyar 2011) but have not (yet?) taken steps that lead to gesture–speech units.

6.2.2   Self-aware agency, Mead's Loop natural selection and instruction

Essential for the natural selection of Mead's Loop was awareness of self as agent (see Hurley 1998). The gesturer had to be sensitive to her "new" gesture-actions as public. Not merely responding to others but awareness of being in public gave self-aware agency its foundational role. The origin of Mead's Loop took place in adults in social encounters, especially in giving instruction to infants. There, Mead's Loop gave the adult, typically a mother, the sense of being an instructor as opposed to being just a doer with an onlooker (the chimpanzee way). Entire cultural practices of childrearing depend upon this sense (Tomasello 1999). The mother must have been sensitive to her own acts as social/public actions, responding to them as by another, and aware of herself as the agent. The children of these mothers then gained an advantage in the emerging cultural life of early humans and inherited the tendency in turn to have Mead's Loop themselves. The ability to engage in the collective infant-rearing that Hrdy (2009) highlighted clearly demands (and also naturally selects) seeing one's own actions as social. Such practices stand in sharp contrast to chimpanzee infant-rearing, where infants left without their mothers are vulnerable to brutal attacks by adults in the same group.

6.2.3   Questions and answers about Mead's Loop

Here are five questions and answers that together help clarify Mead's Loop and what it implies:[3]

1 **Is a second gesture involved?** There is just one as mentioned earlier. It's not that you gesture and then respond. The self-response is part of the gesture intrinsically, part of it from its inception.
2 **Was the self-response needed?** A gesture without it is still a gesture. Why is that not enough to orchestrate speech? Only the self-response brings the gesture face-to-face with speech where they are co-expressive. One gesture lacking in self-response is what Kendon (2008) calls the "tongue-gesture," for example making a smaller mouth opening if you are asked to say "ba" when picking up a small object than when picking up a large one (Gentilucci and Dalla Volta 2007). How does "ba" change size depending on the size of the object the hand grasps? The answer Gentilucci and Dalla Volta offer is shared motor control, and indeed shared motor control is necessary for a Mead's Loop gesture-orchestration of speech

---

[3] From an exchange with Renia Lopez-Ozieblo on Mead's Loop, self-response, and other points in this chapter, as well as the GP concept. The edited exchange will be published in a volume edited by Ruth B. Church, Martha Alibali and Spencer Kelly, "Why gesture? How the hands function in speaking, thinking and communicating" (forthcoming by John Benjamins Publishing Company).

as well. Without a self-response, however, vocalization and gesture, even though sharing motor control, stay on separate paths. This is revealed in that the "ba" was not a meaningful vocalization and the hand-grasp was an "old" action-action of picking up an object. Self-response is needed because without it the gesture is not co-expressive with speech. Precisely what "ba" and hand-grasp lacked was self-response and co-expressiveness, and so no foundation for gesture–speech unity.

3 **Can't a straight-response pantomime also have a self-response?** It can but it has a different effect. A self-response to a pantomime is contradictory. It is both the action of another made as one's own and one's own action responded to as by another. The contradiction forces the self-response and the straight-response to separate. The gesture repels speech (its "straight" response) while it also orchestrates the resulting silence (its self-response). A pragmatic effect is to stop speech and call attention to the gesture:

[S]ilence … is an integral element of discourse, and constitutes a socially significant act when it is voluntarily performed during a conversation. Such acts are generally intended to address some aspect of the relationship between the parties involved in the interaction, by way of establishing, maintaining, curtailing, or clarifying the personal connections that exist between them. (R. McNeill 2010, pp. 69–70)

4 **Where did the Mead's Loop self-response come from?** We can imagine several origins. It might have evolved from straight mirror neurons. However, Hickok's **"eight problems"** appear to undermine the use of mirror neurons to explain language origins, since they "reflect sensory-motor associations that are devoid of meaningful conceptual content" (Hickok 2009, p. 1240). Without meaningful conceptual content, with just sensory-motor conditioning, the mirror system loses contact with co-expressiveness. This contact, however, it is what Mead's Loop provides. Mead's Loop could have evolved out of straight mirror neurons and leave the "eight problems" behind.

Alternatively, Mead's Loop might have evolved from other psychological/neural systems, and then separately developed mirror-like self-responses under the self-response natural selection. This avoids the "eight problems" as well. Two features of Mead's Loop suggest this path: (a) It circumvents goal-directedness—gesture-actions are not action-actions. To evolve this feature from straight mirror neurons would have required Mead's Loop somehow to undo goal-directedness. (b) It crucially depends on awareness of personal agency. Natural selection of the self-response is possible only with this feature. These suggest a separate evolution selected for socially referenced self-agency. It is thus possible that Mead's Loop pegs language to a different source, self-response and self-aware agency—the two pillars of language according to the Mead's Loop hypothesis—and so again moves out of range of the "eight problems."

Which source of the Mead's Loop self-response is closer to the truth is unknown, but they demonstrate that Mead's Loop is not entangled by the "eight problems" problem.

5 **Finally, why isn't the inflexibility of non-human primates vocalization an argument for gesture-first?** It is, but Mead's Loop undercuts it. The gesture-first argument is that, because of inflexibility, our speech could not have evolved out of primate vocalization but instead evolved from gestures (Corballis has invoked this several times; Gentulicci and Dalla Volta invoke it as well, whose formulation I have just paraphrased). However, the inference does not recognize gesture–speech equiprimordiality as a possibility. Equiprimordiality in the form of Mead's Loop accepts, in fact, *predicts* that non-human primates lack speech control. *They lack it because they cannot orchestrate speech with gesture.* An argument for gesture-first in the rigidity of non-human primate vocalization is therefore undercut by this alternative hypothesis that predicts it.

6.2.4   Mead's behaviorism

Mead called himself a social behaviorist—as he said in other words, "Gestures become significant symbols when they implicitly arouse in an individual making them the same response which they explicitly arouse in other individuals" (Mead 1974, p. 47). This behaviorist vocabulary, however, seems not intrinsic to his underlying idea of a self-response. The gesture–speech unity and gesture-orchestrated speech effects that Mead's Loop creates, without any behaviorist presuppositions, moreover seem not remote from Mead's own "act upon this gesture, as the other" in the long quote given earlier.

6.3   Origin of syntax

Words are arbitrary, Saussure said, and we add are readily forgotten, but syntax is not arbitrary: it is a template for action and is never forgotten apart from neurological injury. "Syntax" covers a range of phenomena but for our discussion it is understood as *systems of socioculturally mandated templates or schemes— "constructions"—for orchestrating the actions of the vocal tract*—lips, tongue, velum, larynx, lungs and diaphragm that originally were vegetative and which speech co-opted, a view developed by Peter MacNeilage (2008). The cohorts that *langue*-feelings provide for instant unpacking arise here. A non-obvious implication of Mead's Loop is that in part *the origin of syntax was rooted in gesture–speech unity.*

We seek its origins, the *ability* for it, in three places—the nature of the GP and its unpacking; the new paths this opened; and in "shareability," a concept to be defined. These in turn suggest three kinds of adaptive advantages. First, syntax is crucial for a GP dialectic. Without morphs and combinations of morphs there cannot be a semiotic opposition to gesture imagery. Second and linked, syntax stabilizes the dialectic. It is the resting point *par excellence*. Third, syntax is the "stop-order" of the dialectic in simultaneous awareness, ending the gesture-orchestrated speech cycle. Fourth, syntax is crucial in sociocultural encounters. Any or all of these factors could have favored an ability to form syntactic patterns, creating meaningful wholes out of patterned, segmented part, establishing and meeting standards of form, providing cultural identity, and transmitting and maintaining all this system over geographic space and developmental time. The result is our ability to inhabit constructions, quickly find them via *langue*-feelings, summon them in cohorts, orchestrate speech and create awareness.

An important concept for this origin is "shareability" (from a 1983 paper by Jennifer Freyd). She wrote,

It is easier for an individual to agree with another individual about the meaning of a new "term" (or other shared concept) if that term can be described by: (a) some small set of the much larger set of dimensions upon which things vary; and (b) some small set of dimensional values

creating in this process a **discreteness filter**, such that the discreteness properties of words (the syntagmatic values of word combinations) arise and with them the analytic/combinatoric semiotic opposition of linguistic forms to gestures in GPs. Gesture in the guise of a social other in Mead's Loop naturally offers a home for shareability and its discreteness filter.

An area of life where shareability exerted this force is **the cultural and social encounter**. The term "encounter" is taken broadly, from migrations to interpersonal interactions. Presumably no current-day language descends from the original inhabitants of where it is spoken now; it descends instead from migrants who encountered earlier languages.

How could encounters shape syntax? Trudgill (2011), speaking of pidgins, which are simplifications by any measure, sees encounters simplifying language. However, not all encounters result in pidgin or trade languages. We are thinking of two existing languages encountering each other, and here one or both may gain features. This encounter adds complexity. An example from Thomason (1997, 2011) hints at what happens. The situation she describes models later-comers encountering earlier-comers. In Thomason's example, Russian is the resident language and Finnish the incoming language. Incoming Finnish speakers acquired resident Russian but also introduced a distinction not in the host Russian out of their Finnish. For these speakers, then, the encounter sparked a new, enriched form of Russian. If we imagine this process repeating in encounter after encounter over thousands of years, a gradual accumulation of features takes place and the language drifts into greater complexity, eventually reaching the synthetic and polysynthetic territories that Sapir (1921) defined.

A different proof that encounters enrich syntax is the elaborations of Nicaraguan sign language as successive cohorts encountered earlier ones (Senghas 2003).

How does an encounter accomplish any of this? In the Russo–Finnish example, the speakers of one language imported a distinction into the other language, and its syntax grew in complexity (for them). But the sheer fact of an encounter also can lead to complexity. We do not know the exact situation with Thomason's Finnish speakers but we can invent an encounter and imagine its effects. Unpacking a GP is via objects in *langue*. The GP calls for one or more *langue* objects. Simultaneous and successive awareness are essential. The "call" is part of the speaker's awareness of the sentence. It takes the form of something lacking. Awareness of the GP and field of equivalents is simultaneous; gesture-orchestrated speech is successive but there is nothing the simultaneous awareness of the "call" connects to successively. It comes up a blank. Here is a sense of something in simultaneous awareness and an expectation of resolving it in the successive. This is the pressure the emerging syntax feels and leads to changes that add complexity.

Now imagine a language that does not have a way to unpack agency even though speakers have a sense of agency and make gestures like that with "it down" that include it. The language can refer to objects moving along paths but nothing more; it has no constructions with which to unpack the idea of an object being made to move; this is among the ineffable. This improbable language will be the incomer of our example. The tribe encounters another tribe and the idea of agency becomes important (disputes about things being taken and withheld, for example). Unlike the Finns, who imported a new form, here shareability and discreteness bring pressure to create something new to analyze and resolve the words "it" and "down" plus gestures with this significance. This is a new construction that orchestrates speech with agency the focus.

I don't suppose in the origin of syntax there was gesture, then syntax; this is gesture-first again. We proceed from the hypothesis speech and gesture were equiprimordial and from this came syntax. The smallest step from GP speech-orchestration is a syntax of temporal order (isolating/analytic in Sapir's 1921 terminology). The agency-innovation might be simply a new significance for the temporal order of "Tweety" and "it down"—the latter becoming a result of the former. Temporal order captures new syntagmatic values and constituents, and behind the temporal order new structures. This is no ur-language. Any temporal order would serve, subject–verb–object or subject–object–verb or any other (see Dunn et al. 2011; cf. Armstrong et al. 1995). Even these constituents are products of encounters. This is what the discreteness filter produces: words and sequences of words attached to meanings. The orchestration is not iconic to any real-world action. New discretenesses spread and became stabilized in the tribe. Then speakers of other languages appear and two stable languages again encounter each other, triggering further changes.

Embedding—the ability to embed one construction within another, accruing syntagmatic values as it goes, which Hauser et al. (2002) nominated as the sole linguistic universal in "the narrow sense"—would likewise be coordinated at temporally fixed loci in primitive speech-orchestrations—the embedded parts temporally isolated from the embedding parts, which in turn are continuous in time except for other embeddings. This creates levels of embedding but always holds the temporal sequences together. Thus a language in which embedding is handled by holding pieces in memory until an embedded piece is complete is a candidate for an early form. Notice that both the embedding and the basic mapping mechanisms assume that the creatures employing them have some way to know when a form is "complete" or "incomplete"—that is, have standards of form. Elaborations of this basic plan would be correlated with migration and encounters. Also, as we have seen with Corballis, embeddings enter into gesture–speech unities, and so could have been part of the earliest syntax.

More derived are morphological complexes that dissociate meanings from temporal order, releasing syntax from the grip of sequence and opening the way to what Sapir called synthetic and polysynthetic languages. Perhaps there is this correlation—the farther a language's forebears migrated, the more encounters the language absorbed, both of preceding languages and of latecomers' more remote languages. Then, more outlying areas from the presumed starting point—the Arctic, the southern ocean, the New World, with longer histories of encounters, encountering more others as they moved and as others moved onto them—are less dependent on temporal sequencing. The ultimate result is the most complex of Sapir's types, the polysynthetic—such as the Warlpiri in Australia, at a far tip-end of a migration track, which is characterized by departures from time-based unpacking that Hale (1983) termed "non-configurational."

Conversely, languages spoken close to the presumed origin point would tend to be time-based even now. Atkinson (2011) deduces on different grounds this point to have been the southwest corner of Africa. A hint that languages there lean toward the isolating type appears in Greenberg (1970), who reports that some 70 percent of noun, verb and adjective roots in the Khoikhoi (Hottentot) language begin with clicks—an exceptionally rigorous time-based orchestration. And the Wikipedia article on the Khoisan languages of the region summarizes that they: "are generally fairly isolating, with word order being more widely used to indicate grammatical relations than is inflection."[4] This is the

---

[4] http://en.wikipedia.org/wiki/Khoisan_languages (accessed January 6, 2014).

prediction of Mead's Loop when there have been historically comparatively few encounter events.

6.4   Evolution timeline

The phrase, "the dawn of language," suggests that language burst forth at some definite point, say 150–200 kya (thousand years ago), when the pre-frontal expansion of the human brain was complete. But the origin of language has elements that began long before—5 mya (million years ago) for bipedalism, on which things gestural depend, and 1 mya, based on humanlike family life dated to then, for starting the expansion of forebrain and the selection of self-responsive mirror neurons and the resulting reconfiguration of areas 44/45. I imagine this form of living was itself the product of changes in reproduction patterns, female fertility cycles, childrearing, neotony—all of which may have been emerging over long periods before.

So this says that language as we know it emerged over one to two million years and that not much has changed since the 150K–200 kya landmark of reconfiguring Broca's Area with the mirror neurons/Mead's Loop circuit (although this date could overlook continuing evolution: there are hints that the brain has changed since the dawn of agriculture and urban living; see Evans et al. 2005). Levinson and Holler (2014) add a further idea, that language is the product of multiple evolutions that have converged. The timeline that follows can be regarded in this light. "Convergence" of the multiple evolutions I attribute to the Mead's Loop trigger: its evolution brought them together.

The Mead's Loop model doesn't say what might have been a protolanguage before 2 mya—Lucy and all. It would have been something an apelike brain is capable of. There are many proposals about this—Kendon (1991), for example, proposed that signs emerged out of ritualized incipient actions (or incomplete actions). Natural gesture signals in modern apes have an incipient quality as well, the characteristic of which is that an action is cut short and the resulting action-stub becomes a signifier (see Figure 6.2 in which truncated shoving was a deictic/pantomime gesture).

This slow-to-emerge precursor could have produced gesture-first from 5 mya to 2 mya, a gesture language from "old" action-actions and points. It would have been the blind alley described earlier, an evolution not reaching human language. But the human brain evolved a new thought–language–hand brain link in which gesture came to orchestrate speech.

A proposed timeline for Mead's Loop and the thought–language–hand brain link origin is as follows:

(a)   (b)

Figure 6.2 Bonobo pantomimic/deictic gesture. Left bonobo induces right bonobo to move. Thanks to Amy Pollick.

1 To pick a date, the evolution of the thought–language–hand link started 5 mya with the emergence of habitual bipedalism in *Australopithicus*. This freed the hands for manipulative work and gesture, but it would have been only the beginning. Even earlier there were preadaptations such as an ability to combine vocal and manual gestures (Hopkins and Cantero 2003), to perform rapid sequences of meaningful hand movements, and the sorts of iconic/pantomimic gestures we see in bonobos (Pollick 2006), but not yet an ability to orchestrate movements of the vocal tract by gestures. The bonobo in Figure 6.2 was silent during this and other of her gestures (not shown).

2 The period from 5 to 3–2 mya—Lucy and the long reign of *Australopithicus* —would have seen the emergence of various other precursors of language, such as the protolanguage Bickerton (1990) attributes to apes, young children and aphasics; also, ritualized incipient actions becoming signs as described by Kendon. These are not yet Mead's Loop and dual semiosis.

3 At some point after the 3–2 mya advent of *H. habilis* and later *H. erectus*, there commenced the crucial selection of self-responsive gestures and the reconfiguring of areas 44 and 45, with a growing co-opting of actions by language to form speech-integrated gestures, this emergence being grounded in the appearance of a humanlike family life with a host of other factors shaping the change (including cultural innovations such as the domestication

of fire and cooking). The timing of this stage is not clear but archeological findings suggest that hominids had control of fire, had hearths, and cooked 800 kya (Goren-Inbar et al. 2004).

4 The family was the scenario for the thought–language–hand link.

5 Another crucial factor would have been the physical immaturity of human infants at birth and the resulting prolonged period of dependency giving time for cultural exposure and GPs to emerge, an essential delay pegged to the emergence of self-aware agency (Neanderthals, in contrast, appear to have had a short period of development, Rozzi and de Castro 2004).

Along with this sociocultural revolution was the expansion of the forebrain from 2 mya, and a reconfiguring of areas 44 and 45, including Mead's Loop, into what we now call Broca's Area. This development was an exclusively human phenomenon and was completed with *H. sapiens* about 200–100 kya. If there was a "dawn" it was here.

At least two other human species have existed: Neanderthals and the recently discovered *Denisova hominin*, and each may have had a gesture-only form of communication. Our species developed Mead's Loop. These other humans went extinct, one factor in which could have been limitation to pantomime and a consequent inability to reach dual semiosis and new forms of language when faced with rival creatures who possessed them.

Figure 6.3 shows two timelines differing in when Mead's Loop evolved. According to the timelines, language with dual semiosis came into being over the last one or two million years. Considering protolanguage and then language itself, the timeline extends back more than five million years. Meaning-controlled manual and vocal gestures that combine under imagery emerged over the last two million years. The evolution of self-aware agency would be one critical step unleashing Mead's Loop and may not have emerged until 800 kya or more recently. The entire process may have been completed not more than 100 kya, a mere few thousand human generations, if it is not continuing.

6.4.1   Neanderthal "cognition" under version B

What might Neanderthal cognition looked like if Mead's Loop evolution was version B, and to what can we compare it today? The Neamdethal genome project (Pääbo and colleagues, see news focus in *Science* 2009 323: 866–871) shows that this extinct form of human had FOXP2, and also may have been capable of fine motor control. Whether this control covered the vocal tract is unknown but speech seems not impossible (and in itself points to version A).

However, the Neanderthal brain, although large, may have had a different developmental time course (much briefer, see Rozzi and de Castro

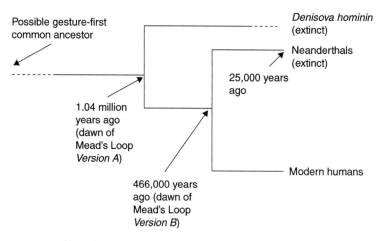

Figure 6.3 Two versions of gesture-first extinction and Mead's Loop origin.

Version A: The branch leading to modern humans and Neanderthals and away from the newly discovered *Denisova hominin* was the emergence of Mead's Loop. *Denisova* was the continuation of the gesture-first creature, and went extinct some 30,000 to 40,000 years ago—the date of the fossil finger bone from which its mtDNA was recovered by Krause et al. 2010. In this version, Neanderthals and modern humans share Mead's Loop but differ in other brain areas (the temporal lobes and possibly the prefrontal area) and ontogenesis (Neanderthals, according to Rozzi and de Castro 2004, developing markedly faster, leaving less time for GPs to emerge before any critical period shutdown).

Version B: Mead's Loop arose instead at the 466 kya split between modern humans and Neanderthals, and in part defines this separation of lines. In this version, neither of the extinct *hominin* species evolved Mead's Loop, which may have been a factor in their extinctions. In an alternate version, the split at the 1 mya point separated the common ancestor of the Neanderthal and the *Denisova hominin* from that of modern humans. The Neanderthal and *Denisova* ancestors later left Africa while the ancestors of modern humans remained behind (possibly in the southwest, Atkinson 2011), evolving Mead's Loop and carrying it out of Africa in their turn. Diagram based on Brown (2010), Mead's Loop annotations added. Cambridge University Press, reprinted with permission.

2004) and did not sustain robust activity of the prefrontal cortex (Wynn and Coolidge 2008). These factors suggest version B and a lack of Mead's Loop. A short ontogenesis meant less time for Mead's Loop development (which does not appear before age three or four in contemporary human children). An early critical period cutoff would have truncated any GP-like developments. The prefrontal cortex, among other functions, arranges and selects alternatives. The formation of fields of equivalents is a place in language where this ability is tapped. Weakened fields of equivalents could have yielded cognitive inflexibility and repetitiveness. Other than this rigidity, which appears in many contexts, including methods of hunting that never developed throwing spears and required close-in stabs of large, dangerous prey, a highly adaptive intelligence was also present (as described by Wynn and Coolidge 2011).

The simplest statement of version B Neanderthal language and thought is that it would have been a **single semiotic**, lacking an imagery–language dialectic. The human model it most closely resembles is **Down's syndrome**. If we imagine a Down's linguistic capability yet also a quick, adaptive intelligence that carried the species through harsh environments and built cultures, we can use Down's as the model. Down's speakers, children at least, may not experience thinking-for-speaking in the form it takes in normal speakers, their gestures with speech semantically redundant—for example, POINT AT CHAIR + "chair" = "chair." In typically developing children of the same mental ages, speech–gesture combinations are "supplementary"—POINT AT CHAIR + "daddy" = "daddy's chair." The elements semiotically equivalent in DS GPs have little scope for cognitive movement; are rigid and apply in narrow contexts. The impression one gets is of stasis, immobility, with little potential for fueling a dynamic dimension. The nearest modern human glimpse of what, linguistically, Neanderthals achieved would be words and redundant gestures with possibly "pivot-grammar" type constructions (Braine 1963).

Language–thought redundancy would hamper those aspects of cognition that depend on the thought–language–hand link: psychological predicates, dual semiosis and gesture–speech unity, all would be depleted. A creature like this would seem to us very strange.

6.5   Models and modules

Popular culture aside, I have the impression that AI is less regarded now than it once was as replicating natural human intelligence or language but more as forming artificial versions of each. Indeed, as things have developed the artificial–natural gap seems ever wider, even unbridgeable. I am inspired to take the plunge and understand it by Herbert Simon's 1996 *The Sciences of the Artificial*, a work exploring the foundations of artificial intelligence and other computational domains, which he begins by insightfully contrasting the "natural" to the "artificial." The natural sciences, he writes, "make the wonderful commonplace, show that complexity, correctly viewed, is only the mask for simplicity [and] finds patterns hidden in apparent chaos ... [aiming at] knowledge about natural things and phenomena"(Simon 1996, p. 1). The aims of this book stand under this ample umbrella, to find patterns hidden in apparent chaos, make the wonderful if not commonplace at least comprehensible, make the complexity of thought, language and context as far as possible simple, and analyze not synthesize them. Various computational models, on the other hand, are recognizably sciences of the artificial.

Artificial science is knowledge about artificial things and phenomena ... Some artificial things are imitations of things in nature, and the imitation may use the same basic materials as the natural object or quite different materials. As soon as we introduce 'synthesis as well as 'artifice,' we enter the realm of engineering. For 'synthetic' is often used in the broader sense of 'designed' or 'composed.' We speak of engineering as concerned with 'synthesis,' while science is concerned with 'analysis.' (Simon 1996, pp. 3–4)

Design and composition is the mode of AI models. Indeed, they work in the very domain that Simon was announcing as the new science of the artificial. We can use the natural–artificial distinction to understand the divide and discover why it seems so unbridgeable. Symptomatic of the unbridgeability is the incompatibility of gesture–speech unity with two major tenets of artificial design: the **module** and the **model**. Neither grasps it.

6.5.2   Mental modules

The concept of a **mental module** dates to Fodor (1983). A module is a hypothetical self-contained mental "device" that carries out specific (not necessarily simple) functions. Its inputs are from a restricted set of the other devices (possibly just one) and its outputs go to a restricted set of different devices (again possibly just one). The input/output contacts are formed in advance and do not change as a result of the module's own activity. The parallel is with the modular design of computers and stereo equipment, although the idea of separate "faculties" of the mind, as Fodor points out, goes back to the nineteenth century and phrenology. Like their electronic exemplars, modules are said to have self-containment such that, when a breakdown occurs, the damage is limited and repairs, including self-repairs, can be accomplished on a limited scale. Because of this supposed advantage, modules are thought to have had a selective advantage in evolution and thus have come to permeate the mind/brain. In Fodor's original form, it was an inspired idea with which to explain how certain illusions are impervious to correction (such as the Müller-Lyer). Which is longer? We know that tip-to-tip the lines are equal, and yet they look different and refuse to look otherwise no matter our knowledge. It plausibly taps a module:

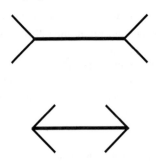

Such examples are compelling. It is equally compelling however that the synchrony of co-expressive speech and gesture in psychological predicates contradicts modules of language and gesture. Whatever one may think of modularity in general, gesture and speech fly in the face of it. Anything on the dynamic dimension that combines imagery and linguistic form and is inseparable from context contradicts it. The GP, this unity of imagery and language form differentiating fields of meaningful oppositions, is the flat opposite of it. Speech–gesture unity, psychological predicates and the inclusion of context into the GP are further contradictions. The "inhabiting" of language and gesture with thought and being are still more contradictions. Modular theories impose a rigid thought-first, symbolic expression-after order, and this too the GP contradicts.

6.5.3   Mental models

While modules can be likened to devices this section argues that artificial devices of any kind do **not model GPs** and their global-synthetic semiotics (for other arguments against the computer model metaphor, see Gigerenzer and Goldstein 1996). As a result, they do not model gesture-orchestrated speech, gesture–speech unity or an imagery–language dialectic. The systems model gestures in a bottom-up, features-to-whole, language-like way that, even if synchronized with speech, is incapable of forming a gesture–speech unit.

The problem is not just adjusting models to include imagery. Mead's Loop is beyond them because action, which speech fundamentally is and which the linguistic system evolved in part to orchestrate, does not exist as a unit in these artificial systems. They instead construct actions using a feature-based mode wherein the features are the units and the actions the outcomes (in a GP, features are outcomes, actions are the units). The inherent context-boundedness of action is responsible for this.

I can propose two ways for bringing artificial systems within the Mead's Loop orbit—most importantly, having coordinative structures attracted to idea units and spreading activation devices—but doing so we find they have problems of their own, suggesting some sort of fundamental incompatibility of systems designed for artificial devices and the evolved biological systems of language on its dynamic dimension.

Foremost of these difficulties is the dual semiosis global-synthetic imagery of the GP, essential for the dialectic. The problem is that the design of computational models forces the process of gesture creation to be combinatoric, to move from parts to whole rather than whole to parts; and this is the opposite semiotic from that of imagery. Once created we can usually identify form and meaning features, for example, enclosure means interiority, and so forth. But we must not conclude from this observation that composition was the process of creation; it is the result of our analysis. Features are products. This is the paradox of natural gestures—they work in the opposite direction from modeling based on features.

6.5.4   Coordinative structures

Coordinative structures may provide a partial way out. They are "flexible patterns of cooperation among a set of articulators to accomplish some functional goal" (anonymous Yale linguistics handout found on Google; accessed February 14, 2007). The approach would be to exploit the inherent flexibility of coordinative structures in such a way that the significance of gestures and speech activates and shapes them.

This process could indeed work from global meaning to forms. It still seems however that form features need meanings of their own. Coordinative structures substitute one obstacle for another. Form features need their own meanings for global meanings to find them, meanings like "spherical," "interior," "downward" and "effort." Such a requirement again bottom-up and does not grasp the global property.

A coordinative structures model, however, if modified to have GPs as attractors, seemingly could skirt this problem. Here is a sketch of how a model might try to do so:

1 Suppose that global significances ("thrusts-bowling-ball-down") trickle down and the author of "it down" improvised something that, after the fact and upon examination, we interpret to mean "spherical," "downward" and "effort"—what does she need in order to do this?
2 She needs to perform an action that embodies the global meaning. Does this imply form–meaning features? Or is it enough to "act"? Is the idea of propelling a bowling ball downward sufficient to generate a gesture with the significance that we are after, without positing a preexisting "spherical" feature?

3   A stab at resolution, given a thought–language–hand link, is that ideas or significances can be the "attractors" of coordinative structures; coordinative structures then zero in on these significances, the properties of the significance bringing out features in the coordinative structures interactively: in this way, gesture features are outcomes, not initial conditions, with significances that derive from the action as a whole: and this is the global property. There is no lexicon of feature–meaning pairs (no "facing down → force downward" and the like). The features arise during the action itself. Each coordinative structure is an "action primitive," but the critical difference from a feature (or morpheme) is that coordinative structures do not in themselves have significances like a standard feature (rounded shape = spherical).

4   So far, then, so good. While coordinative structures with ideas as attractors may avoid the bottom-up problem they create a new problem. One problem disappears only to be replaced by another, a symptom of an unbridgeable divide. The coordinative structures approach imposes a distinction between "image" and "gesture" (the attractor is the image and coordinative structures fashion a gesture to embody it). This distinction is again because there is no concept of global-synthetic action. It creates a new contradiction, now with the concept of a gesture as a material carrier. In a material carrier the gesture *is* the image—the image in its most material form—not a representation of it. That we have exchanged one contradiction for another, and are no closer to a model of the GP and imagery–language dialectic, is the "proof" that the designed and composed artificial does not substitute for the evolved natural.

6.5.5   Spreading activation

Spreading activation is another popular model of the artificial that may seem at first glance to provide a solution. In this scheme, two systems—say gesture and speech—mutually activate each other, the energy of one spreading to the other and vice versa. Then co-expressive gesture and speech can link up. However, the effect is not to produce a gesture–speech unit but to force one system to supplant the other or, avoiding this, to maintain the separation of systems after their mutual activation. Again, absence of action as a global-synthetic whole is the reason. Either way, there is no room for gesture-orchestrated speech. A modern model created along these lines has been placed on Research Gate by Stefan Kopp et al. (2013) of Bielefeld University. It has mutual activation but no gesture–speech unity and again shows the limits of the artificial (see Figure 6.4).

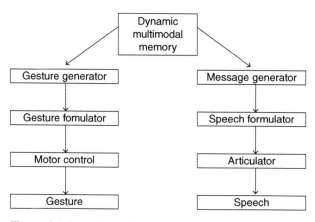

Figure 6.4 Spreading-activation scheme produces neither gesture–speech unity nor gesture-orchestrated speech, after Kopp et al. (2013).

6.5.6   Robots

Robotics is a third approach. Here, at least, there is a "body" with which gesture–speech unity could potentially form, but the direction of effort again seems fundamentally artificial. A radically different approach has some potential to make artificial systems compatible with the GP. The approach, as described to me by Michita Imai (pers. comm.)—computer scientist and robot-designer at Keio University, Japan—is based on a form of logic explored by Yukio Pegio Gunji of Kobe University. While I cannot evaluate the technical limits of the following, I mention it as a new and remarkable idea. It is based on a form of logic described as "True and False" (not True or False, which is tautology). Imai is currently applying this logical form as a way to get robots to behave spontaneously. He writes: "When we try to prove the logical form of 'True and False,' an eternal proving loop appears. It never stops … This loop continues forever" (thus capturing instability). However, it is not a dialectic opposition. Its chief difference is that the spontaneity of the system does not differentiate fields of equivalents or open a place for them, and again is symptomatic of an unbridgeable gap between the natural and the artificial.

6.5.7   Mentally controlled devices

Even closer to a bridge, theoretically, is the development of **mentally controlled prosthetic devices**, surgically connected to neural inputs from the user. A major issue facing these devices is finding neural inputs that can be controlled voluntarily, and in which areas of the brain this is achieved. Fetz (2007), reviewing physiological studies of this topic, notes a dearth of information, but if in developing it studies were to include gesture-orchestrated speech, they could possibly uncover clues that may help to bridge the artificial–natural gap. Of course, it is also possible that these devices need not consider, even when performing gestures, orchestrations or the thought–language–hand brain link at all but merely borrow them out of the speech of the user, in which case we would be no closer to bridging the gap in our understanding.

6.6.8   *Summary*

Summarizing, we learn from these experiments, thought and real, that artificial models do not match an evolved biological/psychological process in several areas or head in the right direction to reach the GP—most crucially, that the semiosis must include a global component (to drive the dialectic), that there is a dialectic, and that finally the process is embodied in and tied to action (specifically coordinative structure units) and requires accordingly a "body" that is the embodiment of meaning. Robots have "bodies" but the computations controlling them are still without global-synthetic wholes. Mentally controlled prosthetic devices may show more promise but currently seem to reflect little of inner processes. Further, the whole differentiates a context and the context and its differentiation are "a meaning." Finally, all these models conflict with Quaeghebeur's "all-at-onceness," in that in their logic they are sequential. Conversational agents can simulate many of these properties, but the basic difference between an artificial system, designed by rational intelligence, and what has naturally evolved remains a root fact in the contrast of the GP with modeling schemes.

6.6   **Overall summary and discussion of phylogenesis**

Gesture–speech unity is felt across a spectrum of dynamic effects—prosody (the peak being a part of the GP), the formation and differentiation of contexts, and the energizing of communicative dynamism and, with it, the amount of coding material in both gesture and speech in motion together in a positive relationship. Pulling the threads together, we have a new idea of how language works and began. How Mead's Loop works in outline:

- Gestures emanating from Broca's Area are mirrored by it.
- The gestures acquire significance by being responded to in the same way they are responded to by others.
- The self-response imparts a sense of social/public reference.

- The gesture is now ready to orchestrate actions of the vocal tract (or hands in the case of a sign language).
- Thus speech (or signing) acquires dual semiosis—imagery orchestrating symbols that are themselves codified by sociocultural conventions.
- The locus of this selection would be adults—language evolved in this scenario, with women in particular ("man the toolmaker," etc. being a recipient, not a source).

7 Ontogenesis

Picking up a thread from Chapter 6 that "Acquisition 1" recapitulates gesture-first and then its extinction, we take up "Acquisition 2" and its effects on current-day language ontogenesis. The earliest steps that infants take toward language are like those of a gesture-first creature. This language then extinguishes in children, as it did in the gesture-first creature, and is followed by a second acquisition in the same children. The second acquisition is for gesture–speech unity and is the language we actually evolved as a species. Gesture–speech unity emerges when the thought–language–hand link brain structures underlying it mature at age three or four, as neurological and psychological data suggest. Gestures now relate to speech in a new way—the single semiosis of speech–gesture combinations replaced by the dual semiosis of gesture-orchestrated speech.

7.1 Two to three acquisitions

A "two-acquisitions" portrayal is the topic of the current chapter. Importantly, the first acquisition leaves few traces in the second; extinction wipes them out, as though the two languages appear with no relationship. Only words carry forward but the Pivot-Open grammars vanish. There is also a "third acquisition" of speech adapted to attract adult attachment that actually begins before Acquisitions 1 and 2. It provides continuity through the ontogenesis and extinction of Acquisition 1 and then merges with Acquisition 2. These stages include not only the development of human language but also that of a long-gone human precursor, an archetype brought back to life for a time. For current-day children, the argument implies, contrary to a longstanding assumption that children develop more or less continuously (perhaps with stages, but earlier acquisitions still carrying forward), that ontogenesis is not cumulative; it is a mixture of continuity and discontinuity. Discontinuities come from the recapitulation of the two origins. Continuities come from the autonomous development of speech control. Autonomous development could be due to other evolutionary pressures, such as speech control to garner parental attachment ("baby-talk" being the adult half of the adaptation; it is automatic and unthinking, and the mere sight of an infant or a surrogate infant triggers it; all qualities that suggest a built-in response. I was once introduced to a *Bunraku* puppet. It happened to be the figure of an old woman, but as I held the approximately infant-sized doll in my arms, to my astonishment, not to mention embarrassment—minimized only because I was doing it in a language foreign to the puppet-master—I found myself speaking to it in baby-talk).

First I need to say more about the role of **the ontogeny-recapitulates-phylogeny hypothesis** in this discussion. That ontogeny recapitulates phylogeny has often been derided when considered at all, but it has value as a heuristic. Such arguments are useful for sorting out steps in phylogenesis. Taking an ontogeny-recapitulates-phylogeny perspective lets us see where different evolutions influence and then cease to influence the developing child. When something emerges in current-day ontogenesis only at a certain stage, we reason (in this way of arguing) that the original natural selection of the feature (if any) took place in a similar social-psychological milieu in phylogenesis. We exploit the fact that children's intellectual status is not fixed; it is changing. Using this argument, we look at the ontogenesis of gesture–speech unity and formulate possible landmarks—both in phylogenesis and ontogenesis—packages of phenomena that evolution has created and that now re-emerge when the relevant brain processes mature. We see in this way landmarks of the two origins, reappearing in current-day acquisition. The earliest steps are identifiably gesture-first. This language is replaced by a second language, recognizably having gesture–speech unity. Bridging the discontinuities of two origins is the third acquisition, upon which each recapitulation rides. I will comment on the third "speech-for-attachment" acquisition after explaining Acquisitions 1 and 2.

7.2   "Acquisition 1" (again)—gesture-first

Acquisition 1 was described in Chapter 6 as part of the gesture-first discussion. Now it reappears as the effect of Mead's Loop, or its absence, on children's language. Children's first gestures consist of pointing. Indexicality seems to be the cognitive mode. Pointing appears in the form of action-stubs, compatible with a gesture-first mind. Next to appear are gesture "names," also compatible with gesture-first. Pivot grammars are the highest achievement of Acquisition 1 (see Table 6.2). Gesture-orchestrated speech, if "orchestration" is an appropriate concept for this stage, takes a different form from later. The gesture fills an empty slot in a construction—point + "want" as a proto-pivot, for example. All of this fits the gesture-first theory quite well. There are no gesture phrases or kinesic signatures such as Kendon observed (2004), suggesting that gesture–speech unity is absent. Awareness, insofar as one can guess, is indexical—the awareness of fascinating, desired and shareable objects and actions.

Table 7.1 Single and dual semiosis by a child of two years and four months, seconds apart describing the bowling ball episode (Gale Stam data; used with permission).

1. Gesture-first example.	and h[e* **he went** <a>and<u><d></u><u><uuhm uuh></u> // down /]
	a b
	(a) pantomimic: full body, both arms rise, hold overhead, and then body goes down with one hand landing on the floor,
	(b) gaze down and retracts to sitting.
Mom	what did he do with the ball?
2. Gesture–speech unity example	he<e> d[u* **dunk it** in] iconic: right hand rises and then lowers <Tweety dropping ball into drainpipe>

7.3 "Dark age"—extinction

Not a separate acquisition phase, the "dark age" of extinction is continuous with Acquisition 1 and is singled out because here gesture-first disappears from children's language. It is "dark" because of the accompanying disappearance of gesture, in keeping with a gesture-first supplantation by speech. Pantomime is the dominant gesture type. Gesticulation (gesture unified with speech) is at first minimal and increases gradually. Single and dual semiosis overlap but no organic or developmental link connects them, just two overlapping curves, one up and one down, the old system dwindling while the new emerges. This is extinction; the gesture-language disappearing, marginalized as gesture-first says, but what results is limited and shallow (Bannard et al. 2009) and unity does not emerge out of it.

We see the lack of gesture-first/gesture–speech unity linkage vividly in Table 7.1, which snapshots the co-occurrences of the two language systems in the same sentence. They alternate but not influence each other. A child of two years and four months, describing the cartoon, is gesture-first one moment, unified gesture–speech the next. The modes do not combine. The child wavers, first an "old" action-action, next a "new" gesture-action. The gesture in (1a) is a classic pantomime. It has a semi-verbal accompaniment beginning with a verb, but this is abandoned for garbled speech, showing the mutual repulsion of speech and pantomime. In (2) is a true growth point (GP). Gesture and speech synchronize. The gesture has a preparation phase and a stroke, the latter timed with "it," cohesively linking the gesture–speech unit to the mother's question. The gesture provides a psychological predicate differentiating the context the mother's question has established. Speech is one moment repelled by a pantomime, the next orchestrated by a "new" gesture, bouncing between languages, the replicated ancient and the incoming modern. I cite the example to show the impossibility of finding bridging links from the gesture-first performance in (1) to the gesture–speech unity performance in (2). They do not link up. They are qualitatively different. To get from (1) to (2), a shift in linguistic cognition takes place, and this is the emergence of dual semiosis and gesture–speech unity.

Further insight comes from the role of cohesion, or its lack, in the genesis of the hallmarks of gesture–speech unity. Levy (2008, 2009–2010, 2011; Levy and McNeill 2015), using Levy's repeated narrations experiment, observed an inverse relationship of pantomime and discursive fluency—as fluency increased, pantomime decreased. This shows that pantomime is removed from speech orchestration. What drives cohesion is the emergence of gesture–speech unity, the imagery unifying across utterances.

Cohesion shows up in another form that also suggests gesture-first's last gasp as it overlaps but does not connect with an emerging gesture–speech unity. Özçaliskan and Goldin-Meadow (2009) discovered that two-argument constructions first appear as gesture + speech: "I paint" + GIVE, with a conventional extended supine palm to request a crayon (Özçaliskan and Goldin-Meadow 2009, Table 1, note h). This two-argument gesture–word combination is followed, a few weeks later, by the same construction in speech alone: "I want to draw with a crayon." The picture fits the gesture-first model: speech coming later and supplanting a use in gesture. In three-argument cases, however, there is no gesture-first phase, no case where the third argument appears first in gesture and then "forecasts" (is supplanted by) speech; third arguments appear in both speech and gesture and at the same developmental point. This is explained if GPs are also emerging, and the third argument is being added to a GP, not to a dying gesture-first hybrid. Then gesture–speech unity accommodates gesture and speech equally. That the two-argument-forecasting combinations and the three-argument-non-forecasting combinations exist side-by-side in ontogenesis again shows the two semiotic modes overlapping but not connecting.

7.4   "Acquisition 2"—gesture–speech unity

Here, finally, is "language" as we know it. Gestures become more adult-like, less pantomimic. Acquisition 2 reveals itself in changes across a wide front that remove the "shallowness" that Bannard et al. (2009) describe. These include a gesture explosion, the advent of gesticulation, motion event decomposition, gesture phrases (preparations, strokes, holds and retractions), fields of equivalents tailored to make differentiations possible, "new" gesture-actions, the onset of self-aware agency, this last underpinning the rest (and explained in Section 7.6), and now, at last, gestures orchestrating speech. Each item possesses dual semiosis. These widespread changes, amounting to a rebuilding of the child's language, occur around age three or four.

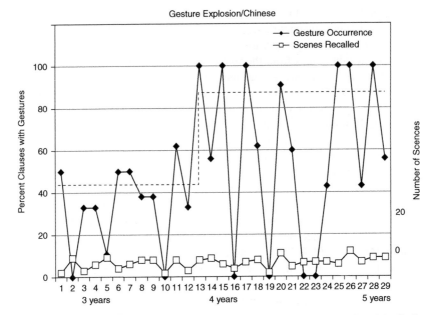

Figure 7.1 "Gesture explosion" between the ages of three and four. Mandarin data collected by Susan Duncan. Graph plots 29 individual children. Dotted summary line by eye. In contrast to gesture upsurge, recall of cartoon scenes increases little with age. Used with permission of University of Chicago Press.

7.4.1   The gesture explosion

In keeping with a gesture-first regime where speech supplants gesture, two-year olds, once they have begun to combine words, produce few gestures. Then between three and four years, gesture output suddenly rises (Figure 7.1). The upsurge is a signature of the imagery–language dialectic. More than before, gestures are combining with the child's verbal output. The explosion relates to a dialectic in two ways. First, an abundance of gesture makes a dialectic more accessible; there are more gesture–speech co-occurrences in which it can develop. Second, a dialectic itself can cause the upsurge, since an imagery–language dialectic requires, for the first time, that gestures be part of speaking.

7.4.2   Advent of gesticulation

Gesture-first pantomimes tend to engage the whole body. The principle is more parts, a better show. However, once Mead's Loop has matured, the hands/forearms become the focus, the rest of the body orchestrated under them. (In the gross anatomy of the brain, adjacent areas control speech and

(a)   (b)

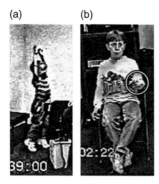

Figure 7.2 Gesture-first whole-body pantomime at the age of three compared to dual semiosis single-hand gesticulation in older child. From McNeill (2014b).Used with permission of John Benjamins Publishing Company.

hands, which could be the ultimate reason for the special role for the hands in gesture–speech unity.) Figure 7.2 shows two children depicting Sylvester's ascent of the drainpipe, a three-year-old on the left, an older child (about six or seven) on the right. The three-year-old shows a gesture-first pantomime of the kind we expect before Mead's Loop matures. Speech likewise is uncoordinated (a screech). Word knowledge is not the difficulty—the single word "up" could have joined a GP if one existed. By six or seven years, gesture and speech have changed dramatically—symbolization is all in the hands and combined with speech in a dual semiotic package ("he goes up," synchronous with the gesture). The gesture is adult-like and part of a GP. The older child also spoke synchronously with his gesture stroke. The gesture orchestrated the speech.

7.4.3   Advent of motion event decomposition

In languages as different as English, Mandarin and Spanish, beyond three years, children **decompose motion events** that are fused in the cartoon stimulus, and are fused again by adult speakers of the same languages. While seemingly regressive, decomposition is actually a step forward. As in other areas, the child at first overdoes newfound powers, here the power to analyze complex events, and zeroes in on one component at a time (Karmiloff-Smith 1979). It reveals that the new semiotic of gesture has moved beyond pantomime to pull motion event components apart. A scene depicting Sylvester rolling down the street with the bowling ball inside him includes, in one event, a Path (along the street), a Manner of motion (rolling), as well as the Figure (Sylvester). Adults speaking a range of languages (English, Spanish, Mandarin) produce descriptions of such scenes with two kinds of gestures, either Path only (the hand moving down) or Manner

Table 7.2 Percentage of gestures showing Manner–Path combination or decomposition at three ages. Decomposition percentages for the viewpoint congruent with the motion event component (C-VPT with M; O-VPT with P).

Age Group	M+P Combined (both viewpoints)	M Decomposed (of C-VPT)	P Decomposed (of O-VPT)
Adults	31%	5%	0%
7–11 years	0%	25%	31%
3–6 years	0%	24%	47%

and Path together (the hand rotating as it goes down). Moreover, for these adults, when Matter is present it always merges with Path. Children of three of four match adults in having Path-only gestures but, unlike adults, have a large number of pure Manner gestures (the hand rotating but not moving down) and very few Path + Manner gestures. A child saying, "he rolls away with it," speech incorporating both Path ("away") and Manner ("rolls"), has a gesture with Manner only. Younger "gesture-first" children do not decompose motion events this way. If anything, on the indexical principle that the more moving parts the better, they add extra copies of Manner or Path to gesture-first-like pantomimes of interesting objects and events. Table 7.2 summarizes these differences.

7.5   Discrepancy of findings, resolution

However, there is a conflict of evidence. Children learning verb-framed languages (Talmy 2000) such as French (Gullberg et al. 2008; Hickmann et al. 2011) and Japanese or Turkish (Kita and Özyürek 2003) show separate Manner gestures and, crucially, Path + Manner gestures. Spanish, also verb-framed, is thus an exception. Figure 7.3 shows four children, all with pure Manner gestures where adults would have combined Path and Manner—satellite-framed Mandarin and English and verb-framed Spanish (monolingual, resident of Guadalajara, Mexico), who contrast with Kita and Özyürek, Gullberg et al. and Hickmann et al.[1]

A factor separates the "decomposition" and "no-decomposition" studies, however, that has nothing to do with the respective languages but with the design of experimental materials. The "no-decomposition" studies used purpose-designed stimuli to highlight Path and Manner. There was no storyline and a child responding to a motion event could focus on it alone. This single focus could divert speech from the gesture–speech unity of Acquisition 2, where context and its differentiation are the key factors. Our cartoon, naturally, had no such design. It presented action-packed scenarios with characters doing things that happened to include Path and Manner. Acquisition 2 children could

[1] Guadalajara experiments carried out by Lisa Miotto and Karl-Erik McCullough.

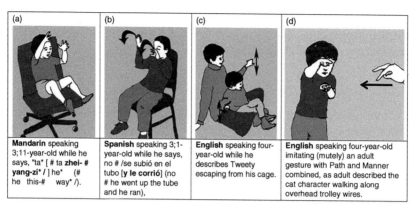

(a)	(b)	(c)	(d)
Mandarin speaking 3;11-year-old while he says, "ta* [# ta **zhei-** # **yang-zi*** /] he* (# he this-# way* /).	**Spanish** speaking 3;1-year-old while he says, no # /se subió en el tubo [**y le corrió**] (no # he went up the tube and he ran),	**English** speaking four-year-old while he describes Tweety escaping from his cage.	**English** speaking four-year-old imitating (mutely) an adult gesture with Path and Manner combined, as adult described the cat character walking along overhead trolley wires.

Figure 7.3 Motion event "decompositions" to pure Manner in three languages. Computer art by Fey Parrill. Transcriptions/translations by S. Duncan (Mandarin), Karl-Erik McCullough and Lisa Miotto (Spanish). Used with permission of the University of Chicago Press.

then form GPs and differentiate fields of equivalents with psychological predicates. The result would be two different portrayals of children's motion event cognitions. The purpose-designed materials are pure in an experimental sense, but less able to reveal children's changing semiotics during Acquisition 2.

Nonetheless, a possible Acquisition 2 signal is also apparent in the Gullberg et al. (2008) and Hickmann et al. (2011) studies. Four-year-old French speakers gestured both Path and Manner while their speech conveyed Path alone, especially in the control condition of the experiment where Manner was highlighted. This may be *hyper-composition*. The right-panel English speaker of Figure 7.3 is perhaps a satellite-framed counterpart—this English-speaking child shows *hyper-decomposition*. The child, a four-year-old, was attempting to imitate (spontaneously) a Path + Manner gesture from an adult, reducing it to pure Manner (arms rotating in a running motion, no Path). In the adult's gesture the Path component was prominent—his hand was right in front of the child, moving directly toward her (Path), while his fingers moved back and forth for running (Manner)—and was ongoing as the child began her imitation. Nonetheless, the child dropped the Path component, standing rock still. The two experiments may be tapping the same signal of Acquisition 2, with the verb-framed and satellite-framed directions reversed. In each case, signals could reflect Karmiloff-Smith's principle of overdoing the components of newly acquired systems, filtered now through the verb-framed and satellite-framed typologies. The directions of overcompensation (hyper-composition versus hyper-decomposition) seem to be dynamic versions of Whorf (1956): signals that tap the motion-worldviews encased in the languages—"motion" is movement along paths (French et al.) *versus* "motion" is movement in different manners (English and Mandarin). Both worldviews intrude, the verb-framed leading to uninvited Path and hyper-composition, and the satellite-framed to too-quickly deleted Path and hyper-decomposition; basically, however, the signals of Acquisition 2 are the same.

7.5.1   Advent of gesture-speech orchestration

Gestures gaining power over speech, joining it not as a constituent of the sentence, as in a gesture-first language, but as a template to organize speech is another hallmark of Acquisition 2. We see its first glimmerings in this example from Ella, aged two years and seven months (from Michael Forrester on CHILDES; example from Levy and McNeill 2015; see also Forrester 2014):

> (7.1) (*eating*) I like Thomas xxxxx much ...
> mm xxxx [$_a$xxxx /$_b$ xx Trucks /$_c$on the- /$_d$ on television /
> (a) *BH move out*
> (b) *start to move in toward each other*
> (c) *BH hold in midair*
> (d) *BH in fists, come together*

Levy and I proposed that Ella here illustrates one of her first orchestrations of speech by gesture. Her psychological predicate was not referential. The gesture then would be expected with Trucks, but in (b)–(c) she rejected this. It was, rather, discourse-relevant. The whole conversation with her father was about her activities the day before, comparing her enjoyment of watching *Troublesome Trucks* on television to another child's dislike of it (Thomas is the name of an animated steam engine character). The imagery contributes to the production of the utterance and articulates the core meaning, the trucks crashing. The whole was organized around this imagery. There was preparation at (a), showing the GP flashing on. Then an interruption and hold at (b) and (c), suggesting speech getting out of step. This was so despite the word "trucks" referring to the colliding objects. Then the stroke at (d) with the phrase "on television." This last is the telling detail. We see here a true psychological predicate. Ella's field of meaningful equivalents was something like *on television*, and her psychological predicate *trucks hitting*. Further proof comes from the form of the gesture stroke. It has the global and synthetic semiotic—the hands (trucks), motion (moving) and contact (collision) do not have these meanings on their own; they are dependent on the whole. This was perhaps the earliest recorded instance of the global-synthetic semiotic in Ella's case (Figure 7.4).

At two years old, just seven months earlier, Ella was completely in gesture-first mode, as in this further example from Levy and McNeill (Figure 7.5). Her meaning is something like, "the moon is here—where I'm touching," and then up in the sky:[2]

---

[2] Examples and transcript thanks to Elena Levy. The table is from Levy & McNeill (2015).

(a)  (b)

Figure 7.4 Ella's dual semiosis gesture–speech unity. Images recorded by Forrester (2008), deposited on CHILDES (the use of TalkBank data is governed by the Creative Commons License). Drawings by Dusty Hope. Cambridge University Press, reprinted with permission.

Figure 7.5 Ella's single semiosis pantomime at two years exactly. Image recorded by Forrester (2008, 2014), deposited on CHILDES (the use of TalkBank data is governed by the Creative Commons License). Drawing by Dusty Hope. Cambridge University Press, reprinted with permission.

(7.2)	where's the moon?
(a) F:	
	F glances to right, as if looking for the moon
(b) E:	[**'ere**]
	Left hand points up; gazes at extended finger
(c) F:	ohhh (pause)
	E returns to eating
(d) E:	[$_1$**an' look up** /$_2$ **u u sky**] (nods head)
	1: pantomime: E moves head back and looks up
	2: E moves head to right, still looking up
(e) F:	did we look up high in the sky and saw the moon? (E: yeah)

The gesture with "here" shows the primitive form of pointing that Vygotsky described as the first points, a modified, truncated grasp based on a classic "old" action-action. It is seen in how Ella turns her head to gaze at *the point itself.* Where her finger is, is the limit of her pointing, as if grasping. She improves her response with another pantomime as she says, "look up" and "u u sky." This differs from the collision gesture 7 months later in lacking a global and synthetic semiosis. There are no parts; or the "parts" *are* the whole; either way a part/whole distinction is absent. Rather than gesture–speech unity, there are two single semiotics laid side-by-side.

7.5.2   Dawn of the gesture phrase

As we have seen, Ella at two years and seven months distinguished preparation and stroke and had the internal structure of Kendon's gesture phrase—a pre-stroke hold, showing that the gesture had significance as a semiotic unit synchronized with speech. This came at the start of her genesis of gesture phases appearing with speech through the gesture's orchestrating power.

7.5.3   Creating fields of oppositions

The unity of gesture–speech appears around the age of three or four but its development continues well into school age, when an ability emerges to go beyond environmental givens and shape fields of meaningful equivalents to fit GPs. This last is an important further step. A GP is both a point of differentiation *and* the context it differentiates. The context is an indispensable part of meaning, since without it differentiation cannot exist. For adults context is dynamically adjustable by the speaker to make the GP's differentiation meaningful (the "it down" speaker formed a context for the bowling ball that had to do with its role as a force against Sylvester, and this made the GP meaningful not just as an object to be dropped but as an agent for Good in the moral battle). Kazuki Sekine (2009a, 2009b) has observed the beginning of this ability in children's gestures as they describe how they walked to and from school. His four-year-olds "matched" gestures to actual routes, known geographically, while the six-year-olds "mismatched"—that is, "produced gestures as if making a virtual space in front of themselves, without regard for orientation to the actual environment." In other words, the younger children created gestures to fit a map, while older children created a map to fit a conceptual environment—shaping fields of equivalents to make differentiations meaningful.

"New" actions are intrinsic to Acquisition 2. Orchestrating speech with gesture is the kind of "new" action described in Chapter 3, a form of action that exists only in language, only when speaking (or thinking in inner speech).

To summarize, language in ontogenesis first recapitulates gesture-first, then plateaus at the pivot grammar level. It extinguishes while dual semiosis arises, sometimes the two modes of language alternating in the same sentence. The changeover is established around age three or four. Gesture–speech unity continues to develop, as in the six-year-olds' tailor-made fields of meaningful oppositions.

I will explain a final Acquisition 2 signature—**self-aware agency**—in the section on gesture–speech unity timing. But first we consider the third acquisition.

7.6   Third acquisition

Continuity bridges the discontinuities the first and second acquisitions recapitulate from the two origins. Werner and Kaplan (1963, p. 42) caught that young children's speech evokes adult attachment when they wrote of symbolic actions with "the character of 'sharing' experiences with the Other rather than of 'communicating' messages to the Other." Sharing with, as opposed to communicating and representing to, would be what we see in the gestures of two-year-olds, but the adaptation appears much earlier. It is not beyond reason to imagine the first speech developments are shaped by it, infants from babbling onward developing the ability to orchestrate their vegetative anatomy for speech—lips, mouth, tongue, velum, larynx and diaphragm all coordinated for speech (rather than ingestion and breathing) (MacNeilage 2008). Even newborns have distinctive neural responses to the rhythmic patterns of speech (versus speech played backwards), suggesting the perception of rhythmic pulses at this early age (Peña et al. 2003). And the birth cries of the newborns of French-speaking mothers and those of German-speaking mothers have different "melody contours," rising for the French, falling for the Germans (Mampe et al. 2009)—suggesting intrauterine speech perception and motor orchestration matches. This is orchestration, third-acquisition style, the "significance" of vocal action movements of the anatomy itself and its audible effects.

While the gesture-first Acquisition 1 and gesture–speech unity Acquisition 2 are taking place, an infant's speech follows its own development, disconnected from inhabitance by thought and control by gesture, but plausibly adapted to adult attachment. It would be the beginning of the micro-level of speech control. Later acquisitions adapt it for their own uses. Discontinuity, however, implies that the child cannot get to gesture-first orchestration from attachment-speech or to gesture–speech unity from gesture-first orchestration. Instead, speech-for-attachment carries gesture-first along as a free-rider. The first gesture "names" and later gesture–speech supplements are not continuations of babbling; they ride on it and impose new orchestrations climaxing in pivot grammars. Then the gesture–speech unity of the third and fourth years is not a continuation of pivots but again rides on attachment-speech as it merges finally with gesture to form gesture-orchestrated speech.

7.7   Timing of gesture–speech unity

When gesture–speech unity develops it reflects the maturation of the thought–language–hand brain link. What matures at age three or four?

7.7.1   Prefrontal cortex

Part the thought–language–hand link is the prefrontal cortex. It is engaged for comparing and choosing alternatives. There it may construct the fields of equivalents that psychological predicates differentiate. The prefrontal cortex develops slowly, not reaching levels of synaptic density matching that of the visual or auditory cortex until about the age as the second acquisition, four years (Huttenlocher and Dabholkar 1997). This maturation, while still not complete for many years more (see Sowell et al. 1999; Diamond 2002), could be one reason to fix the second acquisition timing at three or four years of age.

7.7.2   Self-aware agency

We can also draw on the ontogeny-recapitulates-phylogeny heuristic. We seek an ontogenetic hallmark to which the proposed evolution can be tied. If we find it, then we propose that evolution installed this connection, and its maturation now in ontogenesis fixes the three/four-years timing. We expect the two timings to agree even if they are in separate areas of the thought–language–hand brain link. We shall see the prefrontal cortex and the one we identify next do.

The ontogenetic hallmark is the emergence of **self-aware agency**. It underlies all the other ontogenetic hallmarks. A selective advantage of the Mead's Loop gesture self-response depends on awareness of one's own agency. The term "self-aware agency" in this discussion means *the condition of being aware of oneself as an agent*. Susan Hurley (1998, p. 141) wrote that self-awareness is taking a unified perspective, keeping track of what is seen and what is done, and how this engenders awareness of your own agency. We presume our ancestors had the ability to take this unified perspectives on things. It was from it the adaptive advantages of new-form "twisted" mirror neurons could be felt. Self-aware agency does not mean that you know you are gesturing, are teaching something or are orchestrating your vocal tract around a gesture. Some people may be aware of some of these things and others not, but this is not the meaning. The term signals that if you gesture, you feel that something has crystalized in the world of

Table 7.3 Proposed Acquisition 1–dark age–Acquisition 2 succession.

Gesture type	Period 1 (Acquisition 1)single semiosis in gesture-speechcombinations	Period 2 (Dark Age extinction)transition	Period 3 (Acquisition 2)dual semiosis in gesture–speech unity
Representational gestures	Loose hand waving	Large iconic gestures	Typical iconic gestures
Nonrepresentational gestures		Large beats	Typical beats

After Levy and McNeill (2015).

meanings, and *this crystallization is your doing*. Self-aware agency is the feeling of being the agent of this new meaningfulness. Your awareness does not necessarily include the *form* of the symbol, and typically one is not aware of having made a gesture (goal (b) is the relevant fact, (a) not being part of it). Other developments at age four also depend on self-aware agency, such as Tomasello's (2008, 2014) shared intentionality and Wimmer and Perner's (1983) theory of mind, and all emerge at the same developmental point, and do because of a shared maturation.

7.8   Summary

Table 7.3, based on a similar table in Levy and McNeill (2015, Table 8.1), summarizes the gesture-first Acquisition 1 → "dark-age" gesture-first extinction → gesture–speech unity Acquisition 2 succession this chapter has described. The table suggests four conclusions with implications for current-day ontogenesis study.

First, we can see why Acquisition 2 occurs when it does, around age three or four. In theory, dual semiosis and the GP become available in ontogenesis when the thought–language–hand link created at the origin matures in the child's brain. This occurs around three or four because several of its aspects—the prefrontal cortex, the new-form mirror-neuron adaptation of Mead's Loop, and the child's recapitulation of its phylogenetic adaptation to self-aware agency—all proposed to come to life then.

Second, the perspective researchers take on child language changes when a more complete vision of language as a dynamic process is taken into account. With this view, it is reasonable to say that the acquisition of human language occurs at three or four (not at one or two: which is gesture-first acquisition with "old" action-actions), with a separate evolution of vocal attachment carrying the child forward. The new perspective can open fresh ways of looking at ontogenesis. To search for ontogenetic hallmarks of phylogenetic recapitulations and when they mature is one such perspective, bringing together neurocognition with the study of child language corpora.

Third, the first steps of syntax should differ in predictable ways in Acquisition 2 from Acquisition 1. As Levy and I point out, Werner and Kaplan (1963) saw this in their portrayal of symbol formation—a shift from *parataxis* to *hypotaxis*, which we linked to the semiotics of symbol formation—the shift from a *single* to a *dual semiotic*. The syntax of parataxis is summarized by pivot grammars and their lack of depth and that of hypotaxis by gesture–speech unity and its depth.

Finally, the adaptation of Mead's Loop to inculcate adult-to-child culture suggests a line of study of how this interchange works. Here we can enlarge upon Corballis's (2011) and Arbib's (2012) insights without falling back into the gesture-first trap. Thinking first of phylogenesis, after the origin we see Mead's Loop leading each later generation to inculcate culture a bit more successfully. And with each turn of the screw culture increased the selection pressure for Mead's Loop itself until reaching some equilibrium. In this way Mead's Loop enabled more and more complexity of culture, and more complexity of culture favored Mead's Loop. Via the interactions of mothers and infants, culture and biology lifted each other, and this could have happened quickly. Can current-day mothers and infants be understood in part as recapitulating this process, their interactions at various points echoing the mutual dependence of gesture–speech and cultural inculcation? The new perspective described here sees them in the light of a growing gesture–speech unity. For example, using the ontogeny-recapitulates-phylogeny heuristic, it should be possible to predict the kinds of cultural innovations adults impart at different stages, adults timing them intuitively to meet the maturation points of gesture–speech unity. The way that dual semiosis and GPs are timed could be just the tip of the iceberg, with much more sorting out in the realm of adult-child interaction, adults and children unknowingly following the recapitulated order and linking themselves to specific intellectual abilities when as forged by evolution they mature.

8   Brain

We now look at the thought–language–hand brain link itself and consider some of its properties. A brain model is the first topic; then evidence from cases of aproprioception, commissurotomy and speech disorder; finally, a working memory that evolved in the origin of language specifically for gesture-orchestrated speech in gesture–speech units.

8.1   Brain model

The thought–language–hand link is a neurogesture–speech system criss-crossing the brain to engage the right and left sides as well as the anterior and posterior parts of the brain in a choreographed operation.

Wernicke's Area is not limited to comprehension. It supplies categorial content, not only for comprehension (as classically supposed) but for the creative production of verbal thought. If this content crosses to the right hemisphere, which seems particularly adept at creating *sui generis* metaphors and imagery and capturing discourse content (McNeill and Pedelty 1995), the right hemisphere could play a role in the creation of growth points (GP), which require content from context, imagery and *sui generis* metaphors—the right hemisphere specialties to which Wernicke's Area sends linguistic categories. Kelly et al. (2004) observe evoked response effects (N400) in the right brain when subjects observe speech–gesture mismatches.

All this could recross to Broca's Area to create a GP. A germane result is Federmeier and Kutas (1999), who found through evoked potential recordings different information strategies in the right and left sides of the brain—the left they characterized as "integrative," the right as "predictive." These terms relate to the hypothesized roles of the right and left hemispheres in the generation of GPs. Broca's Area is the site of Mead's Loop and self-response, an integrative process. The GP is integration *par excellence*. The right hemisphere for its part offers the left hemisphere imagery, cohesive discourse and linguistic content related to imagery, and fits the predictive role.

The prefrontal cortex has a role in forming fields of equivalents and psychological predicates. Language depends on processes of choice and differentiation and these the prefrontal cortex provides. This too could go to the right and left hemispheres.

Finally, rhythmicity (Duncan 2005) and interactional entrainment (Gill 2007) point to a circulation in and out of the cerebellum (see Lieberman 2002).

The GP itself would form in Broca's Area. The particular Broca's Area specialty is the ability to use these other brain areas to create the GP, to call for constructions and words by which to unpack them, to form intuitions of formal completeness that provide "stop orders" to the dialectic, and to orchestrate the vocal tract and hands by gesture under significances other than those of the vocal tract itself. It is likely here also where mimicry and the metaphoricity semiotic reside (which Broca's Area can send to the right hemisphere and receive back *sui generis* metaphoric packages using the semiotic).

All parts of the model—left (front, rear), right, prefrontal, cerebellar—can be called the thought–language–hand brain link. It is not just that these brain areas are borrowed but the origin of language included the evolution of a dedicated link running through them. I do not imagine a series of causal steps but rather a violin string or piano wire. Striking it anywhere causes it to sound, and so the thought–language–hand brain link can be set in motion at any point. Recall here Liesbet Quaeghebeur's dictum that the experience of language is by the "all-at-onceness" principle (2012), and Michael Silverstein's "complex and mediated absorption of indexically linked values and presuppositions" (2003, p. 195).

The language centers of the brain have classically been regarded as just two—Wernicke's and Broca's Areas—but if we are on the right track, metapragmatic and contextual background information must be present to activate the broader spectrum of brain regions the model describes. Typical item-recognition, memory and production tests would not tap these other brain regions but discourse, conversation, play, work and the exigencies of language in daily life, where language originated, would.

8.2   Evidence of aproprioception

Mr. Ian Waterman, sometimes referred to as 'IW', suffered at age 19 a sudden deafferentation of his body from the neck down—the near total loss of all the touch, proprioception and limb spatial position senses that tell you, without looking, where your body is and what it is doing. The loss followed a never-diagnosed fever that is believed to have set off an autoimmune reaction. The immediate behavioral effect was immobility, even though IW's motor system was unaffected and there was no paralysis.

The problem was not lack of movement per se, but lack of control. Upon awakening after three days, IW nightmarishly found that he had no control over what his body did—he was unable to sit up, walk, feed himself or manipulate objects; none of the ordinary actions of everyday life, let alone the complex actions required for his vocation. To imagine what deafferentation is like, try this experiment suggested by Shaun Gallagher (personal communication): sit down at a table (something IW could not have done at first) and place your hands beneath the surface; open and close one hand, close the other and extend a finger; put the open hand over the closed hand, and so forth. You know at all times what your hands are doing and where they are but IW would not know any of this—he would know that he had willed his hands to move but, without vision, would have no idea of what they are doing or where they are located. The IW case is a fascinating study of a person who has lost his body schema (to use the Gallagher's 2005 terminology), "his body" in the title of the 1998 BBC *Horizon* program about his case. The neuronpathy destroyed all sensory neurons at roughly the neck level in proportion to their myelination and conduction speed. The initial prognosis was that IW would spend the rest of his days confined to a wheelchair. Not one who takes setbacks lightly, IW commenced a rigorous self-designed and administered program of movement practice with the aim of learning to control movement again, endlessly performing motions over and over in different combinations, different trajectories, different distances and velocities, until he could, by thinking about the motion and using vision as his guide, plan and execute movements flawlessly, so nearly so that observers find nothing unusual about them. The original description of IW and his self-administered recovery was called *Pride and a Daily Marathon*, a title that captures in a nutshell the rigor and determination of IW's battling the catastrophe that had befallen him (Cole 1995). After more than 30 years, IW has developed an entirely new way of initiating and controlling movement. He has perfected this style to an astonishing degree. His movements depend on having constant visual contact with the environment, including the surrounding space, objects to be manipulated and any other objects in the immediate vicinity. Every movement is planned in advance, the force and direction calculated intuitively, and the movement monitored as it is taking place. Given all these requirements, it is impressive to see IW move at normal speeds without visible flaw. Although his gait seems somewhat lumbering, his arm and hand movements are indistinguishable from normal. However, if vision is denied, IW can no longer control his hands and arms accurately.

Thanks to the BBC, IW, Cole, Gallagher and the University of Chicago, researchers gathered at the university for filming in July 1997. We wanted to record IW under a variety of conditions, both with and without vision. IW cannot be simply blindfolded, since then he would be unable to orient himself and be at risk of falling over. We devised the tray-like blind, pictured in Figure 8.1,

Figure 8.1 IW seated at the blind designed for gesture experiments. Computer art in this and the remaining illustrations of this chapter (except Figures 8.6 and 8.7) by Fey Parrill, now on the faculty of Case Western University. Used with permission of University of Chicago Press.

Figure 8.2 IW iconic gesture with vision.

which could be pulled down in front of him, blocking vision of his hands, while allowing him space in which to move and visual contact with his surroundings.[1] IW was videotaped retelling the usual animated cartoon. He also was recorded under the blind in casual conversation with Jonathan Cole. In 1997 we did not appreciate the importance of testing IW's instrumental actions without vision but we had an opportunity to test his performance on this kind of task in April 2002, when IW, Cole and Gallagher came back for a second visit to Chicago.[2]

To have a systematic approach to IW's gestures, we pay specific attention to the following variables:

---

[1] Nobuhiro Furuyama suggested the blind experiment. The blind was designed and built by David Klein.

[2] The second round of experiments was supported by a grant from the Wellcome Trust to Jonathan Cole and by funds from Ian Waterman.

(a)   (b)

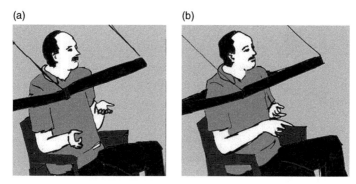

Figure 8.3 IW coordinated two-handed iconic gesture without vision.

Timing: synchronization with co-expressive speech.
Morphokinesis: the shape of the gesture in terms of hand forms and use of space.
Topokinesis: the location of hands relative to each other in space, including but not limited to the approach of one hand by the other.

IW's gestures with vision look much like those produced by normal speakers, although they are fewer in number and tend to be isolated, performed one by one, in keeping with his self-conscious constructed-gestures strategy. Figure 8.2 shows such a narrative gesture with vision. IW was describing Sylvester after he had swallowed the bowling ball. Both morphokinesis and topokinesis are indistinguishable from normal. IW's hand appears to bracket a small figure in the central gesture space and move it downward, wobbling right and left slightly as it went down. The motion is co-expressive with the synchronous speech: [//**he** // **wiggles his way down**]. The only clue that control is other than normal is that IW looks at his hand during the gesture.

It is important to recognize a distinction introduced by IW himself. Some gestures, he says, are **constructed**—planned in advance, launched at will and controlled in timing and motion throughout; in other words carried out exactly as he carries out practical, world-related movements. The gesture in Figure 8.2 was of this type. IW's constructeds may be close to "old" action-actions. They are planned, executed and monitored just as pragmatic actions are. And they are purposeful. IW believes his constructeds give him the appearance of "normalcy" and are essential elements of self-presentation. They are performed with this goal. Then, how IW orchestrates speech with gestures that ordinarily repel it is by visual monitoring—essentially two actions, manual and spoken, kept in alignment by a third, visual monitoring.

The other type he calls **throw-aways** (IW's term)—"ones that just happen. Sometimes I'll be aware of them because there may be something around me

Figure 8.4 Lack of topokinetic accuracy without vision.

(a)   (b)

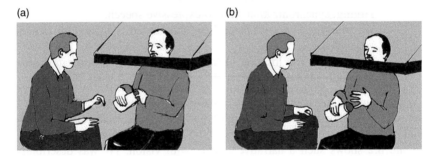

Figure 8.5 IW attempts to perform an instrumental action (removing cap from thermos).

... but most are just thrown away." Throw-aways are not explicitly planned and monitored. Although to IW they are incidental, for us they are of primary interest and our focus. Throw-aways are "new" gesture-actions. To contrast under the blind the constructed and throw-away gestures is our main observation for seeing the effects of aproprioception on "new" gesture-actions.

When vision is denied, "constructed" gestures disappear but "throw-aways" remain. Without vision, in other words, gestures of the "old" action-action type and those of the "new" gesture-action type diverge sharply. This implies that the thought–language–hand link that carries the "new" type does not draw upon the "old " type. Neurologically, they are on separate tracks, such that "throw-aways" are not affected by a lack of feedback. An explanation is that goal-directedness directs speech away from the thought–language–hand link. We learn from the IW case that the thought–language–hand link is neuronally separate from "old" action-actions, as Mead's Loop evolution posits.

Figure 8.3 illustrates a throw-away gesture without vision, a coordinated two-handed tableau, in which the left hand is Sylvester and the right hand is a streetcar pursuing him. IW was saying, "[and the ₐtram ᵦ**caught** him up]"—with (a) and (b) referring to the first and second panels of the illustration. His right hand moved to the left in exact synchrony with the co-expressive "caught." Moreover, a poststroke hold (underlining) extended the stroke image through "him" and "up" and thus maintained full synchrony of the meaningful configuration in the stroke with still unfolding co-expressive speech. It is important to recall in viewing these examples that synchrony and co-expressivity were achieved without any kind of visual, proprioceptive, temporal or spatial feedback.

Figure 8.3 demonstrates how similar IW's "throw-aways" are to normal non-impaired gestures. The gesture is complex, two hands doing different things in relation to each other, the whole is imagery depicting a situation in which the entities identified in speech are changing their relationships in time and space. Such complexity contributes to communicative dynamism; that is the case with Figure 8.3—the event is the denouement of a buildup and the main discursive point.

The gesture in Figure 8.3 however was affected by IW's aproprioception at one level. While accurate morphokinetically it was off topokinetically; as the right hand approached the left, the right and left hands did not line up. Figure 8.4 illustrates another topokinetic approximation as IW sketched a square in gesture space. The illustration captures the misalignment of his hands as he completed the top of the square and was about to move both hands downward for the sides. Similarly, when denied vision actual instrumental actions are difficult for IW. Figure 8.5 shows steps in IW's attempt to remove the cap from a thermos bottle without vision. The first is immediately after Jonathan Cole placed the thermos in IW's right hand and his left hand on the cap (IW is strongly left-handed); the second is a second later when IW began to twist the cap off. As can be seen, his left hand fell off and turned in midair. Similar disconnects without vision occurred during other real-world "old" action-actions (threading a cloth through a ring, hitting a toy xylophone, etc.—this last of interest since IW could have made use of acoustic feedback or its absence to know when his hand had drifted off target, but he still could not perform the action).

During a conversation with Jonathan Cole, while still under the blind, IW reduced his speech rate at one point by about one-half (paralinguistic slowing), and gesture slowed to the same degree, so that it and speech and remained in synchrony: **normal** = "and I'm startin' t'use m'hands now"; **slow** = "because I'm startin' t'get into trying to explain things." This is a striking demonstration of the thought–language–hand link and how it merges gesture with speech. IW, without vision, can modulate the speed at which he presents meanings in both speech and gesture, and do this in tandem (Figure 8.6). As speech slows, so too does gesture and to the same extent, so that speech–gesture synchrony is preserved. This is what the Warlpiri speech-sign bilingual (Chapter 6), putting together two codes, could not do. If IW is forming cognitive units comprised of co-expressive speech and gesture imagery, in synchrony, this joint modulation of speed with gesture-orchestrated speech is explicable. He does it based on his sense (available

Gestures	(a) Hands move outward, then inward from the position shown.	(b) Hands again move outward, starting to move out of phase.	(c) At Slow speed, hands out of phase, left hand rotates max in, right hand max out, corresponding	to both hands max in phase at normal speed. (d) Hands back in phase, both move outward
Normal (bracketed material=0.56 sec., 5 syllables) **"and [I'm startin' t'] use m'hands now"**	and I'm ⇓	startin' ⇓	t' use m- ⇓	-y hands now ⇓
Normal speed image				
Slow (bracketed material=0.76 sec., 5 syllables) **"-cuz [I'm startin' t'] get into"**	'cuz I'm ⇓	startin' ⇓	t' get in- ⇓	-to try(in') ⇓
Slow speed image				

Figure 8.6 IW changes rate of speech and gesture in tandem, maintaining synchrony. Motion of hands outward and inward occurs at same speech points, although hands are in phase at normal speed, out of phase at reduced speed. Cambridge University Press, reprinted with permission.

to him) of how long the joint imagery-linguistic cognitive unit remains "alive"; peripheral sensory feedback need not be part of it. The gestures are of a familiar metaphoric type in which a process is depicted as a rotation in space (see the similar rotation metaphor for computer operations in Chapter 5). IW executes the metaphor twice; first at normal speed, then at slow speed. The crucial observation is that the hand rotations are locked to the same landmarks in speech where the words were the same despite the different speeds. IW's hands rotate in phase at normal speed, in opposite phases at slow speed. Nonetheless, if we look at where the hands orbit inward and outward (in the out-of-phase case, the left hand especially), we find rotations at both speeds coinciding with the same lexical words and stress peaks. This agreement across speeds shows that whatever controlled the slowdown, it was exactly the same for speech and gesture.

Bennett Bertenthal (pers. comm.) proposed a possible micro-level mechanism for this tandem reduction. Speech and gesture, slowing together, could reflect the operation of a pacesetter in the brain that survived IW's deafferentation; for example, the hand moves outward with a prosodic peak, an association that could be maintained over a range of speeds. The rotating hands as noted were metaphors for the idea of a process. The pacesetter accordingly could be activated by metaphoricity on the thought–language–hand link and co-opt hand movements by a significance other than rotation itself. This metaphoric significance is consistent with the timing, since *the hands rotated only during the metaphors* while IW was saying "I'm starting to … " There was actually a cessation of movement between the first (normal speed) and second (reduced speed) rotations, indicating that the rotation and any phonetic linkages it claimed were specifically organized around the idea of a process as a rotation in space. It is another example of gesture shaping the micro-level.

The following points summarize what we have seen of IW's gestures in the absence of visual, proprioceptive or spatial position feedback:

1 Gestures preserve morphokinetic accuracy while they lose topokinetic accuracy.
2 Gestures are co-expressive and synchronized with speech, even as speech rate varies.

Morphokinesis is accessed via the thought–language–hand brain link and is accessible for "new" gesture-action while topokinesis depends on pragmatic action. Gesture–speech synchrony depends on GPs and is accessed via the thought–language–hand brain link while it is inaccessible from "old" action-actions.

Ramachandran and Blakeslee in *Phantoms in the Brain* (1998) describe Mirabelle, a young woman born without arms. Yet she experiences phantom arms and performs "gestures" with them—non-moving gestures, but imagery in actional-visual form.

Dr: How do you know that you have phantom limbs?
M: Well, because as I'm talking to you, they are gesticulating. They point to objects when I point to things. When I walk, doctor, my phantom arms don't swing like normal arms, like your arms. They stay frozen on the side like this (her stumps hanging straight down). But when I talk, my phantoms gesticulate. In fact, they're moving now as I speak. (Ramachandran and Blakeslee 1998, p. 41)

Mirabelle's case points to a conclusion similar to IW's—dissociation of gesture from practical actions. In Mirabelle's case, moreover, goal-2 intentions create the sensation of gestures when no motion is possible. Presumably, again, the same thought–language– hand link is responsible.

The IW and Mirabelle cases suggest that control of the hands and the relevant motor neurons is possible directly from the thought-linguistic system. Without vision, IW's dissociation of gesture-action, which remains intact, and instrumental action-action, which disappears, implies that the "know-how" of gesture is not the same as the "know-how" of instrumental movement (to use Shaun Gallagher's terms, pers. comm.). In terms of brain function, this implies that producing a gesture cannot be accounted for entirely with the circuits for instrumental actions; at some point the gesture enters a circuit of its own and there is tied to speech. This thought–language–hand link connection circumvents the goal-directedness of instrumental action. A likely locus lies in part in Broca's Area.

8.3   Evidence of the "split-brain"

Other evidence of the thought–language–hand link comes from the effects of the surgical procedure of commissurotomy, the complete separation of the two hemispheres at the corpus callosum (popularly known as the "split brain"). The operation has been performed in selected cases of intractable epilepsy, where seizures would have led to severe brain injury (see Levy and Trevarthen 1976). The cases have intrigued generations of neuropsychologists. The patients seem to have two sensibilities, each isolated in a half brain, each with its own powers, personality and limitations. I was very curious to see what the gestures of these patients were like, and had an opportunity to test two of the original Sperry and Gazzaniga patients, LB and NG (LB has since died). Colwyn Trevarthen introduced me to Dalia Zaidel, a psychologist at UCLA, who was studying and looking after the patients.

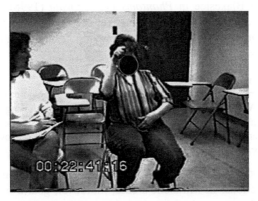

Figure 8.7 NG's gesture, preceding, not overlapping, co-expressive speech, "through the window."

(a)   (b)   (c)   (d)

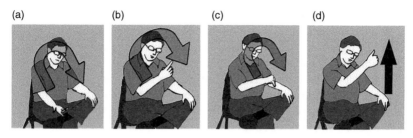

Figure 8.8 LB's iconic depiction, totally without speech, of Sylvester throwing a weight and launching himself. From McNeill (2005). Used with permission of University of Chicago Press.

Dalia graciously agreed to videotape them retelling our standard animated cartoon stimulus.

The split-brain procedure would interrupt the thought–language–hand link's left-right hemisphere crossing and recrossing. Straightforward organization of speech orchestrated by gesture should not be possible, the commissurotomy having isolated the left hemisphere's specialty of gesture-orchestrated speech from the right's specialties of imagery and context. The two patients, LB and NG, follow different strategies to cope with the split-brain problem. LB makes little use of his right hemisphere. NG, in contrast, seems "bicameral," using her left hemisphere for speech and her right for gestures. To orchestrate speech, NG communicated to herself *externally*—her left hemisphere watching her right hemisphere's gestures and her right hemisphere listening to her left hemisphere's speech. In other words, NG restored the severed interhemisphere link by watching her own gestures and listening to her own speech. Speech often followed its co-expressive gesture by about a second, which is close to the amount of time gesture-orchestrated speech would take once the left hemisphere has registered the right hemisphere gesture.

Figure 8.7 shows NG's gesture for Sylvester clambering into Tweety's window. The screenshot is just as the stroke ended. Her hand had by then risen and arced forward; then, after about a second of poststroke hold, NG said "through the window." Her poststroke hold is a significant detail. It shows that the right hemisphere maintained the gesture until it heard the left hemisphere speak. The gesture's self-response in the left hemisphere to its visual presence from the right could be brought face-to-face with speech in memory and orchestrate it. Simultaneous awareness would span this temporally separated gesture and co-expressive speech.

In contrast to NG, LB had few gestures. Most were beats or simple conduit-like metaphors in the lower center gesture space near his lap. The absence of iconicity is consistent with a left-hemisphere origin. He could make bimanual gestures, almost always two similar hands of the palm-up or palm-down open hand type with conventional metaphoric significances. *Sui generis* metaphoric gestures were totally lacking, consistent with the absence of right hemisphere information. The open-hand gestures may have been emblems. Two similar hands could be managed from the left hemisphere via bimanual motor control. His narrative style seems list-like, a recitation of steps from the cartoon, sometimes accompanied by counting on his fingers, also consistent with a left-hemisphere organization. It seems likely that his Wernicke's and Broca's Areas intercommunicated. This decontextualized style and minimal gesturing may be what the left hemisphere is capable of on its own. LB never found an alternative thought–language–hand brain link like NG's and indeed LB never showed NG's asynchronies. Equally consistent with the lack of left–right contact, contextual embodiment was missing for LB.

LB and NG jointly illustrate one of the elements of the brain model—how the right hemisphere (available to NG, not used by LB) is necessary for situating speech in context and orchestrating linguistically categorized significance around imagery; the left hemisphere (exclusively relied upon by LB, accessible from NG's right hemisphere after a delay) orchestrates well-formed speech output with gesture but otherwise has minimal ability to apprehend and establish discourse cohesion.

Figure 8.8 shows one of LB's rare iconic gestures, depicting Sylvester in another scene launching a weight. It reveals the left and right hemispheres' functional separation in a way that only a split-brain patient could. It also shows LB's inability to restore the thought–language–hand brain link the way NG did. Unlike NG, his gesture and the flanking speech were not co-expressive and the gesture could not have orchestrated it. Indeed LB's entire performance was *in silence*, as if the right hemisphere source was unable to reach the left hemisphere. The instant the gesture ended speech resumed. LB was saying, "he had a plan," then speech stopped and the Figure 8.8 gesture commenced (the elapsed time of the whole gesture was a bit more than a second). Then as his right hand reached its peak (right panel) speech returned with "to get up," completing the clause. It is as if the left hemisphere had switched off while the right hemisphere had switched on.

Considered together, the split-brain patients show the interhemisphere routes of the thought–language–hand brain link, and something of the particular roles each hemisphere plays—iconicity from the right, constructions from the left.

8.4   Evidence of language disorders

The origin of language seemingly left a process with cracks. The cracks open disorders, in the examples to be reviewed—Broca's and Wernicke's aphasia,

Down's syndrome, Williams syndrome, childhood autism, and stammer—they reveal the thought–language–hand brain link in yet another way (McNeill and Duncan 2010).

8.4.1 The aphasias

Dysfluent or **Broca's aphasia** arises from a more or less severe disruption of unpacking. The GP itself seems intact. There is still gesture-orchestrated speech with what remains on the speech side. A Broca's aphasic differentiates psychological predicates in fields of equivalents but has difficulty unpacking them. In the following the speaker performed two well-synchronized, co-expressive gestures. With speech they constituted a likely (repeated) GP:

(8.1) [a- and **down**] [(pause) **t- d- down**]

The strokes were downward thrusts of the right hand synchronized closely with the two occurrences of the co-expressive path particle, "down," the second stammered (Figure 8.9).

The difficulty of finding constructions, however, is not absolute. Broca's aphasia does not prevent catchment formation. Given time and catchment support, even unpacking into multiple clauses is possible. A different patient began with only single nouns and a gesture. Over the next two and a half minutes, speech gradually expanded accompanied by the same gesture in various elaborations to become eventually a two-clause, embedded sentence—"he saw the el train comin'," a construction that did not appear before. Figure 8.10 shows the stages of this gradual unpacking.

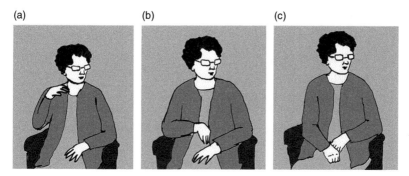

(a) (b) (c)

Figure 8.9 Downward gestures by Broca's speaker timed with "an' down" (a–b) and "t- d- down" (c). Used with permission of University of Chicago Press.

(a)   (b)   (c)

(d)   (e)   (f)

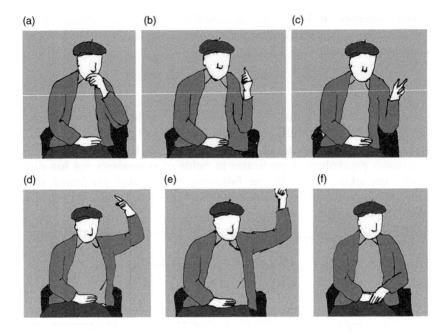

Figure 8.10 Catchment from Broca's speaker made of repeated gestures in upper space. Used with permission of University of Chicago Press.

Figure 8.11 Wernicke's gesture with "to-it." Used with permission of University of Chicago Press.

Table 8.1 Wernicke's unpacking.

1	a little tooki tooki goin to-it to him
2	looki' on a little little tooki goin' to him
3	it's a not digga not næ he weduh
4	like he'll get me mema run to-it they had to is
5	then he put it sutthing to it takun a jo to-it
6	that's nobody to-it
7	I mean pawdi di get to-it she got
8	got got glasses she could look to-it
9	to set something to in to-it to a to a got in to-it
10	to a duck to-it
11	hit on hit him on nice to him
12	then she just sent to 'im
13	to ah my knowledge anyway
14	she trie to get the little little ah ak it t- t- tush t- t- take it
15	the part of the gun ta- take a part of a gun she's tryin' a take up a he got into a puky
16	she was trying to be that she was going to take
17	to make d- her take the part of the little ton't litle the gar gen to-it little little
18	little little like puss to-it
19	that's all I tooki
20	an' run someplace
21	she dropped hi baggage up
22	she 'member that she was to-it
23	nothin' but a byum that's all
24	'n I lef' the whole damn the whole damn
25	side look bloorep 'n to-it I use to
26	look I look at it way day way took
27	I look to-it
28	ju' a little ol' toy
29	with tappn'
30	why he ed take the part of 'im
31	an' they give 'im away to 'im
32	they gvme him an' they they find out who it was
33	it was a no no 'n that was
34	bammed up
35	an'
36	that was all to-it

Transcription by Laura Pedelty, now on the medical faculty of the University of Illinois.

Conversely, **Wernicke's aphasia** appears as a failure of the GP itself and/ or of its field of equivalents but spares unpacking. Gesture-orchestration is robust. Unpacking takes place but because GPs and fields of equivalents are distorted as a result of injury, the result is unbridled speech with odd loops and weak constraints. Gestures trigger a word, and then the word plus the gesture become a new field of equivalents and (very odd) *also* the next GP. It is a field of equivalents differentiating itself. This is one explanation of the common observation that Wernicke's speech seems "empty." It is not the absence of GPs and fields of equivalents but self-differentiating ones. As a result, gesture-orchestrated speech is unconstrained. The role of Wernicke's Area seems clear from its absence in these breakdowns—the very core of thought is disrupted. Table 8.1 contains the complete Canary Row narration of one Wernicke patient. Figure 8.11 shows one of the "to-it" gestures that illustrate the kind of garbled, repeating GPs self-differentiation (something like *arrives: arrives*), not contextless but circularly self-differentiating.

The conclusion of Table 8.1 and Figure 8.11 is that GPs and fields of equivalents depend on a semantic coherence from Wernicke's Area. It is more than a lexicon. We learn from both anterior and posterior aphasias that GPs open two avenues of breakdown, unpacking or the GPs themselves.

8.4.2   Non-typical development

Here we consider three patterns of abnormal development in children, Down's syndrome, Williams syndrome and childhood autism. Each shows, through its particular absence, a part of the thought–language–hand brain link.

Down's syndrome
Down's syndrome (DS) reveals through its absence the maxim that "one meaning is two things." DS are unable to meet it. They lag in language but are relatively spared in visuospatial and visuomotor abilities (Iverson et al. 2003, Stefanini et al. 2007). It is not surprising that they show a "gesture advantage"— a preference for and receptivity to gesture over vocal speech, a phenomenon first noted by Abrahamsen et al. (1985) with taught signs and words.

Typically developing children (TD) also show a gesture advantage at early ages but with a revealing difference. As we have seen, TD gestures combine with words to encode semantic relations (child points to chair and says "daddy" = "daddy's chair"). For DS, word-gesture combinations tend to be redundant (child points to chair and says "chair"). Second, the TD gesture advantage occurs before the two-word threshold, and in fact predicts with what semantic relations this threshold will be crossed (Butcher and Goldin-Meadow 2000; Goldin-Meadow and Butcher 2003) while for DS it *is* the threshold, and suggests a different ontogenesis despite being called the same "gesture advantage." These differences, when examined, shed light on the DS linguistic deficit itself.

To put the difference into GP terms, redundancy and the exclusion of semantic connections between gesture and speech suggest that DS growth points, in whatever form they exist, are narrowly constrained. The opposition of semiotic modes within these narrow limits would give them little traction. Metaphoricity, intrinsic to gesture in normal development after Acquisition 2 when it emerges, is absent. The type of example in Figure 1.2, in which the underlying idea of Sylvester moving up inside a pipe is symbolized in two semiotically opposite forms, may accordingly be beyond their reach. Imagining them recounting this episode, they may say "pipe" and gesture its shape; or "sidewalk" (where Sylvester paced before going up the pipe) and gesture a flat surface; or "ball" and make a circle; but not "rising hollowness" or even "down" if, as we suppose, the Broca's speaker in Figure 8.9 was differentiating the idea of a downward force in a context of things that Tweety and Sylvester were doing. In DS, narrowness in turn could impact the GP's differentiation. DS growth points, redundantly welded, would differentiate only equally narrow contexts where synonymy of gesture and speech is meaningful. Verbalized thought, for DS, would then be confined in at least two ways—growth points with little dynamic push, and contexts cramped to make minimal differentiation significant: in this way coming up short on the dynamic dimension. The aphasic speaker who after two arduous minutes reached a two-clause, embedded sentence was sustained throughout by his spatially configured catchment, and this kind of achievement, and any benefit of catchment formations in general, may be out of reach for a DS speaker. Finally, a lack of GP semiotic opposition could impair the unpacking step, limiting access to constructions that fit with minimal *langue*-feelings. So the picture is of limited GP potential, lessened dynamism of thinking-for/while-speaking, limited contextual scope, and limited potential to form gestural (catchment) discourse segments. In a way, DS seems trapped in Acquisition 1 and in a world not unlike that of gesture-first so that the full development of Acquisition 2 never can take hold. Bellugi et al. (1999) describe older DS responses to vocabulary tests as often involving perseverations or category errors (e.g., "horsie, dog, ice cream" to one picture), which could be manifestations of this linguistic-cognitive narrowness and truncated development.

Given that DS speakers have comparatively good visuospatial and visuomotor cognition, it is telling that the gestures they do produce, after considerable experience, are not ones likely to foster dual semiosis. Volterra et al. offer an interesting suggestion which we can set down to "old" action-action:

children with DS may be able to make use of actions produced in the context of object-related activities and social routines as communicative gestures. Once this happens, they may begin to develop relatively large repertoires of gestures and make enhanced use of gesture to compensate for poor productive language. (Volterra et al. 2005, p. 32)

These are "old" action-actions, not co-equal participants with encoded language that a GP demands; in fact, such gestures are substitutes and doubly

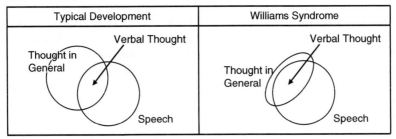

Figure 8.12 Representations in the manner of Vygotsky (1987) of the relationship between thought, speech and verbal thought, adapted for Williams syndrome children.

so—not only for deficient language, but also for deficient gestures (see Chan and Iacono 2001).

Williams syndrome (WS) is often pictured as the inverse of Down's syndrome. WS children also have cognitive deficits, IQs in the 50–70 range, yet seem to have greater language skills than the cognitive deficits would allow. They are also highly engaged socially, musical and lively.

WS poses an interesting challenge to the GP theory: how can language be orchestrated without thought? The sparing of language has made WS the poster child of purported language modules (see Brock 2007 for a critical review). From a non-modular GP perspective, however, another interpretation is possible. Although it may seem perverse to say that better-than-predicted language is a "disorder," I shall say just this. My argument refers to how this linguistic superiority is achieved. Social engagement is a key to language as well. It shows the social resonance of Mead's Loop. In WS, *good language arises from GP disruption*, a disconnect between the social framing of thinking-for-speaking in Mead's Loop, of which WS speakers are clearly capable, and what Vygotsky (1987) termed "pure thought," of which they are deficient. WS speakers can connect idea units to the social context of speaking via what has been termed "hypersociability" (Bellugi et al. 1999). This can be likened to the mimicry we have seen at several places (recall TOT mimicry—loss of speech in this case, but showing the power of mimicry). They can create *joint GPs* with interlocutors, as do unimpaired speakers (Figure 5.4), but are unable to shape thinking outside this social interaction, and this is their disorder, paradoxically creating superior language for their IQs.

For the project of this chapter, the aspect of gesture-orchestrated speech WS reveals is this social aspect. Vygotsky visualized thought and speech as overlapping circles, one for thought, one for speech, and inner speech the overlap (Figure 8.12); the GP is a theory analyzing this overlap, and what we propose for WS is truncation or inaccessibility of the thought circle. An important factor in this flattening could be a WS weakness at global organization in the visual domain (Bellugi et al. 1999). If WS are unable to create visual global wholes they would gain little from the global-synthetic imagery created in their socially merged GPs as part of the speaking process. The result leaves little room for the GP to shape cognition.

Childhood autism. Elena Levy (2007, 2008; Levy and Fowler 2005) has developed a method by which to observe the emergence of spoken discourse cohesion over short intervals—short, but extended enough to permit observation of the emergence. A child is shown a classic film, *The Red Balloon*, and tells the story to a listener. Specific to the method is that the child tells the story repeatedly, over several days (sometimes on the same day), to the same or different listeners. In this way, changes, which typically are consolidations that enhance cohesion, can be tracked as they emerge. While many differences from typically developing children are found in childhood autism, following Levy, I focus on the catchment and fields of equivalents.

In the first attempts at retelling by one ten-year-old ("D") speech was fragmented and gestures few. From this fractured starting point, fully encoded descriptions gradually emerged and—equally striking—also gestures that look typical for such speech. GPs apparently arose in appropriate fields of equivalents and with them coherence became possible by way of catchments. An example analyzed in detail by Levy involves two catchments at early points in the child's narrative attempts—flying gestures, and holding gestures—that resulted eventually, after several retellings, in a correctly narrated sequence of events (i.e., corresponding to the film's sequence). As fields of equivalents, we can see in these catchments how the narrative order was finally straightened out. Initially, the boy described flying with balloons, then, immediately following, holding onto the balloons, and finally the sequence in Table 8.2 (compiled from Levy 2008, p. 23).

Although starting with an out-of-sequence airborne reference, the child had the holding gesture in the correct narrative order (holding first). The GP at this point would be something like that suggested in the table: differentiating what could happen while the boy was holding—floating. The child continued with the correct sequence: holding followed by flying. Achieving temporal coherence stemmed from catchments and the boy's realization, eventually, that the holding and flying catchments interrelate, one continuing what the other began. This is a kind of imagery-enactment version of

Table 8.2 Speech, gesture and estimated fields of equivalents in autistic boy's narration.

Narrative order	Speech	Gesture	Field of Equivalents and GPs something like:
1	he floated	start of holding gesture	What Happened While Holding: floating
2	he hanged on tight	continuation of holding gesture	Still What Happened While Holding: holding tight
3	[no speech]	flying gesture	The Thing That Happened: flying

Based on Levy (2008).

the logical relationship of an enabling cause/resultant, which the boy could achieve in this form even if not with a clear vision of the logical connections themselves.

8.4.3   Stammer

Mayberry and Jaques (2000) discovered an incompatibility of gesture and clinical stammering. The onset of a gesture prevented stammering onset, and if a gesture was in progress the onset of stammering would immediately stop the gesture.

Stammering may come from the nature of the GP. I draw upon data from an experiment by Richard Mowery and William Pagliuca, at the University of Ottawa, that I was a part of in the late 1980s (described as "DAF Experiment 2" in McNeill 1992; none of us clinical stammerers). "DAF" stands for delayed auditory feedback—a crucial feature of the experiment. In DAF, the subject hears his own speech played back after a short delay. The delays in the experiment varied from one-tenth up to several full seconds. DAF often causes speech to slow down and even stop. The experience is to wait for the speech "to catch up," which it never does. This slowdown and interruption are features of clinically stammered speech (whether with a waiting experience I cannot say).

But another stammer-like effect appeared in this experiment. Speech continued without interruption but was severely disrupted and disengaged from gesture. The disruption was in the form of multiple repetitions, a stammer-like feature. The amount of speech correlated with the amount of delay. At the shortest delays repetitions were phonetic ("t-t-t-t-take" etc.); at slightly longer delays syllables ("ta-ta-ta-take" etc.); at the longest words and even phrases ("take the cake-take the cake-take the cake and cut it"). Given this observation, we can hypothesize that a stammerer experiences something like a self-created DAF. The repetitions moreover became wildly disconnected with co-expressive speech. This suggests that stammerers, if this models them correctly, may also experience breakdowns of gesture-orchestrated speech, which is the second half of Mayberry and Jacques's finding, the onset of stammering stopping an ongoing gesture. Individual stammerers may differ in the level they recycle, either characteristically or episodically producing different forms of stammer—phones, syllables, words, phrases, etc.

In the middle range of delays, not far from the 300ms interval during which Levelt et al. (1999) concluded the process of normal speech runs ballistically and cannot be altered, the repetitions in the Ottawa experiment took on the quality of clinical stammering. If in this range speech is self-mimicked mimicry can open another 300ms capsule before the current one closes just in time to seal the process off again, and so stammering starts.[3]

8.4.4   Conclusions

The five language disorders show different sides of the GP.

The aphasias preserve and lose different aspects of the GP. Broca's keeps the psychological predicate and loses unpacking. Wernicke's preserves unpacking but garbles psychological predicates. As often noted, the two aphasias are mirror images, but now we see why this is so in a new light, relating to gesture–speech unity.

Down's syndrome speakers may not experience thinking-for-speaking in anything like the form it is encountered by normal speakers. The elements in GPs are redundant, there is little scope for cognitive movement, and the contexts comparably narrow.

Williams speakers unusually seem to have half the normal complement of thinking-for-speaking, missing the other half. Their language reveals the power of mimicry and social/public references of Mead's Loop.

Autism reveals an imbalance of enactment and catchment formation that, with repetition, can be overcome. In contrast to the aphasic, once balance is reached, speech and discourse approach something like normalcy.

Stammerers have repetitive unpacking, an interruption of gesture-orchestrated speech, and possibly a self-inflicted DAF—all features arising from the nature of the GP itself.

---

[3] Susan Duncan alerted me to the relevance of the 300ms constant.

8.5   Specific memory

8.5.1   A new form of memory

Memory obviously permeates language performance. Speech requires it, but memory for gesture-orchestrated speech may not be the usual short-term memory for outside events. Gesture-orchestrated speech appears to use a memory *tied to one's own speech*. Neurological insults spare it the impairments the usual memory suffers. We experience it every moment we speak. It is the vessel of simultaneous awareness, opening and closing with it, and the succession of words in sequential awareness takes place within its span. It carries feeling and the cohort of inhabited *langue* constructions to be winnowed for unpacking. It is complex yet extremely fast within its narrow one- to two-second window and seems adapted to gesture-orchestrated speech. When simultaneous awareness ends (the gesture reaching the end of its retraction, the hand if necessary creeping forward until its closure), the memory window slams shut and information moves into a more permanent state. This abrupt, non-continuous change is a key feature of the specific memory. Without this quick-to-change system, thinking in terms of language could not have evolved into Mead's Loop; the action orchestration it provides would have clogged and not been naturally selected. The state change at the end of the cycle is an active step, part of the continuation of the discourse. The GP then loses cohesion and identity. The pieces do not disappear and may be swept up into the next GP, for example, as part of the next field of equivalents. The "natural experiment" (Chapter 2) showed this kind of recycling.

Built into this linguistic memory are thus the workings of the GP. The truism that memory is better in context misses the deeper fact that the special linguistic memory *does not exist outside a context*. It includes a psychological predicate differentiating the context; context is intrinsic to it, it does not form without it. The usual decontextualized memory tests do not tap it at all.

The special memory is far from a passive receptacle. It is dynamic, as we see in its adjustments to action, speech and perspective, yet it is rapid, effortless and mostly free of error, and has the hallmarks of a special memory evolved as part of language.

Here in outline is how it is proposed to operate:

1 It is discrete, not gradual.
2 It has capacity to cover the GP and the field of equivalents it differentiates, and winnowing a cohort of constructions and words in unpacking.
3 It is marked at the end of the retraction phase whereupon it empties, these contents passing into some other form.

A provocative approach in this domain that helps to understand the specific linguistic memory was launched by Cowan (2001) and continued by Oberauer

(2005). The essence of their approach is that there is but one memory, a long-term storehouse, which is functionally differentiated into working memory and within working memory into a focus of awareness. It is a view that contrasts to the modular separations proposed by Baddeley and Hitch (1974), for whom working memory is a product of separate processors, an executive, a phonological loop and so forth. I see no natural mapping of memory so described onto the dual semiotic of language conceived dynamically. Cowan's non-modular, function-based approach, on the other hand, especially as particularized by Oberauer, adapts well to the GP and Wundt awarenesses. The GP adds simultaneous awareness to memory and the focus of successive awareness within it. Oberauer diagrams his "embedded-component model of working memory" as a net (illustration thanks to Klaus Oberauer, personal communication):

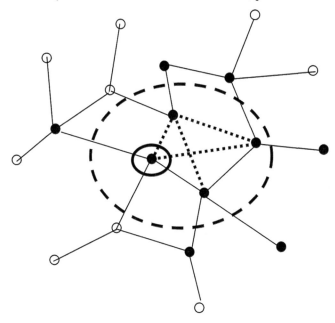

This net can be aligned with GP properties. The formation of a gesture–speech unit during gesture-orchestrated speech would produce:

- Large dotted oval = gesture imagery (an inhabited "new" gesture-action unit).
- Small solid oval = the GP surfacing in successive awareness.
- Black nodes = field of meaningful equivalents.
- Black node links = field of meaningful equivalents structured to make the GP possible.
- White nodes = potential next field of equivalents or GPs (depending on speaker intentions, dialog and environment factors).

Memory researchers are classically interested in capacity questions whereas our interest is in the evolution of the dual semiotic of language, and how memory adapted to it; how, in terms of Oberauer's diagram, the emergence of linguistic dynamism influenced what is "white" and "black," where the large and small ovals appear and the black nodes link to fields of meaningful equivalents.

8.5.2   Applying the new memory

Example 1: speech errors A cohort will often have more than one construction. Thus the possibility of error arises. Within constructions, word errors also occur. Construction error involves simultaneous awareness, word error successive. Spoonerisms are of the successive type ("the queer old dean" for "the dear old queen," or "you hissed all my mystery lectures" for "you missed all my history lectures"). The same applies on various levels in examples collected by Fromkin (1973)—"Rosa always date shranks" [Rosa always dates shrinks"—disordering past tense], "muddle" [blend of "mud" and "puddle"]. "Omnipicent" is a kind of hybrid of the simultaneous and successive: two words from the same equivalence class in simultaneous awareness blending rather than one surviving in successive awareness ("omnipotent" and "omniscient").

Errors with constructions entirely in simultaneous awareness also occur. An instance is the "nurturing" example (Dray and McNeill 1990), where a cohort winnowed to a wrong construction, which the speaker rejects:

(α) The fact [that she's ...] [she's nu- uh]
(β) [... she's somehow ... she's] [done this nurtur] [ing] [thing and here you]

Brackets are the winnowing gestures—repeated spatial metaphors of rearrangement. The speaker was describing the nurturing actions of a third party that she found cloying and intrusive, and this feeling of uselessness led her into a cohort. The problem was a mismatch at (α) of the transitive construction to the field of meaningful equivalents. Transitivity means, roughly, that the action has a direct transformative impact via nurturing on the recipient of the action. However, this meaning distorted the idea the speaker wanted to convey—something that would differentiate a field of meaningful equivalents more like *her otiose acts*. Further winnowing led to the slight but successful updating in (β) that separated effect from act.

Example 2: gesture improves memory A discovery by Goldin-Meadow et al. (2001), that **gestures enhance memory**, that one's memory for something improves if you talk about something else and perform gestures as you do, shows an important property of the specific linguist memory, namely, that *it opens and closes with a gesture*. It corresponds to one cycle in the gesture-orchestration of speech. In the experiment, speakers described one thing while holding in memory incidental, unrelated information. More of the incidental information was recalled in a later test if the speaker had gestured while talking about the other topic. If linguistic memory changes state when the window closes at the end of the gesture phrase, then information can be lost and the incidental information in general purpose memory benefits. When there is no gesture, memory undergoes less or no state change, either because the sentence has low communicative dynamism or because no end of a gesture phrase is reached, and incidental information receives less benefit. Since incidental information is not in a GP-cycle it does not take part in this state change. So, paradoxically, it is not lost and more incidental information is retained when there is a gesture than when there is not, and this is the Goldin-Meadow et al. finding.

The experiment makes clear, moreover, that the explanation is because linguistic memory promptly empties when the gesture finishes and not because of low communicative dynamism. The experiment compared spontaneous non-gestures, those that likely occurred with minimal communicative dynamism, to imposed non-gestures, which would be distributed randomly with respect to communicative dynamism, and found the same reductions of incidental memory. So the effect is uncorrelated with communicative dynamism, which leaves discrete forgetting of linguistic memory at the end of the temporal window as the main factor sparing incidental information.

In addition, Cook et al. (2010) found that making a gesture along with speech is followed by better memory for the information encoded in the speech, compared to speech where no gesture occurred. Here the benefit was for direct information, not incidental information. Again, gestures were suppressed either by instruction or spontaneously, and memory was poorer in both cases. As earlier, this suggests the effect was not due to low communicative dynamism information when gestures were absent. Enhanced memory for direct information also could be the work of the specific gesture–speech memory. The gesture, when present, opens the memory and, more to the point, closes it when the gesture ends. Part of closing it is to shift the information to a different, more permanent store. Hence it is better recalled at a later time. No gesture in contrast, as described earlier, does not open the specific memory (or opens it less often or less strongly). The new point is that the benefit of the transfer to a more permanent memory also is weakened; hence recall is lessened. Thus both incidental and focal information are affected by the specific memory's closure when a gesture ends.

The two experiments, covering respectively incidental and direct information, show gestures enhancing memory, as Goldin-Meadow and colleagues have long argued. Our conclusion adds that gesture enhancement is a natural consequence of a specific linguistic memory active during gesture-orchestrated speech.

Example 3: aphasia Conceivably, the two aphasias involve in part different impairments of a specific gesture-orchestrated speech memory. Wernicke's loss is of simultaneous awareness with successive spared: having successive awareness without simultaneous the *memory fails to close*. Fluency with unbridled content flow could result. Broca's loss is of successive awareness with simultaneous spared: *the memory closes with the GP but unpacking is incomplete*. Gesture–speech unity with disfluency results. A catchment builds simultaneous awareness continuity and this can forestall the Broca's too-early closure, as we have seen.

Example 4: second language A step to mastery of a new language would be when the student can use the linguistic memory, which she has for L1, now in L2. Thinking in a new language is classically said to be a hallmark of mastery. This seems to require the simultaneous awareness of the sentence in L2. However, there are subtleties. Successive awareness is equally part of thinking, since the GP is also anchored there, not to mention the unpacking, which has its own role in thinking but may have a different learning time-course. Simultaneous memory is filled with GPs, the constructions that unpack them and the *langue*-feelings that recover them. The result is a sense of inhabiting the new language. Once inhabitance is reached the language in some sense has been "mastered." Successive memory, however, may be incomplete. It depends on vocabulary size and appropriateness. Immersion may do the trick here. It seems that high levels of "mastery" of simultaneous and successive awareness are needed as well to produce the mutual construction-word assistance the "it down" example demonstrated. Finally, with good simultaneous awareness and inhabitance but blocked successive awareness, a sense of a bottleneck arises where the speaker knows what to say but frustratingly not how to say it. "Mastery" in any case is a vague concept, the two awarenesses coming to L2 on their own time scales with their own different aspects of the new language, their interactions yielding a host of mastery points.

8.6   Another look at the brain link

1   The brain must be able to combine motor systems—manual and vocal/oral—in a systematic, *meaning-controlled* way.
2   There must be a convergence of two cognitive modes—visuospatial and linguistic—and a locus where they converge in a final motor sequence. Broca's Area is a logical candidate for this place. It has the further advantage of orchestrating actions that can be realized both manually and within the oral-vocal tract. MacNeilage (2008) relates speech to cyclical open–close

patterns of the mandible, and proposes that speech could have evolved out of ingestive motor control.

3 More than Broca's and Wernicke's Areas support language—there is also the right hemisphere and interactions between the right and left hemispheres, as well as possibly the prefrontal cortex.

4 Wernicke's Area serves more than comprehension—it also provides categorization, might initiate imagery and might also shape it.

5 Imagery arises in the right hemisphere and needs Wernicke-originated categorizations to form GPs. Categorial content triggers and/or shapes the imagery in the right hemisphere.

6 The GP is unpacked in Broca's Area. GPs may take form in the right hemisphere but they are dependent on multiple areas across the brain (frontal, posterior left, as well as right and anterior left).

7 The frontal area of the brain establishes fields of oppositions and differentiates psychological predicates. This functionality implies access to the context of thinking and speaking in the right and left hemispheres by the frontal area and feedback from the frontal area to these other brain areas.

8 Catchments and GPs specifically are shaped under multiple influences—from Wernicke's Area, the right hemisphere, and the frontal area—and take form in the right hemisphere.

Throughout the model, information from the posterior left hemisphere, the right hemisphere and the prefrontal cortex converge and synthesize in the frontal left hemisphere motor areas of the brain—Broca's Area and the adjacent premotor areas. This circuit could be composed of many smaller circuits—"localized operations [that] in themselves do not constitute an observable behavior … [but] form part of the neural 'computations' that, linked together in complex neural circuits, are manifested in behaviors" (Lieberman 2002, p. 39).

Broca's Area in all this is the unique point of (a) convergence and (b) orchestration of manual and vocal actions guided by GPs and semantically framed language forms. The Mead's Loop evolutionary model is specifically aimed at explaining orchestration in this brain area and how it co-opted language and thought.

Part III

The last page[*]

[*] Thanks to Nobuko McNeill for this title.

9 Why we gesture (again)

We have found several answers to our question, why do we gesture? Speech is inseparable from gesture. Gesture orchestrates speech. For an individual speaker, embedded in context, his/her cognitive Being is a gesture–speech unity. Language is dynamic through a dialectic with gesture, and takes on life with it. Behind this dialectic, gesture has been in language at the start. At the origin, language was a unity of gesture and speech. If for some reason it is suppressed, the inner gesture, imagery in actional form, remains and leaks out though some other part of the body. Gesture takes Humboldt's *Ergon*—language viewed as structure—and as *Energeia*—language as an "embodied moment of meaning" (quoting Glick 1983) and fuses them. The effects are felt far beyond language and into every corner of life. I was tempted to embark on a rant against the computerization of Being, how it rests on assumptions this book disputes, but the topic belongs to another day. If ever I have the time, energy and inclination, I may try to write on it; but for now, we have reached the last page.

References

Abrahamsen, A., Cavallo, M.M. and McCluer, J.A. 1985. "Is the sign advantage a robust phenomenon? From gesture to language in two modalities." *Merrill-Palmer Quarterly* 31: 177–209.

Acredolo, L.P. and Goodwyn, S.W. 1990. "Sign language in babies: the significance of symbolic gesturing for understanding language development." In R. Vasta, (ed.), *Annals of Child Development, Vol. 7*, pp. 1–42. London: Jessica Kingsley Publishers.

Arbib, M. 2005. "From monkey-like action recognition to human language: an evolutionary framework for neurolinguistics." *Behavioral and Brain Sciences*, 28: 105–124.

2012. *How the Brain Got Language: The Mirror System Hypothesis*. Oxford: Oxford University Press.

Armstrong, D., Stokoe, W.F. and Wilcox, S.E. 1995. *Gesture and the Nature of Language*. Cambridge: Cambridge University Press.

Atkinson, Q.D. 2011. "Phonemic diversity supports a serial founder effect model of language expansion from Africa." *Science* 332: 346–349.

Baddeley, A. and Hitch, G.J. 1974. "Working memory." In G. Bower (ed.), *Recent Advances in Learning and Motivation, Vol. VIII*, pp. 49–89. New York: Academic Press.

Bakhtin, M.M. 1981. *The Dialogic Imagination*, ed. M. Holquist, trans. C. Emerson and M. Holquist, trans. Austin, TX: University of Texas Press.

Bannard, C., Lieven, E. and Tomasello, M. 2009. "Evaluating constructivist theory via Bayesian modeling of children's early grammatical development." Abstract posted on the International Cognitive Linguistics Conference website, accessed 30 March 2009 (since removed). See, Bannard, C., Lieven, E. and Tomasello, M. 2009. "Modeling children's early grammatical knowledge." *PNAS* 106: 17284–17289, for a published version, but lacking the pithy quote of the abstract.

Bates, E. and Dick, F. 2002. "Language, gesture and the developing brain." In B.J. Casey and Y. Munakata (eds.). Special issue: converging method approach to the study of developmental science. *Developmental Psychobiology* 40: 293–310.

Bellugi, U., Lichtenberger, L. Mills, D. Galaburda, A. and Korenberg, J. R. 1999. "Bridging cognition, the brain and molecular genetics: evidence from Williams syndrome." *Trends in Neuroscience* 22: 197–207.

Bickerton, D. 1990. *Language and Species*. Chicago: University of Chicago Press.

Blumenthal, Arthur (ed.). 1970. *Language and Psychology: Historical Aspects of Psycholinguistics*. New York: John Wiley and Sons Ltd.

Boesch, C. and Tomasello, M. 1998. "Chimpanzee and human cultures." *Current Anthropology* 39: 591–604.

Bolens, G. 2012. *The Style of Gestures: Embodiment and Cognition in Literary Narrative*. Baltimore: John Hopkins University Press.

Braine, M.D.S. 1963. "The ontogeny of English phrase structure: the first phase." *Language* 39: 1–13.

Bressem, J. 2010. *Pounding the Verbal Utterance: Forms and Functions of Beats*. International Society of Gesture Studies, Conference Talk, Frankfurt/Oder, Germany.

Bressem, J., Ladewig, S.H. and Müller, C. 2015. "Ways of expressing action in multi-modal narrations—the semiotic complexity of character viewpoint depictions. In A. Hübl and M. Steinbach (eds.), *Linguistic Foundations of Narration in Spoken and Sign Languages*. Amsterdam and Philadelphia: Benjamins.

Brock, J. 2007. "Language abilities in Williams syndrome: a critical review." *Development and Psychopathology* 19: 97–127.

Browman, C.P. and Goldstein, L. 1990."Tiers in articulatory phonology, with some implications for casual speech." In J. Kingston and M.E. Beckman (eds.), *Papers in Laboratory Phonology I: Between the Grammar and Physics of Speech*, pp. 341–376. Cambridge: Cambridge University Press.

Brown, R. and Lenneberg, E. 1954. "A study in language and cognition." *Journal of Abnormal and Social Psychology* 49: 454–462.

Brown, T.A. 2010. "Stranger from Siberia." *Nature* 464: 838.

Brown, P. and Levinson, S. 1990. *Politeness: Some Universals in Language Usage*. Cambridge: Cambridge University Press.

Bühler, K. 1982. "The deictic field of language and deictic words." In R. Jarvella and W. Klein (eds.), *Speech, Place, and Action*, pp. 9–30. New York: Wiley.

Butcher, C. and Goldin-Meadow, S. 2000. "Gesture and the transition from one- to two-word speech: when hand and mouth come together." In D. McNeill (ed.), *Language and Gesture*, pp. 235–257. Cambridge: Cambridge University Press.

Chan, J.B. and Iacono, T. 2001. "Gesture and word production in children with Down Syndrome." *AAC Augmentative and Attentive Communication*. 17: 73–87.

Chase, W.G. and Eriksson, K.A. 1981. "Skilled memory." In J.R. Anderson (ed.), *Cognitive Skills and Their Acquisition*, pp. 227–249. Hillsdale, NJ: Erlbaum.

Clark, A. 1997. *Being There: Putting Brain, Body and World Together Again*. Cambridge, MA: MIT Press.

Cohen, A.A. 1977. "The communicative function of hand illustrators." *Journal of Communication*, 27: 54–63.

Cole, J. 1995. *Pride and a Daily Marathon*. Cambridge, MA: MIT Press.

Cook, S.W., Yip, T.K. and Goldin-Meadow, S. 2010. Gesturing makes memories that last. *Journal of Memory and Language* 63: 465–475.

Corballis, M.C. 2002. *From Hand to Mouth: The Origins of Language*. Cambridge, MA: Harvard University Press.

2011. *The Recursive Mind: The Origin of Human Language, Thought, and Civilization*. Princeton, NJ: Princeton University Press.

2014. The word according to Adam: the role of gesture in language evolution. In M. Seyfeddinipur and M. Gullberg (eds.), *From Gesture in Conversation to Visible Action as Utterance*, pp. 177–197. Amsterdam and Philadelphia: Benjamins.

Cowan, N. 2001. "The magical number 4 in short-term memory: A reconsideration of mental storage capacity." *Behavioral and Brain Sciences* 24: 87–185.

Daniels, P.T. and Bright, W. 1996. *The World's Writing Systems*. Oxford: Oxford University Press.

Dennett, D.T. 1991. *Consciousness Explained*. Boston: Little, Brown & Company.

de Ruiter, J. 2000. "The production of gesture and speech. In D. McNeill (ed.), *Language and Gesture*, pp. 285–311. Cambridge: Cambridge University Press.

Diffloth, G. 1994. "i: *big* a: *small*." In L. Hinton, J. Nichols and J.J. Ohala (eds.), *Sound Symbolism*, pp. 107–114. Cambridge: Cambridge University Press.

Diamond, A. 2002. "Normal development of prefrontal cortex from birth to young adulthood: cognitive functions, anatomy, and biochemistry." In D.T. Stuss and R.T. Knight (eds.), *Principles of Frontal Lobe Function*, pp. 466–503. Oxford: Oxford University Press.

Donald, M. 1991. *Origins of the Modern Mind: Three Stages in the Evolution of Culture and Cognition*. Cambridge, MA: Harvard University Press.

Dray, N. and McNeill, D. 1990. "Gestures during discourse: the contextual structuring of thought," in S.L. Tsohatzidis (ed.). *Meanings and Prototypes: Studies in Linguistic Categorization*, pp. 465–487. London and New York: Routledge.

Dreyfus, H. 1994. *Being-in-the-World: A Commentary on Heidegger's Being and Time, Division I*. Cambridge, MA: MIT Press.

Dunbar, R. 1996. *Grooming, Gossip, and the Evolution of Language*. Cambridge, MA: Harvard University Press.

Duncan, S. 2005. "Gesture in signing: a case study in Taiwan Sign Language." *Language and Linguistics* 6: 279–318.

Duncan, S. and Fiske, D.W. 1977. *Face-To-Face Interaction: Research, Methods, and Theory*. Hillsdale, NJ: Erlbaum.

Dunn, M., Greenhill, S.J., Levinson, S.C. and Gray, R.D. 2011. "Evolved structure of language shows lineage-specific trends in word-order universals." *Nature*, www.nature.com/journal/vaop/ncurrent/full/nature09923.html (accessed April 19, 2011).

Duranti, A. and Goodwin, C. 1992. *Rethinking Context: Language as an Interactive Phenomenon*. Cambridge: Cambridge University Press.

Emmorey, K., Borinstein, H.B. and Thompson, R. 2005. "Bimodal bilingualism: code-blending between spoken English and American Sign Language." In J. Cohen, K.T. McAlister, K. Rolstad and J. MacSwan (eds.). *Proceedings of the 4th International Symposium on Bilingualism*, pp. 663–673. Somerville, MA: Cascadilla Press.

Enfield, N.J. 2001. "Lip-pointing: a discussion of form and function with reference to data from Laos." *Gesture* 1: 185–211.

Engle, R.A. 2000. *Toward a Theory of Multimodal Communication: Combining Speech, Gestures, Diagrams, and Demonstrations in Instructional Explanations*. Unpublished PhD dissertation, Stanford University.

Evans, P.D., Gilbert, S.L., Mekel-Bobrow, N., Vallender, E.J., Anderson, J.R., Vaez-Azizi, L.M., Tishkoff, S.A., Hudson, R.R. and Lahn, B.T. 2005. "Microcephalin, a gene regulating brain size, continues to evolve adaptively in humans." *Science* 309: 1717–1720.

Federmeier, K.D. and Kutas, M. 1999. "Right words and left words: electrophysio-logical evidence for hemispheric differences in meaning processing." *Cognitive Brain Research* 8: 373–392.

Fetz, E.E. 2007. "Volitional control of neural activity: Implications for brain-computer interfaces." *The Journal of Physiology* 579: 571–579.

Fillmore, C., Kay, P. and O'Connor, C. 1988. Regularity and idiomaticity in grammati-cal constructions: the case of let alone. *Language* 64: 501–538.

Firbas, J. 1971. "On the concept of communicative dynamism in the theory of func-tional sentence perspective." *Philologica Pragensia* 8, 135–144.

Fodor, J.A. 1983. *Modularity of Mind: An Essay on Faculty Psychology*. Cambridge, MA: MIT Press.

Forrester, M. 2008. "The emergence of self-repain: a case study of one child during the preschool years." *Research on Language and Social Interaction* 41: 97–126.
    2014. *Early Social Interaction: A Case Comparison of Developmental Pragmatics and Psychoanalytic Theory*. Cambridge: Cambridge University Press.

Freyd, J. 1983. "Shareability: the social psychology of epistemology." *Cognitive Science* 7: 191–210.

Fromkin, V.A. 1973. *Speech Errors as Linguistic Evidence*. The Hague: Mouton.

Furuyama, N. 2000. "Gestural interactions between the instructor and the learner in origami instruction." In D. McNeill (ed.), *Language and Gesture*, pp. 99–117. Cambridge: Cambridge University Press.

Furuyama, N. and Sekine, K. 2007. "Forgetful or strategic? The mystery of the sys-tematic avoidance of reference in the cartoon story narrative." In S.D. Duncan, J. Cassell and E.T. Levy (eds.), *Gesture and the Dynamic Dimension of Language*, pp. 75–81. Amsterdam and Philadelphia: Benjamins.

Gallagher, S. 2005. *How the Body Shapes the Mind*. Oxford: Oxford University Press.

Gelb, A. and Goldstein, K. 1925. "Über Farbennamenamnesie." *Psychologische Forschung* 6: 127–186.

Gentilucci, M. and Dalla Volta, R. 2007. "The motor system and the relationship between speech and gesture." *Gesture* 7: 159–177.

Gigerenzer, G. and Goldstein, D.G. 1996. "Mind as computer: birth of a metaphor." *Creativity Research* 9: 131–144.

Gill, S. 2007. "Entrainment and musicality in the human system interface." *AI & Society*. 21: 567–605.

Givón, T. 1985. "Iconicity, isomorphism and non-arbitrary coding in syntax." In J. Haiman (ed.). *Iconicity in Syntax*, pp. 187–219. Amsterdam and Philadelphia: Benjamins.

Glick, J. 1983. "Piaget, Vygotsky, and Werner." In S. Wapner and B. Kaplan (eds.), *Toward a Holistic Developmental Psychology*, pp. 35–52. Hillsdale, NJ: Erlbaum.

Goldberg, A. 1995. *Constructions: A Construction Approach to Argument Structure*. Chicago: University of Chicago Press.

Goldin-Meadow, S. 2003a. *The Resilience of Language: What Gesture Creation in Deaf Children Can Tell Us About How All Children Learn Language*. New York: Psychology Press.
    2003b. *Hearing Gesture: How Our Hands Help Us Think*. Cambridge, MA: Harvard University Press.

Goldin-Meadow, S. and Butcher, C. 2003. "Pointing toward two-word speech in young children." In S. Kita (ed.), *Pointing: Where Language, Culture, and Cognition Meet*, pp. 85–107. Hillsdale, NJ: Erlbaum.

Goldin-Meadow, S., McNeill, D. and Singleton, J. 1996. "Silence is liberating: removing the handcuffs on grammatical expression in the manual modality." *Psychological Review* 103: 34–55.

Goldin-Meadow, S., Nusbaum, H., Kelley, S.D. and Wagner, S. 2001. "Explaining math: gesturing lightens the load." *Psychological Science* 12: 516–522.

Goren-Inbar, N., Alperson, N., Kislev, M.E., Simchoni, O., Melamed, Y., Ben-Nun, A. and Werker, E. 2004. "Evidence of hominid control of fire at Gesher Benot Ya'aqov, Israel." *Science* 304: 725–727.

Greenberg, J.H. 1970. *The Languages of Africa*. The Hague: Mouton.

Glucksberg, S. and Keysar, B. 1990 "Understanding metaphorical comparisons: beyond similarity," *Psychological Review* 97: 3–18.

Gullberg, M. 2013. "So you think gestures are compensatory? Reflections based on child and adult learner data." In A.F. Mattsson and C. Norrby (eds.), *Language Acquisition and Use in Multilingual Contexts: Theory and Practice*, pp. 39–49. Lund: Travaux de l'Institut de linguistique de Lund 52.

Gullberg, M., Hendricks, H. and Hickmann, M. 2008."Learning to talk and gesture about motion in French." *First Language* 28: 200–236.

Hale, K. 1983. "Warlpiri and the grammar of non-configurational languages." *Natural Language and Linguistic Theory* 1: 5–47.

Hauser, M., Chomsky, N. and Fitch, W.T. 2002. "The language faculty: what is it, who has it, and how did it evolve?" *Science* 298: 1569–1579.

Haviland, J. 2013. "Where did 'where do nouns come from?' come from?" *Gesture* 13: 245–252.

Herder J.G. 1986 [1772]. *Essay on the Origin of Language*. J.H. Moran and A. Gode (trans.). Chicago: University of Chicago Press.

Hickmann, M., Hendricks, H. and Gullberg, M. 2011. "Developmental perspectives on the expression of motion in speech and gesture: a comparison of French and English." *Language, Interaction & Acquisition* 2: 129–156.

Hickok, G. 2009. "Eight problems for the mirror neuron theory of action understanding in monkeys and humans." *Journal of Cognitive Neuroscience* 21: 1229–1243.

Hoetjes, M., Krahmer, E. and Swerts, M. 2015. "On what happens in gesture when communication is unsuccessful." *Speech Communication* 72: 160–175.

Hopkins, W.D. and Cantero, M. 2003. "From hand to mouth in the evolution of language: the influence of vocal behavior on lateralized hand use in manual gestures by chimpanzees (Pan troglodytes)." *Developmental Science* 6: 55–61.

Hrdy, S.B. 2009. *Mothers and Others: The Evolutionary Origins of Mutual Understanding*. Cambridge, MA: Harvard University Press.

Humboldt, W. 1999. *On Language*. Trans. P. Heath, ed. M. Losonsky. Cambridge: Cambridge University Press.

Hurley, S. 1998. *Consciousness in Action*. Cambridge, MA: Harvard University Press.

Huttenlocher, P.R. and Dabholkar, A.S. 1997. "Regional differences in synaptogenesis in human cerebral cortex." *Journal of Comparative Neurology* 387: 167–178.

Iverson, J.M., Longobardi, E. and Caselli, M.C. 2003. "Relationship between gestures and words in children with Down's syndrome and typically developing children in the early stages of communicative development." *International Journal of Language and Communicative Disorders* 38: 179–197.

Jakobson, R. 1960. "Concluding statement: linguistics and poetics." In T. Sebeok (ed.), *Style in Language*, pp. 350–377. Cambridge, MA: MIT Press.

James, W. 1890. *Psychology (Vol. 1, Chap. IX)*. New York: Holt.

Karmiloff-Smith, A. 1979. "Micro- and macrodevelopmental changes in language acquisition and other representational systems." *Cognitive Science* 3: 91–118.

Kelly, S., Kravitz, C. and Hopkins, M. 2004. "Neural correlates of bimodal speech and gesture comprehension." *Brain and Language* 89: 253–260.

Kendon, A. 1980. "Gesticulation and speech: two aspects of the process of utterance." In Key, M.R. (ed.), *The Relationship of Verbal and Nonverbal Communication*, pp. 207–227. The Hague: Mouton and Co.

1988. *Sign Languages of Aboriginal Australia: Cultural, Semiotic and Communicative Perspectives*. Cambridge: Cambridge University Press.

1991. "Some considerations for a theory of language origins." *Man* 26: 199–221.

2004. *Gesture: Visible Action as Utterance*. Cambridge: Cambridge University Press.

2008. "Some reflections of the relationship between 'gesture' and 'sign.'" *Gesture* 8: 348–366.

2009. "Manual actions, speech and the nature of language." In D. Gambarara and A. Givigliano (eds.), *Origine e sviluppo del linguaggio, fra teoria e storia. Pubblicazioni della Società di Filosofia del Linguaggio*, pp. 19–33. Rome: Aracne editrice s.r.l.

2010. *Accounting for Forelimb Actions as a Component of Utterance: An Evolutionary Approach*. Plenary Lecture. International Society for Gesture Studies, Frankfurt/Oder, July 25.

Kimbara, I. 2006. "On gestural mimicry." *Gesture*, 6: 39–61.

Kita, S. 2000. "How representational gestures help speaking." In D. McNeill (ed.), *Language and Gesture*, pp. 162–185. Cambridge: Cambridge University Press.

Kita, S. and Özyürek, A. 2003. "What does cross-linguistic variation in semantic coordination of speech and gesture reveal? Evidence for an interface representation of spatial thinking and speaking." *Journal of Memory and Language* 48: 16–32.

Kopp, S., Bergmann, K. and Kahl, S. 2013. *A Spreading-Activation Model of the Semantic Coordination of Speech and Gesture*, 35th Annual Meeting of the Cognitive Science Society, Berlin, Germany.

Krause, J. et al. 2010. "The complete mitochondrial DNA genome of an unknown hominin from southern Siberia." *Nature* 464: 894–897.

Krauss, R., Chen, Y. and Gottesman, R.F. 2000. "Lexical gestures and lexical access: a process model," in D. McNeill (ed.), *Language and Gesture*, 261–283. Cambridge: Cambridge University Press.

Kröger, B.J., Birkholtz, P., Kaufmann, E. and Neuschaefer-Rube, C. 2010. "Beyond vocal tract actions: speech prosody and co-verbal gesturing in face-to-face communication." *Cognitive Processing* 11: 187–205.

Lakoff, G. and Johnson, M. 1980. *Metaphors We Live By*. Chicago: University of Chicago Press.

LeBaron, C. and Streeck, J. 2000. "Gestures, knowledge, and the world." In D. McNeill (ed.), *Language and Gesture*, pp. 118–138. Cambridge: Cambridge University Press.

Levitin, D.J. and Menon, V. 2003. "Musical structure is processed in 'language' areas of the brain: a possible role for Brodmann Area 47 in temporal coherence." *Neuroimage*. 20: 2142–2152.

Levelt, W.J.M. 1989. *Speaking: From Intention to Articulation*. Cambridge, MA: MIT Press/Bradford Books.

2013. *A History of Psycholinguistics: The Pre-Chomskyan Era*. Oxford: Oxford University Press.

Levelt, W.J.M., Richardson, G and La Heij, W. 1985. "Pointing and voicing in deictic expressions." *Journal of Memory and Language* 24: 133–164.

Levelt, W.J.M., Roelofs, A. and Meyer, A.S. 1999. "A theory of lexical access in speech production." *Behavioral and Brain Sciences* 22: 1–75.

Levinson, S. and Holler, J. 2014. "The origin of human multi-modal communication." *Philosophical Transactions of the Royal Society B* 369, 20130302.

Levinson, S. and Torreira, F. 2015. "Timing in turn-taking and its implication for processing models of language." *Frontiers in Psychology* 6: Article 731.

Levy, E.T. 2007. "The construction of temporally coherent narrative by an autistic adolescent: co-construction of speech, enactment and gesture." In S.D. Duncan, J. Cassell and E.T. Levy (eds.), *Gesture and the Dynamic Dimension of Language*, pp. 285–301. Amsterdam and Philadelphia: Benjamins.

    2008. *The Mediation of Coherent Discourse by Kinesthetic Reenactment: A Case Study of an Autistic Adolescent, Part II*. Manuscript. Department of Psychology, University of Connecticut at Stamford.

    2009–2010. "The mediation of coherent discourse by kinesthetic reenactment: a case study of an autistic adolescent, part II." *Imagination, Cognition and Personality* 29: 41–70.

    2011. *A New Study of the Co-Emergence of Speech and Gestures: Towards an Embodied Account of Early Narrative Development*. Poster presented at the 2011 Language Fest, University of Connecticut, Storrs, CT.

Levy, E.T. and Fowler, C.A. 2005. *How Autistic Children May Use Narrative Discourse to Scaffold Coherent Interpretations of Events: A Case Study*. Manuscript. Department of Psychology, University of Connecticut at Stamford.

Levy, E.T. and McNeill, D. 2015. *The Narrative Development of Young Children: Explorations in the Embodiment of Cohesion*. Cambridge: Cambridge University Press.

Levy J. and Trevarthen, C. 1976: "Metacontrol of hemispheric function in human split-brain patients." *Journal of Experimental Psychology (Human Performance & Perception)* 2: 299–312

Liebal, K., Bressem, J. and Müller, C. 2010. *Recurrent Forms and Contexts: Families of Gestures in Non-Human Primates*. Conference of the International Society of Gesture Studies, Panel 13: Towards a grammar of gesture: Evolution, brain and linguistic structures, Frankfurt/Oder, Germany.

Lieberman, P. 2002. "On the nature and evolution of the neural bases of human language." *Yearbook of Physical Anthropology* 45: 36–62.

Lieven, E., Salomo, D. and Tomasello, M. 2009. "Two-year-old children's production of multiword utterances: a usage-based analysis." *Cognitive Linguistics* 20: 461–507.

Lopez-Ozieblo, R. 2013. *Exchange on Why We Gesture*. Apply to author at Huddersfield University (UK), School of Linguistics and Modern Languages.

MacNeilage, P.F. 2008. *The Origin of Speech*. Oxford: Oxford University Press.

Mampe, B., Friederici, A.D., Christophe, A. and Wermke, K. 2009. "Newborns' cry melody is shaped by their native language." *Current Biology* 19: 1–4.

Marslen-Wilson, W.D. 1987. "Functional parallelism in spoken word-recognition." *Cognition* 25(1): 71–102.

Mayberry, R. and Jaques, J. 2000. "Gesture production during stuttered speech: insights into the nature of gesture-speech integration." In D. McNeill (ed.), *Language and Gesture*, pp. 199–214. Cambridge: Cambridge University Press.

McCullough, K.-E. 2003. *Gaze, Gesture, and the Construction of Meaning*. Unpublished manuscript. University of Chicago Gesture-Speech Lab.

McCullough, K.-E. 2005. *Using Gestures During Speaking: Self-Generating Indexical Fields*. Unpublished PhD dissertation, Department of Linguistics, University of Chicago.

McNeill, D. 1985. "So you think gestures are non-verbal?" *Psychological Review*. 92: 350–371.

1992. *Hand and Mind: What Gestures Reveal about Thought*. Chicago: University of Chicago Press.

2000. "Catchments and contexts: Non-modular factors in speech and gesture production." In D. McNeill (ed.), *Language and Gesture*, pp. 312–328. Cambridge: Cambridge University Press.

2003. "Aspects of aspect." *Gesture* 3: 1–17.

2005. *Gesture and Thought*. Chicago: University of Chicago Press.

2008. "Unexpected metaphors." In A. Cienki and C. Müller (eds.), *Metaphor and Gesture*, pp. 155–170. Amsterdam and Phliadelphia: Benjamins.

2009. "Imagery for speaking." In J. Guo, E. Lieven, N. Budwig, S. Ervin-Tripp, K. Nakamura and S. Özçaliskan (eds.), *Crosslinguistic Approaches to the Psychology of Language: Research in the Tradition of Dan Isaac Slobin*, pp. 517–530. London: Taylor & Francis.

2012. *How Language Began: Gesture and Speech in Human Evolution*. Cambridge: Cambridge University Press.

2014a. "The emblem as metaphor." In M. Seyfeddinipur and M. Gullberg (eds.), *From Gesture in Conversation to Visible Action as Utterance*, pp. 75–104. Amsterdam and Philadelphia: Benjamins.

2014b. "Gesture–speech unity: phylogenesis, ontogenesis, and microgenesis." *Language, Interaction & Acquisition* 5: 137–184.

McNeill, D. and Duncan, S.D. 2000. "Growth points in thinking for speaking," in D. McNeill (ed.), *Language and Gesture*, pp. 141–161. Cambridge: Cambridge University Press.

2010. "Gestures and growth points in three language disorders," in J. Guendouzi, F. Loncke and M.J. Williams (eds.), *The Handbook of Psycholinguistic and Cognitive Processes: Perspectives in Communication Disorders*, pp. 663–685. New York: Psychology Press/Taylor & Francis.

McNeill, D. and Levy, E. 1982. "Conceptual representations in language activity and gesture." In R.J. Jarvella and W. Klein (eds.), *Speech, Place, and Action*, pp. 271–296. Oxford: Wiley.

McNeill, D. and Pedelty, L. 1995. "Right brain and gesture." In K. Emmorey and J.S. Reilly (eds.), *Language, Gesture, and Space*, pp. 63–85. Hillsdale, NJ: Erlbaum.

McNeill, D., Duncan, S., Franklin, A., Goss, J., Kimbaba, I., Parrill, F., Chen, L., Harper, M. Quek, F., Rose, T. and Tuttle, R. 2010. "Mind-merging." In E. Morsella (ed.), *Expressing Oneself/Expressing One's Self: Communication, Language, Cognition, and Identity*, pp. 143–164. London: Taylor & Francis.

McNeill, R.B. 2010. *"Cum tacent, clamant*: the pragmatics of silence in Catullus." *Classical Philology* 105: 69–82.

Mead, G.H. 1974. *Mind, Self, and Society from the Standpoint of a Social Behaviorist.* Ed. and intro. C.W. Morris. Chicago: University of Chicago Press.

Merleau-Ponty, M. 2007 [1962]. *Phenomenology of Perception.* Trans. C. Smith. London and New York: Routledge.

Mithen, S. 2006. *The Singing Neanderthals: The Origins of Music, Language, Mind, and Body.* Cambridge, MA: Harvard University Press.

Morris, D., Collett, P., Marsh, P. and O'Shaughnessy, M. 1979. *Gestures: Their Origins and Distribution.* New York: Stein & Day.

Montaigne, M. 1958. *The Complete Essays of Montaigne.* Trans. D. Frame. Stanford, CA: Stanford University Press.

Müller, C. 2008. *Metaphors—Dead and Alive, Sleeping and Waking: A Dynamic View.* Chicago: University of Chicago Press.

2014. "Gesture as 'deliberate expressive movement.'" In M. Seyfeddinipur and M. Gullberg (eds.), *From Gesture in Conversation to Visible Action as Utterance*, pp. 127–151. Amsterdam and Philadelphia: Benjamins.

Müller, F.M. 1861. *The Theoretical Stage, and the Origin of Language. Lecture 9 from Lectures on the Science of Language.* Reprinted in R. Harris (ed.). 1996.*The Origin of Language.* Bristol: Thoemmes Press, pp. 7–41.

Morton, J., Marcus, S. and Frankis, C. 1976. "Perceptual centers." *Psychological Review* 83: 105–108.

Nobe, S. 1996. *Representational Gestures, Cognitive Rhythms, and Acoustic Aspects of Speech: A Network/Threshold Model of Gesture Production.* Unpublished PhD dissertation, Department of Psychology, University of Chicago.

Oberauer, K. 2005. "Access to information in working memory: exploring the focus of attention." *Journal of Experimental Psychology: Learning, Memory, and Cognition* 31: 714–728.

Özçaliskan, Ş. and Goldin-Meadow, S. 2009. "When gesture-speech combinations do and do not index linguistic change." *Language and Cognitive Processes* 24: 190–217.

Özyürek, A. 2001a. "What do speech-gesture mismatches reveal about language specific processing? A comparison of Turkish and English." In C. Cavé, I. Guaïtella and S. Santi (eds.), *Oralité et Gestualité: Interactions et Comportments Multimodaux Dans La Communnication.* Paris: L'Harattan.

2001b. *What Do Speech-Gesture Mismatches Reveal About Speech and Gesture Integration? A Comparison of Turkish and English.* Proceedings of the 27th Meeting of the Berkeley Linguistics Society. Berkeley: Berkeley Linguistics Society.

Park-Doob, M.A. 2010. *Gesturing Through Time: Holds and Intermodal Timing in the Stream of Speech.* Unpublished PhD dissertation. Department of Linguistics, University of California, Berkeley.

Peña, M., Maki, A., Kovacić, D., Dehaene-Lambertz, G., Koizumi, H., Bouquet, F. and Mehler, J. 2003. "Sounds and silence: an optical topography study of language recognition at birth." *Proceedings of the National Academy of Science USA* 100: 11702–11705.

Pika, S. and Bugnyar, T. 2011. "The use of referential gestures in ravens (*Corvus corax*) in the wild." *Nature Communications*, 29 November.

Pinker, S. 1994. *The Language Instinct.* New York: Harper Perennial.

Pollick, A.S. 2006. *Gestures and Multimodal Signaling in Bonobos and Chimpanzees.* Unpublished PhD dissertation. Department of Psychology, Emory University.

Quaeghebeur, L. 2010. *A Philosophy of Everyday Face-to-Face Conversation.* Antwerp: University of Antwerp.

—— 2012. "The 'all-at-onceness' of embodied, face-to-face interaction." *Journal of Cognitive Semiotics* 4: 167–188.

Quaeghebeur, L. and Reynaert, P. 2010. Does the need for linguistic expression constitute a problem to be solved? *Phenomenology and the Cognitive Sciences* 9: 15–36.

Quaeghebeur, L., Duncan, S., Gallgher, S., Cole, J. and McNeill, D. 2014. "Aproprioception, gesture, and cognitive being." In C. Müller, A. Cienki, E. Fricke, S.H. Ladewig, D. McNeill and J. Bressem (eds.), *Body—language—communication: an international handbook on multimodality in human interaction*, Vol. 2, pp. 2026–2048. Berlin: De Gruyter-Mouton.

Ramachandran, V. and Blakeslee, S. 1998. *Phantoms in the Brain: Probing the Mysteries of the Human Mind.* New York: William Morrow.

Reddy, M. 1979. "The conduit metaphor—a case of frame conflict in our language about language." In A. Ortony (ed.), *Metaphor and Thought*, pp. 284–324. Cambridge: Cambridge University Press.

Rhodes, R.A. and Lawler, J.M. 1981. "Athematic metaphors." In *Proceedings of the Chicago Linguistic Society*, pp. 318–342. Chicago: Chicago Linguistic Society.

Rieber, R.W. and Carton, A.S. (eds.). 1987. *The Collected Works of L.S. Vygotsky. Volume 1: Problems of General Psychology. Including the Volume "Thinking and Speech."* Intro. and trans. N. Minick. New York: Plenum.

Rizzolatti, G. and Arbib, M. 1998. "Language within our grasp." *Trends in Neurosciences* 21: 188–194.

Rozzi, F.V.R. and de Castro, J.M.B. 2004. "Surprisingly rapid growth in Neanderthals." *Nature* 428: 936–939.

Sacks, H., Schegloff, E.A. and Jefferson, G. 1974. "A simplest systematics for the organization of turn-taking for conversation." *Language.* 50: 696–735

Sahin, N.T., Pinker, S., Cash, S.S., Schomer, D. and Halgren, E. 2009. "Sequential processing of lexical, grammatical and phonological information within Broca's Area." *Science* 326: 445–449.

Sapir, E. 1921. *Language: An Introduction to the Study of Speech.* New York: Harcourt, Brace & World.

—— 1929. "A study in phonetic symbolism." *Journal of Experimental Psychology* 12: 225–239.

Saussure, F. 1959. *Course in General Linguistics.* Ed. C. Bally and A. Sechehaye, trans. W. Baskin. New York: The Philosophical Library.

Schegloff, E.A. 1984."On some gestures' relation to talk," in J.M. Atkinson and J. Heritage (eds.), *Structures of Social Action*, pp. 266–298. Cambridge: Cambridge University Press.

Science Daily. 2010. "New evidence of culture in wild chimpanzees." *Science Daily*, January 4. www.sciencedaily.com/releases/2009/10/091022122321.htm (accessed September 9, 2014).

Sekine, K. 2009a. "Changes in frame of reference use across the preschool years: a longitudinal study of the gestures and speech produced during route descriptions." *Language and Cognitive Processes* 24: 218–238.

2009b. *Creating Context: A Function of Gesture*. Seminar at the University of Chicago, January 21.

Senghas, A. 2003. "Intergenerational influence and ontogenetic development in the emergence of spatial grammar in Nicaraguan Sign Language." *Cognitive Development* 18: 511–531.

Silverstein, M. 1997. "The improvisational performance of culture in real time discursive practice." In R.K. Sawyer (ed.), *Creativity in Performance*, pp. 265–312. Greenwich, CT: Ablex.

2003. "Indexical order and the dialectics of sociolinguistic life." *Language & Communication* 23: 193–229.

Simon, H.A. 1996. *The Sciences of the Artificial*, 3rd edn. Cambridge, MA: MIT Press.

Slobin, D.I. 1987. "Thinking for speaking." In J. Aske et al. (eds.), *Proceedings of the Thirteenth Annual Meeting of the Berkeley Linguistic Society*, pp. 435–445. Berkeley, CA: Berkeley Linguistic Society.

1996. "From 'thought and language' to 'thinking for speaking.'" In J.J. Gumperz and S.C. Levinson (eds.), *Rethinking Linguistic Relativity*, pp. 70–96. Cambridge: Cambridge University Press.

Sowell, E.R., Thompson, P.M. Holmes, C. Jernigan, T.L. and Toga, A.W. 1999. "Invivo evidence for post-adolescent brain maturation in frontal and striatal regions." *Nature Neuroscience* 2: 859–861.

Stefanini, S., Caselli, M.C. and Volterra, V. 2007. "Spoken and gestural production in a naming task by young children with Down syndrome." *Brain and Language* 101: 208–221

Streeck, J. 2009. *Gesturecraft: The Manu-Facturing of Meaning*. Amsterdam and Philadelphia: Benjamins.

Sweet, H. 1971 [1900]. "The history of language." In E. Henderson (ed.). *The Indispensable Foundation: A Selection from the Writings of Henry Sweet*, pp. 1–24. London: Oxford University Press.

Talmy, L. 2000. *Toward a Cognitive Semantics. Vol. 2: Typology and Process in Concept Structuring*. Cambridge, MA: MIT Press.

Thomason, S. 1997. "On mechanisms of interference." In S. Eliasson and E.H. Jahr, (eds.). *Language and Its Ecology: Essays in Memory of Einar Haugen*, pp. 181–207. Berlin: de Gruyter.

2011. *Does Language Contact Simplify Grammars? (No.)* Talk given at the University of Chicago, April 12.

Tomasello, M. 1999. *The Cultural Origins of Human Cognition*. Cambridge, MA: Harvard University Press.

2008. *Origins of Human Communication*. Cambridge, MA: MIT Press.

2014. *A Natural History of Human Thinking*. Cambridge, MA: Harvard University Press.

Trudgill, P. 2011. *Investigations in Sociohistorical Linguistics: Stories of Colonization and Contact*. Cambridge: Cambridge University Press.

Tuite, K. 1993. "The production of gesture." *Semiotica* 93: 83–105.

Van Petten, C., Coulson, S., Rubin, S., Plante, E. and Parks, M. 1999. Time course of word identification and semantic integration in spoken language. *Journal of Experimental Psychology: Learning, Memory, and Cognition* 25: 394–417.

Vendler, Z.. 1967. *Linguistics in Philosophy*. Ithaca, NY: Cornell University Press.

Volterra, V., Caselli, M.C., Capirici, O. and Pizzuto, E. 2005. "Gesture and the emergence and development of language." In M. Tomasello and D.I. Slobin (eds.), *Beyond Nature-Nurture: Essays in Honor of Elizabeth Bates*, pp. 3–40. Hillsdale, NJ: Erlbaum.

Vygotsky, L.S. 1987. *Thought and Language*. Ed. and trans. E. Hanfmann and G. Vakar, revised and ed. A. Kozulin. Cambridge, MA: MIT Press.

Wachsmuth, I. and Sowa, T. (eds.). (2002). *Gesture and Sign Language in Human–Computer Interaction*. Berlin, Heidelberg and New York: Springer-Verlag.

Werner, H. and Kaplan, B. 1963. *Symbol Formation*. New York: John Wiley & Sons Ltd. [Reprinted in 1984 by Erlbaum.]

Whorf, B.L. 1956. *Language, Thought, and Reality. Selected Writings of Benjamin Lee Whorf*. Ed. J.B. Carroll. Cambridge, MA: MIT Press.

Weinreich, U. 1953. *Languages in Contact*. The Hague: Mouton.

Wimmer, H. and Perner, J. 1983. "Beliefs about beliefs: representation and constraining function of wrong beliefs in young children's understanding of deception." *Cognition* 13:103–128.

Woll, B. 2005/2006."Do mouths sign? Do hands speak?" In R. Botha and H. de Swart (eds.), *Restricted Linguistic Systems as Windows on Language Evolution*. Utrecht: Netherlands Graduate School of Linguistics Occasional Series, Utrecht University, http://lotos.library.uu.nl/publish/articles/000287/bookpart.pdf (accessed May 2, 2011).

WSJ. 2009. "Magic flute: primal find sings of music's mystery," *WSJ*, July 3–5, p. A9.

Wu, Y.C. and Coulson, S. 2010. "Gestures modulate speech processing early in utterances." *NeuroReport: For Rapid Communication of Neuroscience Research* 21: 522–526.

Wynn, T. and Coolidge, F. 2008. "Why not cognition?" *Current Anthropology* 49: 895–897.

2011. *How to Think Like a Neandertal*. Oxford: Oxford University Press.

Zbikowski, L.M. 2011. "Musical gesture and musical grammar: a cognitive approach." In A. Gritten and E. King (eds.), *New Perspectives on Music and Gesture*, pp. 83–98. Farnham: Ashgate.

Zinchenko, V.P. 1985. "Vygotsky's ideas about units for the analysis of mind." In J. Wertsch (ed.), *Culture Communication, and Cognition: Vygotskian Perspectives*, pp. 94–118. Cambridge University Press.

Index